We Begin Bombing in Five Minutes

A VOLUME IN THE SERIES
Culture and Politics in the Cold War and Beyond

EDITED BY
Edwin A. Martini and Scott Laderman

We Begin

BOMBING

in Five Minutes

Late Cold War Culture in the Age of Reagan

Andrew Hunt

UNIVERSITY OF MASSACHUSETTS PRESS

Amherst and Boston

ISBN 978-1-62534-576-9 (paper); 577-6 (hardcover)

Designed by Deste Roosa
Set in Minion Pro and DIN Condensed
Printed and bound by Books International, Inc.

Cover design by Charles Brock
Cover photo by Richard Sandler, *Anti Nuclear,* June 12, 1982.
Courtesy of the photographer.

Library of Congress Cataloging-in-Publication Data
Names: Hunt, Andrew E., 1968– author.
Title: We begin bombing in five minutes : late Cold War culture in the age
of Reagan / Andrew Hunt.
Other titles: Late Cold War culture in the age of Reagan
Description: Amherst : University of Massachusetts Press, [2021] | Series:
Culture and politics in the Cold War and beyond | Includes
bibliographical references and index.
Identifiers: LCCN 2020053365 (print) | LCCN 2020053366 (ebook) | ISBN
9781625345769 (paperback) | ISBN 9781625345776 (hardcover) | ISBN
9781613768327 (ebook) | ISBN 9781613768334 (ebook)
Subjects: LCSH: United States—Politics and government—1981–1989. | Cold
War in popular culture—United States. | Antinuclear movement—United
States—History—20th century. | Peace movements—United
States—History—20th century. | Protest movements—United
States—History—20th century.
Classification: LCC E876 .H86 2021 (print) | LCC E876 (ebook) | DDC
973.927—dc23
LC record available at https://lccn.loc.gov/2020053365
LC ebook record available at https://lccn.loc.gov/2020053366

British Library Cataloguing-in-Publication Data
A catalog record for this book is available from the British Library.

Dedicated to Luisa,
with all my love

Contents

Acknowledgments

A book is seldom a solitary undertaking, and this one is no exception. I would like to extend heartfelt thanks to a number of people.

Thank you to a number of my colleagues here at the University of Waterloo who have been so supportive and kind over the years. You have influenced my thinking along the way throughout this project. A round of thank-yous go out to Patrick Harrigan, Lynne Taylor, Gary Bruce, Julia Roberts, Jim Walker, Jasmin Habib, and Sue Roy. A special shout-out to my wonderful posse of Russ Freure, Ryan Van Koughnett, and my brother and dear friend, Dylan Cyr. Finally, I extend my deepest appreciation to John Sbardellati, an amazing colleague and dear friend, who read my entire manuscript and offered invaluable suggestions, nearly all of which I followed in the editing stages. A huge and heartfelt thank you, John!

Thank you to the incredible staff at the Reagan Library in Simi Valley, California, for their gracious support for many years. Thank you to the always magnificent Jane Forgay for all your help here at the Dana Porter Library at the University of Waterloo. And thank you to the scholars who have influenced and inspired me over the years: Christian Appy, Stephen Whitfield, Bradford Martin, Doug Rossinow, William Knoblauch, Patrick Hagopian, Roger Peace, Mike Foley, John McMillian, Mike Davis, the late, great Marilyn Young, and my mentor, Bob Goldberg.

Thank you to the outstanding people at University of Massachusetts Press for your support over the years with this project, with a special tip of the hat to Matt Becker, Sally Nichols, and Rachael DeShano. I couldn't ask for a better copy editor than Nancy Raynor, whose level of engagement, care, patience, and mind-blowing attention to detail left me verklempt and deeply inspired. Finally, thank you to the two anonymous readers for the University of Massachusetts Press, whose superb feedback greatly improved the manuscript. I am beyond grateful.

Thank you to the legendary Richard Sandler, for the breathtaking cover photograph! Meeting you was one of the great highlights of this project.

To my family back in Utah: Kay and Jodie Hunt, Linda Hunt, and my nephew and comrade in history, Spencer Hunt, and his amazing family. Closer home: thank you to Maddox, Charlie, and Aidan, for all of the love, laughter, dinners, gifts, fun, and memorable times here at the Big 20. Thank you, too, to Tony and Ruthie, for being such extraordinary presences. I love you all. You bring magic and wonder to my life.

This book is dedicated to Luisa D'Amato, the woman who captured my heart back in 2002 and still holds it in the palm of her hand. No words can express the depths of my love for you, Luisa. You bring light to my life and warmth to my soul, and you fill my days with happiness. I don't know where I'd be without you. I count my blessings each day that you're with me on this path.

We Begin Bombing in Five Minutes

INTRODUCTION

President Ronald Reagan intended for the joke to be a routine voice check. On Saturday, August 11, 1984, radio engineers arrived at Rancho del Cielo, the president's vacation ranch northwest of Santa Barbara, California, to set up equipment for his weekly address. When a sound man asked the president to speak into the microphone to test it, Reagan improvised a quip: "My fellow Americans, I'm pleased to tell you today that I've signed legislation that will outlaw Russia forever. We begin bombing in five minutes."[1] Reagan's macabre stab at humor was a rewording of comments he read a short time later on the air: "My fellow Americans: I'm pleased to tell you that today I signed legislation that will allow student religious groups to begin enjoying a right they've too long been denied—the freedom to meet in public high schools during non–school hours, just as other student groups are allowed to do."[2] The weekly radio address Reagan delivered that morning about the Equal Access bill for student religious groups was far from memorable and might have slipped into obscurity had it not been for the leak, two days later, of the joke he told about bombing the Soviet Union.[3]

Right away, the joke incited a storm of worldwide controversy and tarnished Reagan's reputation at home and abroad. His approval ratings in the United States declined amid the furor, unnerving his advisers about the upcoming election. For the first time in the campaign, Democratic presidential candidate Walter Mondale had climbed to within single digits of the president in the polls, owing to the fallout.[4] Overseas, one could almost hear the collective facepalms of America's allies as they reacted negatively to the comment. "One just wishes to God—and I think this goes for most Europeans—that it hadn't happened," said Sir James Eberle, director of Britain's Royal Institute of International Affairs. Reagan's joke, lamented the left-leaning French newspaper *Libération*, "can only reinforce his image as a cowboy always ready to push the button for a nuclear attack."[5] Prominent Western European dignitaries—many of whom were already inclined to have

1

negative perceptions of Reagan—heaped scorn on the president. But the harshest condemnation came from the Soviet Union, where officials regarded Reagan's words as incendiary at best, warmongering at worst. High-level figures in the Kremlin took the joke as a threat, coming at a tense time in U.S.-Soviet relations. General Secretary Konstantin Chernenko placed Soviet armed forces on high alert. *Pravda*, the official Communist Party newspaper, editorialized that Reagan's remarks amounted to "a political scandal of an enormous scale."[6] The "monstrous" joke, read an official Soviet statement, "showed the insincerity of U.S. calls for improved relations with Moscow."[7]

The hubbub baffled Reagan. He thought the joke harmless and could not understand why people were being so sensitive. Where was their sense of humor? Meeting with the leaders of prominent American Jewish organizations in the White House on August 16, five days after his radio address, Reagan joked with the men and women in the room that "he certainly was not going to bomb Russia in the next five minutes." Demands for an apology failed to yield the desired result. The closest Reagan came to saying he was sorry was when he groused, "If the press had kept their mouth shut, no one would have known I said it."[8]

As you have no doubt noticed by now, Reagan's gaffe has furnished the title of this book. By explaining the purpose of *We Begin Bombing in Five Minutes: Late Cold War Culture in the Age of Reagan*, I hope also to shed light on why I chose to christen it with Reagan's joke. My desire to write about Cold War culture in the Reagan era dates back to when I was a graduate student in the early 1990s, looking out at a changed world after the Berlin Wall came down, the Eastern Bloc collapsed, and the Soviet Union dissolved into the Russian Federation. At that pivotal moment, I read historian Stephen J. Whitfield's classic *Culture of the Cold War* for the first time in a doctoral seminar and loved it.[9] Whitfield's book—equal parts eloquent, informative, compelling, and persuasive—left me wanting more and nurtured my fascination with Cold War culture. Over the years, I've read extensively about the topic. The Cold War's influence on popular culture in the late 1940s, 1950s, and early 1960s cannot be overstated and has been documented extensively in a number of outstanding books.[10] For years, I sought out a narrative of Cold War culture in the Reagan years that functioned as a sort of sequel to Whitfield's book—something along the lines of *Culture of the Cold War II: Into the Eighties*. When I found out that no such book existed, I set out to write it.

Along the way, I discovered that updating Whitfield's book for the Reagan era was an impossible task, because it explored a dramatically different time and political landscape. Too much had changed by the 1980s. For one thing, the upheavals and cultural transformations of the 1960s and early 1970s had forever shattered America's Cold War consensus, altering the very fabric of the nation. As a result, Cold War culture in the 1980s—which became hotly contested terrain—bore little resemblance to its early postwar era ancestor. Without a doubt, the First Cold War left openings for creative dissent and inspired its own internal ban-the-bomb marches and pop culture critiques.

But in the 1980s, an anti–Cold War culture flourished, oftentimes eclipsing the dominant Cold War culture against which it rebelled. Opponents of the Cold War in the Reagan era brought a passion, a level of commitment, and an underlying sense of mission to their undertakings that its apologists lacked. Their opposition assumed the form of grassroots protest movements and a striking variety of cultural resistance, such as films, music, TV shows, and books. Sure, there are those few famous artifacts of eighties Cold War culture that infamously linger in the memory—the *Red Dawns*, the *Rambos*, the *Rocky IVs*, the *Amerikas*—but they were far fewer in number and lacked the gravitas of the cultural expression generated by the Cold War's foes at the time.

We Begin Bombing in Five Minutes argues that post-détente efforts to revive the Cold War, and all of its cultural manifestations, encountered fierce opposition on a number of fronts. Multiple social protest movements gained traction in the 1980s, focusing on such Cold War–related issues as the disputed legacies of the Vietnam War, the nuclear arms race, U.S. intervention in Central America, sanctuary for Latin American refugees arriving in the United States, and U.S. investments in South Africa. Eighties dissenters posed a more decisive challenge to the Cold War than did their McCarthy era counterparts with their vigor, outspokenness, and creativity and in the sheer size of their critical mass of supporters.

Virtually every facet of the Cold War in the 1980s encountered opposition, putting its proponents on the defensive. The revival of the Cold War created deep fissures in American society, and the general public remained deeply divided on the issue throughout much of the decade. On one side of the rift, President Reagan, Cold Warriors in both parties, assorted anticommunist activists, and conservative cultural figures worked in tandem to revive the Cold War and restore the shattered consensus that buttressed it decades earlier. Theirs, however, proved an onerous uphill struggle. Nationwide polls and surveys taken during the 1980s—as we shall soon see—revealed a lack of public enthusiasm and support for Cold War policies during Reagan's presidency, which made the job of its defenders that much more difficult.

On the opposite side of the spectrum, authors, filmmakers, artists, grassroots political organizers, and a handful of outspoken politicians presented critiques and alternative visions of the Cold War that often had a meaningful impact on American society. Movies with a critical eye depicted such weighty topics as the Vietnam War (*Platoon*, *Full Metal Jacket*), nuclear holocaust (*The Day After*, *WarGames*), U.S. intervention in Central America (*Under Fire*, *Salvador*), and the evils of South African apartheid (*Cry Freedom*, *A Dry White Season*). These films challenged anticommunist narratives that emphasized American exceptionalism and a generally black-and-white worldview.

Elsewhere in the cultural landscape, the 1980s proved to be a renaissance for Vietnam veteran artists, writers, and filmmakers whose contributions contained profoundly antiwar themes. Music offered another pivotal battleground, with a variety of sounds—from Springsteen to punk—subverting dominant Cold War narratives. Central America also came to occupy a central place in the collective American imagination of the 1980s, and cultural and grassroots protests against U.S. policies in the region fueled widespread public skepticism about Washington's Cold War agenda. Meantime, Americans in different religions rigorously debated the meaning and nature of the Cold War, with ideological divides splitting spiritual camps. Right-wing televangelists led crusades against communism abroad and secular humanism at home, while religious figures on the left played vital roles in organizing the peace movement and established sanctuary churches to help Central Americans fleeing persecution in their home countries.

And in the middle of these robust debates about the nation, its purpose in the world, and its future could be found millions of ordinary Americans, experiencing a Cold War culture in which virtually every issue was hotly debated and in which dissenters spoke up without fear of being blacklisted, administered loyalty oaths, or subjected to other forms of McCarthyism. In short, they witnessed an entirely different kind of Cold War culture than the one that loomed so large in the domestic scene a mere thirty years earlier.

Finally, we return full circle to Reagan's joke: "We begin bombing in five minutes." Reagan never understood why words intended to be humorous left so many who had heard them shaken and fearful. That was especially so across Europe, where memories of World War II were still fresh in many people's minds. The president's lighthearted quip about a matter of the utmost gravity reflected a blasé attitude, widely shared by the Cold War's apologists, who seldom defended the global ideological contest with the same level of conviction and emotion as did those who resisted it. Despite a cynicism that underlay their actions, Cold Warriors still sought—with rigor and determination—to revive the bloody and costly contest, with the elusive goal of restoring a consensus destroyed on the battlefields of Vietnam and in the streets of America. The discord that greeted their actions caught them by surprise. Sustained by creativity, tenacity, and a vision of a Cold War–free world, a broad-based protest movement, backed by activists and cultural rebels alike, hunkered down and prepared for a long fight.

CHAPTER 1
Setting the Stage

So thoroughly entrenched is the End of the Cold War, that it has generated an offspring, which is called Bringing Back the Cold War.

—*William F. Buckley,* Detroit Free Press, *November 9, 1979*

Hawks tell us to go back and do it right. But we did it right the first time. Full nuclear development and total ideological suspicion—you can hardly top that for a proper Cold War performance. We made things worse because we performed so well. The moral is not to be a better wife to King Henry VIII, but to give up marrying him altogether.

—*Garry Wills,* Hartford Courant, *January 16, 1980*

Cold War II

At some point in the late 1970s, it became fashionable to declare that the Cold War was on its way back. "As 1975 draws to an end, détente is dead," wrote William Safire, syndicated columnist and former Nixon speechwriter, in the *New York Times.* "The Second Cold War is under way."[1] When Safire's column appeared in the venerable paper of record, it was hard to imagine the Cold War returning to dominate American politics. The once mighty Cold War consensus now seemed unsalvageable in the aftermath of defeat in Vietnam and détente. Televised images of Nixon meeting with Mao Zedong in 1972, as well as the American evacuation of Saigon in April 1975, had left an indelible impression on the public, and few had the stomach to revisit the Cold War conflicts of yesteryear.

Hence, Safire's position was not widely shared when his column ran. Ronald Reagan was one of the few high-profile political figures that publicly concurred with him. In the Republican primaries of 1976, Reagan hammered President Ford from the right, insisting the commander in chief lacked resolve on defense matters. At a campaign stop in Peoria, Illinois, in March 1976, Ford struck back, warning that "returning to a collision course in a thermo-nuclear age can lead to disaster." Without naming Reagan, the president said the nation had "an obligation not to go back to the Cold War."[2]

Before long, others would come around to Safire's way of thinking. Political commentator Kevin Phillips predicted in March 1978 that a "neo–Cold War period, a new anticommunist era, is indeed about to begin."[3] Bespectacled and soft-spoken, Phillips had an authoritative air about him. People on all parts of the political spectrum listened to him and took him seriously. Nine years earlier, Phillips's prescient book, *The Emerging Republican Majority* (1969), had identified political trends favoring a sharp rightward turn in American politics. He popularized the concept of a "southern strategy" in that book, which saw the Republican Party building a powerful conservative coalition in the so-called Sunbelt states—that vast region along America's southern tier, from California to Florida—and abandoning the efforts of moderate Republicans to appeal to more liberal northeastern voters.[4] *The Emerging Republican Majority* became an important go-to book for both political scientists and Republican strategists in the 1970s, and Phillips gained a nationwide pulpit as a syndicated columnist of some renown. Thus, when he forecast the return of the Cold War, his opinion carried weight. "If I had to estimate," he wrote in 1978, "I'd guess that sometime within the next year or two or three, the U.S. will move into another strong anticommunist cycle."[5]

As Phillips wrote these words, worsening regional conflicts in parts of Africa, Latin America, Asia, and the Middle East prompted warnings else-where of a resurgent Cold War. "What is required, and what is difficult for this administration to provide, is an offensive strategy for fighting the second Cold War with the Soviet Union," wrote syndicated conservative columnist and former Nixon speechwriter Patrick Buchanan in April 1979.[6] Alarm bells sounded outside of the United States, as well. "U.S. imperialism is obviously embarking on the path of a new Cold War and creating a situation threaten-ing universal peace and security," warned Soviet president Leonid Brezhnev in 1980.[7] "The enemies of peace have been stepping up their counterattacks against relaxation of tension. In their mass media, the West is longing for a second Cold War," said Erich Honecker, the East German head of state.[8]

"I do believe," wrote Canadian radio host and newspaper columnist Ron Collister in the pages of the *Edmonton Journal* on Valentine's Day 1980, "that the Cold War, with all its horrendous dangers, is back with a bang." Around the same time, on the other side of the Atlantic, Denzil Peiris, the Sri Lankan–born coeditor of the London-based *Guardian Third World Review*, despairingly observed, "With the Soviet move into Afghanistan, the second Cold War is on."[9]

Talk of a "Second Cold War"—or Cold War II, as William Safire called it—suggested that experts in the 1970s thought the Cold War had ended at some point or at least dramatically subsided. But the Cold War never completely vanished from American life. It remained ever present in politics, even in times of improved U.S.-Soviet relations. The arms control treaties signed by Presidents Nixon, Ford, and Carter and their Soviet counterparts did not spell an end to the conflict. Rather, those painstakingly formulated agreements represented attempts to manage tensions and move the superpowers away from the brink of nuclear war arrived at under Kennedy and Khrushchev in 1962. Dividing the Cold War into "first" and "second" phases, as well as using terms such as "Second Cold War" and "Cold War II," offered a useful way of understanding the lull that separated periods of heightened conflict. It also enabled pundits, scholars, and officials to break down complex issues into a more easily digestible narrative for op-ed page readers who did not have the luxury of exploring the Cold War's finer nuances on their own.

The goodwill that characterized détente had evaporated in the second half of the 1970s. The resumption of mutual hostilities between the United States and the Soviet Union was, by decade's end, widely seen as a return to the global ideological contest that had profoundly shaped world affairs since 1945. By the late 1970s and early 1980s, international relations (IR) specialists and diplomatic historians studying recent superpower tensions arrived at a similar conclusion: the Cold War, once on its way to the dustbin of history, was back. For example, renowned IR scholar Fred Halliday, from the London School of Economics, titled his landmark 1983 book on the era *The Making of the Second Cold War*.[10]

Whatever terminology one used, by 1980 there was no question that the Cold War had returned to dominate American foreign policy, as it did prior to détente.[11] Events overseas in the late 1970s drove gloomy predictions of the Cold War's return. In particular, conflicts in three key global hot spots—an Islamic revolution in Iran and subsequent hostage crisis, the Soviet invasion of Afghanistan, and the Sandinista Revolution that ousted pro-U.S.

strongman Anastasio Somoza in the summer of 1979—alarmed American policymakers and coincided with an escalating arms race at home under President Jimmy Carter.

Events in Iran, Afghanistan, and Nicaragua pushed Carter to embrace a more hawkish Cold War approach and to move away from the values of human rights he championed early in his presidency. These were trying times for the thirty-ninth president. At home, a faltering economy left him demoralized. Runaway stagflation, slow job growth, and long lines at gas stations owing to a Mideast "oil shock" combined to whittle Carter's base of support. Unable to repair the ailing economy, Carter set his sights abroad. His heavily publicized success at brokering a peace agreement between Israel's Menachem Begin and Egypt's Anwar Sadat in 1978 did little to stall his downward-sliding reputation. Moreover, his support of a treaty to return the Panama Canal to Panama by 1999 infuriated the right.[12] Some of Carter's critics spoke of a failed presidency. Indeed, the economy's lackluster performance went hand in hand with conservatives accusing Carter of being inconsistent on foreign policy and "soft on communism," a charge that had dogged Democrats in the Oval Office since the days of Harry Truman.[13]

In his transformation to Cold Warrior, Carter relied increasingly on the counsel of his national security advisor, Zbigniew Brzezinski, a former professor of international relations at Columbia University and a hard-line anticommunist. Brzezinski, son of a pre–World War II Polish diplomat, had moved to Canada as a young boy, where his father was posted, and eventually attended Harvard with Henry Kissinger.[14] His disdain for the Kremlin and its policies led him to advise President Carter to take a tough stand against what he believed to be a systematic pattern of ruthless Soviet expansionism.[15]

As a result of the Soviet invasion of Afghanistan, Carter, who had been drifting toward Brzezinski's way of thinking for some time, assumed a firmer Cold War position. He oversaw a huge military buildup in the Persian Gulf and presided over the deployment of SS-20s to Europe, the construction of new cruise missiles, and the preparation of conventional forces for intervention in the Third World.[16] Carter also backed the development of the LGM-118 Peacekeeper, popularly known as the MX Missile (MX stood for "Missile Experimental"), a controversial new missile system. The president gave his blessing for the construction of a hopelessly complex $34 billion network of underground launching facilities, storage shelters, and "racetracks" over which the missiles would be transported, all in an effort to conceal the approximately two hundred Peacekeepers from Soviet tracking systems.

Originally, Air Force planners supervising MX missile system construction intended to build it in remote areas of New Mexico, Utah, and Nevada, but they encountered sustained opposition in those states, which led to the program being scrapped.[17]

The MX fiasco discouraged Carter but did not slow his conversion to Cold Warrior. As the Cold War intensified in 1980, the president further firmed up his position by refusing to sell grain to the USSR until it withdrew troops from Afghanistan and by boycotting the 1980 Moscow Summer Olympics. *Pravda*, the official organ of the Soviet Communist Party, lashed out at Carter's tough line, saying his actions were "drawing the world into an atmosphere of Cold War."[18] Carter insisted such tough measures were necessary, and most congressional Democrats backed his new approach. Those on the left wishing to see a more dovish Democratic Party were disappointed. "For the first time since the Cold War era of communist containment," wrote Princeton international law scholar Dr. Richard Falk, "congressional doves are flocking with their more hawkish brethren in unified support of greater U.S. military spending and a return to interventionism."[19]

In the aftermath of Watergate and defeat in Vietnam, the Cold War's comeback left few surprised. Policymakers from both parties, along with a sizable segment of the American population, shared the view that America had lost its prestige on the world stage. In this souring climate, Republicans took advantage of Carter's perceived weaknesses on foreign policy. When Ronald Reagan began campaigning for the presidency in 1980, he effectively channeled a mix of buoyant optimism, American exceptionalism, and hawkish jingoism. His choreographed speeches, which typically placed him next to large American flags, electrified crowds. On July 17, Reagan delivered his acceptance address at the Republican National Convention in Detroit, warning his audience about the Soviet threat. "America's defense strength is at its lowest ebb in a generation," he told a cheering crowd, "while the Soviet Union is vastly outspending us in both strategic and conventional arms."[20]

Reagan preferred strong language when describing the communist world, especially the Soviets. Since his failed 1976 bid for the presidency, he had routinely borrowed from pre-détente language, using words like "appeasement," "criminal," and "totalitarian." His general outlook dovetailed with the findings of the nonpartisan Committee on the Present Danger, an anticommunist watchdog organization run by a board of luminaries that included former secretary of state Dean Rusk, ex-navy secretary Paul Nitze, and onetime U.S. Army chief of staff General Matthew Ridgway. In January 1980, the committee issued a detailed report, timed to coincide with Carter's State of the Union address. "As the Soviet Union has moved forward, exploiting its growing sea power and airlift capacity, the United States has continued to retreat," the report concluded.[21]

For most ordinary Americans living outside the Capital Beltway, the committee's dire warning held little sway. Most voters—as polls demonstrated—were more concerned with pocketbook issues in 1980 than with foreign policy, and a growing number felt Carter was not managing the economy well. Reinforcing those doubts were the sharply contrasting personalities of the two presidential candidates. On the campaign trail, Reagan appeared confident at every step, yet Carter came across as sullen and pessimistic. The introspective Carter spoke of a national malaise and a crisis of confidence, yet peppy Reagan boasted that it was a good thing to be patriotic again, that free markets would usher in a new era of prosperity, that a strong defense was key to restoring the nation's prestige, and that America could emerge from Watergate and Vietnam a mighty world power. At a campaign stop in Florida, Reagan stood on a high school auditorium stage, waving to cheering crowds while a band played "Stars and Stripes Forever," exuding the same optimism as his onetime hero, Franklin D. Roosevelt. Shadowing Reagan, Elizabeth Drew wrote dispatches for the New Yorker marveling at his appropriation of patriotic symbols. "His rallies are draped in red-white-and-blue bunting," Drew noted. "Reagan's supporters wear straw hats with red-white-and-blue bands that say 'Reagan.' His posters are red-white-and-blue, and this year's shows Reagan smiling his crinkly-eyed smile over a picture of the White House. The slogan is 'Let's Make America Great Again.'"[22] Carey McWilliams, editor of the leftist Nation magazine, observed Reagan on the campaign trail with a sense of grudging respect. In June 1980, one month before he passed away, McWilliams wrote: "The former governor of California is a bright, if not original, thinker. He radiates traditional American values. He is not a hater. He likes people. He appears to feel there is good in almost everyone. He is a very secure man; what you see is what he is."[23]

On Election Day, November 4, 1980, American voters delivered Reagan a stunning victory. Reagan did not simply defeat Carter, he beat him soundly by 51 to 41 percent of the popular vote, which translated to 489 electoral votes to Carter's 44—not exactly the statistical "dead heat" that some polls had been predicting in the weeks leading up to the election.[24] The Senate also went Republican for the first time since 1955. As early as the next day, pundits and commentators recognized the significance of the sea change that had just taken place. "Obviously there has been a conservative sweep of opinion in the nation," opined *New York Times* columnist James Reston.[25] The term "Reagan Revolution" instantly appeared in the press, signaling the shift in American politics.[26] Tip O'Neill referred to the election as a "tidal wave." "The country's politics," writes historian Sean Wilentz, "would begin to look unlike any it had ever known."[27]

Anti–Cold War Culture

The Cold War revival of the late 1970s and early 1980s came after years of domestic upheaval and polarization. A number of unresolved issues and tensions from the late 1960s and early 1970s—a period known as "the Sixties"— had persisted long beyond the era. Much of the rebellion of the times, political and cultural alike, had crystalized in opposition to the Vietnam War, which had been a long, costly, bloody, and divisive conflict for the United States. It also stood as a prime example of a Cold War flashpoint that had exploded into years of war. Even as it ravaged Southeast Asia in combat and a round-the-clock air war, the Vietnam War stoked divisions at home, resulting in a rising tide of antiwar protest. The war also fueled new forms of cultural rebellion and lifestyle experimentation that by the end of the 1960s had earned the label "the counterculture."[28] But the so-called "movement," a name given at the time to a wide range of resistance, was larger than the Vietnam War and its discontents. It also encompassed civil rights coalitions, minority power groups, student revolts, feminism, LGBT activism, environmentalism, and other forms of dissent.

This sweeping and protracted flood of protest contributed significantly to increased openness and tolerance in the United States, emboldening the nation's dissidents. Coincidentally, the Vietnam War, and the widespread opposition it, led to an unraveling the "Cold War consensus." That term, which caught on in the 1970s, had been used to describe a widely held worldview that dominated the halls of power in Washington, D.C., prior to America's ill-fated intervention in Southeast Asia. It rested on the assumption that U.S. foreign policy was, on balance, a positive force in the world that championed democracy, human rights, and a global market economy and formed a barrier to communist expansion around the world. The consensus, writes political scientist Ronald R. Krebs, emerged as "a dominant narrative to which American elites—from policymakers to pundits to even professors—felt compelled to adhere in their public pronouncements, regardless of their private qualms."[29]

Harmony around the Cold War came under withering assault during the Vietnam War in the form of sustained protests, which helped lay the groundwork for the flowering of a movement that opposed the resuscitated Cold War of the Carter and Reagan presidencies. So it was that cycles of dissent continued anew, as efforts by latter-day Cold Warriors to restore the shattered Cold War consensus in the late 1970s and 1980s came under fire once again by resisters of various stripes. Predictably, this pushback, like the diverse rebellions of the Sixties, assumed political and cultural forms. Among its core of insurgents were veterans of uprisings in the 1960s, along with an infusion of newcomers. But these individuals also owed a sizable debt to long-standing traditions of anti–Cold War dissent in America dating back to the 1940s. Groundswells of protest against what President Dwight D. Eisenhower in 1961 presciently called "the military-industrial complex" occurred with regularity before the first American combat troops waded ashore at Da Nang in March 1965. Much of this opposition was cultural in nature, but it also took the shape of grassroots activism. Simply put, as long as there was a Cold War in American society, small clusters of anti–Cold Warriors made films, wrote books, created art, and marched in the streets to show their disapproval of the potentially deadly global ideological contest.

Yet dissent in the First Cold War was slow to mobilize and early on drew only small numbers of intrepid participants. Speaking out too boldly against the excesses of the postwar Red Scare often came with severe penalties. By 1947, the nation was plunging into the swirling tumult of congressional hearings, loyalty oaths, and mass firings, which came about as a result of the coordinated work of thousands of government officials, from presidents down, in cooperation with state and local agencies and private groups, Hollywood studios, labor unions, and public and higher education institutions. In particular, the Cold War's influence on popular culture in the late 1940s and 1950s cannot be overstated and has been documented extensively.[30] In the case of movies, Cold War themes and subtexts permeated different genres, including dramas, science fiction, war movies, and even Westerns. In its most explicit form, outright anticommunism assumed a central place in films such as *Iron Curtain* (1948), *I Was a Communist for the FBI* (1951), *Walk East on Beacon* (1952), *My Son John* (1952), and *Pickup on South Street* (1953); radio shows like *This Is Your FBI* (ABC, 1945–53) and *I Was a Communist for the FBI* (1952–53); and the syndicated television program *I Led 3 Lives* (1953–56).[31]

By contrast, overtly criticizing the Cold War or domestic Red Scare was not an option in the Hollywood entertainment industry in the 1940s and

1950s. There were, however, other, less direct ways of expressing opposition. A recurring approach among dissidents in the arts was to tell stories that were disguised critiques. The 1952 Western *High Noon* exemplified McCarthy-era commentary-by-stealth at is finest. *High Noon* followed Marshal Will Kane around the dusty roads of fictional Hadleyville, New Mexico Territory, for ninety agonizing minutes—one of the first movies to tell a story in real time. Amid frequent shots of clocks, Kane sought help from fearful townspeople to stop four murderous outlaws coming to town to exact revenge. One by one, the men in the community hide away, including Kane's cowardly deputy (Lloyd Bridges). A climactic shootout favors Kane as the victor, helped by his new bride, Amy (Grace Kelly). He guns down his foe, Frank Miller, the man he helped send to prison years earlier, and Miller's bloodthirsty cohorts.[32] *High Noon* opened nationwide in July 1952 to overwhelming commercial and critical success. Not everyone was enthused by the film, though. Its director, Austrian-born Fred Zinnemann, shrugged off John Wayne's criticism that *High Noon* was "un-American" for showing a frightened sheriff and cowardly frontier settlers. "I'm rather surprised at this kind of thinking," Zinnemann said. "Sheriffs are people and no two people are alike."[33] Unlike Zinnemann, the film's screenwriter, Carl Foreman, who was blacklisted by the time of *High Noon*'s release and living in England to obtain work, insisted the movie was an allegory about cowardice in the face of Red Scare repression. In January 1953, six months after the film opened, the liberal *Nation* magazine opined: "There must be times these days when Mr. Foreman feels that he too has been deserted by those who should have helped him stand off the bullies and tough guys whose aggressions have so largely destroyed the moral fiber of the Western town that goes by the name Hollywood."[34]

High Noon was one of many disguised attacks against Red Scare paranoia and persecution. Rarely did Westerns to take such bold risks. By contrast, science fiction—a new and thriving genre in the 1950s—proved friendlier to social commentary by stealth. One of the first films to pave the way for science fiction cinema's golden age, Robert Wise's *The Day the Earth Stood Still* (1951), contained powerful pacifist themes. The film opens with a flying saucer landing in Washington, D.C., greeted by a massive welcoming party of U.S. Army soldiers. Its occupants, Klaatu, a benevolent human-like alien, and his giant robot companion, Gort, emerge from the domed craft after traveling vast distances to warn earthlings about the dangers of the nuclear arms race. Klaatu eventually leaves his government hosts, quietly takes up residence in a local boarding house, and learns the ways of human beings.

He comes to terms with how best to convey his plea for peace to the human race before leaving the planet.[35] Other message-laden sci-fi movies followed, many cautioning against the dangers of nuclear radiation in the form of giant mutant monsters and unforeseen side effects. Hollywood recycled the radiation theme over and over in films such as *The Beast from 20,000 Fathoms* (1953), *Them!* (1954), *The Incredible Shrinking Man* (1957), *The Amazing Colossal Man* (1957), *Beginning of the End* (1957), *The Alligator People* (1959), and others.[36] The famous Japanese kaiju movie *Gojira* (1954) was repackaged two years later in an Americanized version called *Godzilla* (1956), with scenes of rising Canadian star Raymond Burr added. *Godzilla* broke box office records and was widely seen as a metaphor for the atomic bombings of Hiroshima and Nagasaki.[37] Another popular scenario involved aliens taking over human beings and assuming their identities, first in *Invaders from Mars* (1953), followed more memorably by *Invasion of the Body Snatchers* (1956). Such films played on Cold War fears across the spectrum. They functioned as Rorschach tests, which, depending on the moviegoer's politics, could be regarded as warnings against complacency in the face of communist aggression or conformity under the threat of McCarthyism, or simply as escapist entertainment.[38]

Similar dual meanings can also be found in Cold War thrillers of the period. On the face of it, Samuel Fuller's *Pickup on South Street* (1953) appears to be a fairly standard anticommunist film noir, pitting its protagonist, shady pickpocket Skip McCoy (Richard Widmark), against a Red spy ring. The film is that, to be sure, but it is also a frank celebration of an antiauthoritarian criminal antihero, the kind of character who in a more conventional film noir would be done in by his own avarice. But in *Pickup on South Street*, McCoy saves the day by defeating spies that cannot be stopped by the authorities.[39] An even more subversive quality pervades John Frankenheimer's complex conspiracy thriller *The Manchurian Candidate* (1962), about a Korean War veteran sleeper agent Raymond Shaw (Laurence Harvey), who is brainwashed by communists to assassinate an American politician as part of a larger communist plot to take over the U.S. government. Initially, *The Manchurian Candidate* unfolds as a warning about the dangers of the international communist conspiracy and brainwashing. However, one of its chief villains turns out to be Senator John Iselin (James Gregory), a fanatical anticommunist crusader whose witch-hunting demagoguery proves a useful tool for sinister communist conspirators.[40]

Apart from cinema, disguised critiques could be found in other realms of popular culture. On Broadway, Arthur Miller's 1953 stage play *The Crucible* reimagined the Red Scare as the seventeenth-century Salem witch trials, and critics generally responded favorably. *The Crucible*, writes historian Edmund S. Morgan, "was written in the midst of the McCarthy era, and it was intended, I think, to suggest that we were behaving, or allowing our authorized representatives to behave, as badly as the authorities at Salem. There are no overt comparisons. The play is about Salem. But its success depends in part on the shock of recognition."[41] The play had a successful initial run on Broadway and was made into a film in 1957, a coproduction of France and East Germany, scripted by French philosopher Jean-Paul Sartre.[42]

Television also broadcast disguised critiques. The most well known of the medium's social critics-by-stealth, Rod Serling, from Syracuse, New York, got his start writing for network anthology dramas in the fifties. Shows such as *Philco Television Playhouse* (1948–55), *Studio One* (1948–58), *Playhouse 90* (1956–60), and *General Electric Theater* (1953–62) championed dramatic realism, showcasing up-and-coming writers like Stirling Silliphant, Paddy Chayefsky, and Serling.[43] Of all the young Turk TV writers, Serling, a man with strong humanist convictions, utilized the medium most effectively to tell stories that addressed such social ills as war, poverty, racism, and conformity. His science fiction anthology series, *The Twilight Zone*, found a home on the Columbia Broadcasting System (CBS), debuting on October 2, 1959. For five seasons (1959–64), Serling worked with a team of talented writers, including Richard Matheson, George Clayton Johnson, Earl Hamner Jr., and Charles Beaumont. But Serling was the real star of *The Twilight Zone*, both as its on-screen narrator and author of most of its teleplays. Writing perilously close to the heyday of McCarthyism, Serling understood the potential of science fiction to harbor dissent. Multiple episodes contained Cold War or Red Scare allegories, among them "Time Enough at Last" (1959), about a timid, far-sighted bookworm (Burgess Meredith) who survives a nuclear war by hiding in a bank vault; "Third from the Sun" (1960), in which families escape from a planet about to be destroyed by nuclear war; "The Monsters Are Due on Maple Street" (1960), a dark yarn with neighbors turning against neighbors after being manipulated by unseen alien invaders; and "The Shelter" (1961), a tale of hysterical suburbanites trying to break into a kindly doctor's fallout shelter during a Russian nuclear attack. To add balance, Serling took swipes at communism in "The Mirror" (1961), with a bearded Fidel Castro–esque dictator in green fatigues (Peter Falk), who gazes into a magic mirror and sees his enemies trying to kill him, and "The Jeopardy Room" (1964), a taut story of a Soviet defector (Martin Landau) who outwits a pair of KGB assassins.[44]

Humor similarly played a pivotal role in pop culture opposition to the Cold War. On November 19, 1959, the animated television series *Rocky and His Friends* debuted on the American Broadcasting Company (ABC). It would later be renamed the *Bullwinkle Show* when it made the leap over to the National Broadcasting Company (NBC) in 1961.[45] The two main characters were a bizarrely mismatched pair of anthropomorphized animals: a flying squirrel with an aviator's hat named Rocky (voiced by June Foray) and a hulking, deep-voiced moose called Bullwinkle (played by Bill Scott, who also cowrote and coproduced *Rocky and His Friends*). The show, created by producer Jay Ward, with help from his friends writer-producer Bill Scott and cartoonist Alex Anderson, boasted some of the most instantly recognizable voice actors of the era, including Daws Butler, Hans Conried, Edward Everett Horton, Walter Tetley, and June Foray, most of them veterans of Stan Freberg's beloved comedy albums.[46]

Populating the absurdist cartoon were oddballs and eccentrics galore, and the show regularly poked fun at midcentury conventions. Two characters, in particular, stood out. A team of Russian-like spies, Boris Badenov (Paul Frees) and Natasha Fatale (June Foray), emerged as the show's main scene-stealers. The duo hailed from the fictional Eastern European country of Pottsylvania, headed by a monocled, German-accented tyrant, Fearless Leader. "What does Pottsylvania have more than any other country?" asks Fearless Leader on one episode. "Mean! We have more mean than any other country in Europe! We must export mean."[47] Boris and Natasha not only spoofed American stereotypes of Russians, they did so in a brazenly over-the-top fashion. Boris, especially—sharing a similar name with sixteenth-century Russian tsar Boris Godunov—left a memorable impression. A sinister little man with a thin mustache and a matching black fedora and suit, Boris often referred to "fiendish plans" while rubbing his hands together. He carried concealed bombs, pistols, vials of poison, and hangman's nooses, just in case. We never learn why Boris and Natasha are pursuing Rocky and Bullwinkle, but they accepted the mission with unwavering dedication, right down to donning disguises to accomplish their goal.

Boris and Natasha were products of a thaw in the deep freeze of domestic Cold War culture, and *Rocky and His Friends* fit into a body of subversive Cold War–era satire. Satirical magazines of the time, such as *Mad*, Paul Krassner's *The Realist*, and *Monocle*, a left-wing countercultural magazine, routinely attacked Cold War conventions with dry senses of humor and keen eyes for the absurd. In so doing, these publications saw their subscriber lists grow. Enclaves of rebel satirists and stand-up comedians were small, yet robust, and often shared venues with each other. Indeed, *Monocle*'s energetic young founder, Victor Navasky, future editor in chief of the *Nation* magazine, regarded his small rebellious publication "as part of a new ferment that expressed itself . . . through improvisational theater, the Second City group out in Chicago, Mort Sahl . . . Lenny Bruce coming up through the nightclub underground, [and] Paul Krassner doing *The Realist*."[48]

Meantime, in America's newspaper opinion pages, syndicated editorial such cartoonists as Bill Mauldin and Herbert "Herblock" Block routinely lambasted McCarthyism and the perils of unrestrained Cold War policies. Their cartoons, in fact, provided some of the most trenchant political commentary of the early postwar period.[49] In a similar vein, liberal cartoonist Walt Kelly wove social commentary into his syndicated comic strip *Pogo*, which first appeared in newspapers in 1948. Inhabiting the strip was a colorful population of anthropomorphized animals residing in the Okefenokee Swamp, with the protagonist being a kindhearted and philosophical opossum named Pogo Possum. Pogo and his fellow swamp dwellers, Howland Owl, Albert Alligator, and a turtle named Churchill "Churchy" LaFemme, confronted cartoon versions of dilemmas that Americans faced in the postwar era, including racism, ecological challenges, war anxieties, prejudice, and McCarthyism. In a risky move, Kelly introduced a scruffy wildcat named Simple J. Malarkey, a Senator Joseph McCarthy lookalike, who threw his weight around, seeking to intimidate other animals. Some newspapers expressed concerns about *Pogo*'s content and threatened to drop the strip. Kelly refused to ditch his pointed caricature of McCarthy, and *Pogo* remained widely circulated and popular for its quarter-of-a-century run.[50]

By the close of the 1950s, thawing superpower tensions overseas and the waning potency of the Red Scare at home made overt criticisms of the Cold War possible. Bookstore shelves across America began stocking an expanding number of titles about nuclear war and postapocalyptic narratives, among them Leigh Brackett's Hugo-winning *The Long Tomorrow* (1955); Nevil Shute's *On the Beach* (1957); Peter George's *Red Alert* (1958); Helen Clarkson's *The Last Day* (1959); Pat Frank's *Alas, Babylon* (1959); Mordecai Roshwald's *Level 7* (1959); Eugene Burdick and Harvey Wheeler's *Fail-Safe* (1962); and Kurt Vonnegut's *Cat's Cradle* (1963).

Hollywood adapted several of these books into successful films, starting with Shute's *On the Beach* in 1959. In the hands of liberal director and producer Stanley Kramer, the novel became a sensational, big-budget motion picture, filmed in Australia, starring Gregory Peck, Ava Gardner, and Fred Astaire. It depicted an American submarine crew and the residents of Melbourne surviving a global thermonuclear war in the near-future year of 1964, only to eventually succumb to radiation poisoning. During the making of *On the Beach*, Kramer revealed a key spoiler about his "end of the world" picture: "Of course it's sad, because we hope you will get to like these people who, in the end, die."[51] Never before had such a relentlessly grim film come from Hollywood. Not merely one or two or three characters perish. The entire human race dies, which was unheard of in a mainstream studio movie. Scenes of Melbourne's deserted streets at the end of *On the Beach*—streets that had been teeming with life earlier in the film—haunt the viewer. Upon release, *On the Beach* provoked intense controversy. Not surprisingly, Cold Warriors balked at the film. Senator Wallace Bennett of Utah criticized *On the Beach* on the floor of Congress: "In my opinion it paints a distorted picture of what nuclear war would probably be like." Lieutenant General Clarence R. Huebner, head of New York State Civil Defense, insisted *On the Beach* "does not do justice to the theory that there is a 'relatively simple defense against radioactive fallout' and that the end of the world as pictured is not inevitable."[52] By contrast, chemist Dr. Linus Pauling praised Kramer's movie for its realism. "It may be," he said, "that some day we can look back and say *On the Beach* is the picture that saved the world."[53]

In the long run, *On the Beach*'s impact was significant. The film helped inaugurate America's new anti–Cold War culture. Whether Kramer knew it, his cinematic refutation of the concept of nuclear deterrence—a key pillar in America's Cold War strategy—was smashing open a space on the spectrum of dissent previously closed off. *On the Beach* contributed to a more open atmosphere that allowed filmmakers, artists, authors, and entertainers of various stripes to engage in direct forms of cultural resistance against the Cold War. No longer did every critique have to be disguised so as to get movie made, a television show aired, a play staged, or a book published.

After *On the Beach*, a handful of films tackled the previously taboo topic of nuclear war. Early entries in this category were limited by low budgets and weak distribution. For example, Academy Award–winning actor Ray Milland's *Panic in the Year Zero!* (1962) explored a father's struggle to protect his family after a nuclear war levels Los Angeles. American International Pictures, an indie production company famous for drive-in fodder, especially the B movies of director-producer Roger Corman, took a chance on Milland's dark tale of a world wiped out by H-bombs.[54] A more dramatic yet equally modest production followed the next year with director Frank Perry's *Ladybug Ladybug*, a film brimming with understated emotional power, set at a public school in an unnamed small town during an atomic attack. Perry's wife, dramatist Eleanor Perry, wrote the screenplay, infusing it with authentic dialogue, delivered pitch-perfectly by exceptional young actors, all unknown at the time. The Perrys had collaborated on a critically acclaimed drama the previous year, *David and Lisa*, for which they both received Oscar nominations. In *Ladybug Ladybug*, the Perrys hone in on schoolchildren who become increasingly fearful as the prospect of nuclear war grows more real, especially when school staffers cannot contact the outside world. The children make their way to a bomb shelter, but one girl gets separated and locked out. Panicked, she flees through the countryside, arriving at a garbage dump with an abandoned refrigerator. She climbs in the old fridge, pulls the door shut, and it locks from the outside. A boy escapes the shelter to find her, but looks up at the sky and screams "Stop!" as an object roars overhead. It might be an ICBM, it might be a jet airplane—we can only see white condensation trail streaking across the sky. The fate of the children is left unknown as the film goes black.[55]

Strangelove and Beyond

Then came the revolutionary movie that upended everything. No other motion picture about nuclear war has ever come close to rivaling the impact of Stanley Kubrick's *Dr. Strangelove or: How I Learned to Stop Worrying and Love the Bomb*, released in the United States on January 29, 1964. The film remains *the* singular towering achievement of anti–Cold War culture. A cinematic leviathan known by its shortened name, *Dr. Strangelove* arrived in American theaters eight months before its chief rival, director Sidney Lumet's *Fail Safe*, opened in October. *Fail Safe* was a serious movie, a somber thriller starring Henry Fonda as an unnamed president who works against the clock to prevent American nuclear bombers, triggered by a fatal system error, from striking targets in the country.[56] Had there been no *Strangelove*, *Fail Safe* might have been a more singular achievement: the most terrifying motion picture about nuclear war yet made, even more wrenching than *On the Beach*. But Lumet's film premiered in the shadow of *Dr. Strangelove*, which had been a rare achievement—an *event* as much as a *film*. Even in its day, *Dr. Strangelove* came to be regarded as a work of art, ahead of its time, packed with the blackest humor ever found in any movie. *Dr. Strangelove* elevated the humor of American satire's golden age to uncharted planes, treating nuclear warfare as an irrational product of men's violent sexual drives.

Dr. Strangelove can be distilled to a one-sentence log line: Insane American general launches a B-52 nuclear attack against the USSR, and the president and his advisers must act fast to fix the perilous situation. Such a summary, however, fails to capture the film's dark absurdist humor, stark black-and-white cinematography, and richly rendered characters. Kubrick, a relative newcomer, had an idiosyncratic filmography. He directed the racetrack heist noir *The Killing* (1956), the World War I tragedy *Paths of Glory* (1957), the epic *Spartacus* (1960), and *Lolita* (1962), based on the controversial 1955 novel by Vladimir Nabokov. He based *Strangelove* on *Red Alert*, a 1958 novel by Welsh author and former Royal Air Force (RAF) navigator Peter George. Kubrick gave George cowriting credit, despite the author's minimal involvement. A detail-oriented perfectionist, Kubrick spent years researching nuclear weapons, reading roughly fifty books on the topic. He initially set out to write a serious movie but changed his mind. To revamp the script, Kubrick sought the help of writer Terry Southern, known for his absurdist humor. Kubrick opted to film the movie in Great Britain, to escape the control of his employer, Columbia Pictures. During shooting, Kubrick and Southern repeatedly changed the screenplay, working with editor Anthony Harvey to rearrange scenes using index cards tacked to a big corkboard.[57]

The film became legendary for its rogues' gallery of characters. General Jack D. Ripper (Sterling Hayden), cigar-chomping commander of Burpelson Air Force Base, orders a B-52 nuclear strike on the Soviet Union because he's outraged that the communists have "sapped" his "precious bodily fluids" with fluoride. George C. Scott immersed himself in the part of General Buck Turgidson, a he-man member of the Joint Chiefs of Staff, not at all troubled by the prospect of "10 to 20 million killed" in a preemptive nuclear attack. Soviet ambassador Alexei de Sadeski, portrayed by Peter Bull, joins the president to translate for Soviet premier Kissov on the hotline and reveals the existence of a Soviet "doomsday machine," a network of buried nuclear bombs around the world wired to a central computer, set to go off in the event of an attack. Western movie actor Slim Pickens tackled the role of Major T. J. "King" Kong, the Stetson-wearing B-52 commander, reminiscent of John Wayne, who guides his airplane to its primary target and rides a nuclear bomb down to earth, waving his hat and shouting, "Yahoo!" like a rodeo champion. And British actor and comedian Peter Sellers famously played three men in the film: RAF Group captain Lionel Mandrake, assigned to observe General

Ripper at the time of the attack; middle-of-the-roader President Merkin
Muffley, modeled after former Illinois governor, two-time Democratic presidential candidate and UN ambassador Adlai Stevenson; and the titular Dr.
Strangelove, a wheelchair-bound scientific adviser to the president, with an
arm that involuntarily shoots upward in a "Heil Hitler" salute. Strangelove
shares his disturbing theories about the prospects for human survival after
nuclear war with American officials in the fictional "War Room" and twice
refers to the president as "Mein Führer."[58]

Dr. Strangelove left no sacred cows standing. Ultimately, Kubrick's magnum
opus provided an antiauthoritarian framework for future cultural insurgents.
It is impossible to name another film that has done more to dismantle widely
held myths and unexamined assumptions about the Cold War. "*Dr. Strangelove*
helped to unravel the Cold War consensus—at a time when the dichotomy
between good and evil was losing its credibility," observed historian Stephen
J. Whitfield. The timing of the film's release was also crucial, as historian
Christian Appy notes: "On the cusp of major U.S. military escalation in
Vietnam, American filmgoers were already confronted with the possibility
that their nation might engage in unthinkable violence for no rational reason,
in which killing became an end in itself."[59]

By the 1970s, what can be properly be called an anti–Cold War culture
had seeped into the mainstream of American life. Its emergence owed much
to *Dr. Strangelove* and the many other cultural critiques that preceded it.
Reinforcing nonconformist sensibilities in popular culture were years of
turmoil, assassinations, social transformations, war in Southeast Asia, détente,
the Watergate scandal, and a divided population that had grown skeptical of
government authority. Cold War culture, which had been a staple of American
life between 1947 and the early 1960s, had reached a moribund state.

These cultural shifts went hand in hand with an altered political landscape.
Artifacts of the Red Scare, including loyalty oaths, congressional hearings
probing domestic subversion, and anticommunist Hollywood thrillers had all
been consigned to the past. Furthermore, the unraveling of the Communist
Party of the United States of America (CPUSA) made it harder for government officials in Washington to justify continued repression. Years of Smith
Act trials, internecine divisions, congressional hearings, FBI harassment,
revelations of Stalin's crimes, and recurring Soviet imperialism reduced the
Communist Party to a fragment of its old self. By the 1960s, the CPUSA was no
longer the dominant force on the Left. The youthful insurgents of the Vietnam
Era rejected Stalinism and embraced traditions of antiauthoritarianism that
dominated American radicalism before the CPUSA's halcyon years.[60]

On the opposite side of the spectrum, many high-profile anticommunist inquisitors from the fifties were either dead or disgraced by the 1970s or, in some cases, both. Wisconsin senator Joseph McCarthy, whose name epitomized the era, died in 1957 at age forty-eight, brought on by years of chronic alcoholism.[61] Whittaker Chambers died in 1961 at age 60; an ex-Communist and *Time* magazine writer and editor, Chambers gained fame for testifying in 1948 that State Department official Alger Hiss had been a communist. In 1962, Matt Cvetic, a Communist Party infiltrator working with the FBI and subject of the 1951 film *I Was a Communist for the FBI*, died at age 53, after struggles with alcoholism, depression, and electroshock therapy.[62] Representative J. Parnell Thomas, the New Jersey congressman and onetime chair of the House Un-American Activities Committee (HUAC), ended up in a federal penitentiary on fraud charges, dying in obscurity in 1970.[63] And the ultimate Red hunter—and, paradoxically, champion of détente—Richard Nixon, was holed up in his beachfront mansion in San Clemente, tarnished by Watergate, a self-pitying recluse.[64]

While the disgraced former president licked his wounds, the rest of the nation had moved on, leaving behind the excesses he helped create. Popular culture took a more defiant turn as well, with television leading the way. From 1965 to 1970, the sitcom *Get Smart*, starring Don Adams as hapless secret agent Maxwell Smart, poked fun at James Bond movies, *The Man from U.N.C.L.E.* TV series, and espionage films in general. The highly rated TV show *M*A*S*H* (CBS, 1972–83) was adapted from the 1970 Robert Altman hit film (which some critics at the time regarded as a Vietnam War movie disguised as a Korean War film). The show routinely mixed humor and drama to convey the horrors and absurdity of warfare and to attack Cold War assumptions. Likewise, the prime-time adult-themed Hanna-Barbera cartoon *Wait Till Your Father Gets Home* (syndicated from 1972 to 1974) lampooned militant anticommunism with its character Ralph, a John Birch Society–type vigilante who patrols the neighborhood with Sara, his elderly right-wing sidekick. Ralph's mission in each episode is to root out local "commies" and warn the main character, Harry Boyle, about sinister subversives lurking in their midst.[65]

Anti–Cold War themes flourished in cinema as well. Films such as David Miller's *Executive Action* (1973), Alan J. Pakula's *The Parallax View* (1974) and *All the President's Men* (1976), Sydney Pollack's *Three Days of the Condor* (1975), John Schlesinger's *The Marathon Man* (1976), and Francis Ford Coppola's *Apocalypse Now* (1979) recast high-level figures in government, corporations, and the military as malevolent characters involved with sinister conspiracies.[66]

Other films took aim at irrational fears of Russians. For example, James B. Harris's tense submarine drama *The Bedford Incident* (1965) portrays the obsessed captain of a U.S. destroyer (Richard Widmark) engaging in a deadly cat-and-mouse game with a Soviet submarine, even at the risk of starting World War III. On a lighter note, the following year's all-star comedy *The Russians Are Coming, the Russians Are Coming* (1966), directed by Canadian Norman Jewison, depicted a Soviet submarine running aground on a sandbar off a New England island, sparking pandemonium among locals who feared that a large-scale Soviet invasion was imminent.[67] Meanwhile, documentary films such as Emile de Antonio's *In the Year of the Pig* (1968) and Peter Davis's *Hearts and Minds* (1974) delivered harsh verdicts about the conduct and nature of the Vietnam War.[68] The latter film, in particular, an Oscar winner for best documentary in 1975, polarized audiences by explicitly linking the devastation of the Vietnam War to a domestic culture in the United States that emphasized the importance of success and victory at any cost.[69]

But popular culture's bluntest attack on the Cold War in the 1970s came in the form of blistering exposés about the excesses of the McCarthy-era Red Scare in America. A series of books helped nail the lid shut on the coffin of McCarthyism. Columbia Broadcasting System radio host and raconteur John Henry Faulk led the charge in 1964 with his memoir *Fear on Trial*, an account of his Kafkaesque blacklist experience. Faulk's ordeal was caused by private anticommunist agency called AWARE, Inc., a firm founded by the publishers of *Red Channels*, a 1950 witch-hunting booklet that listed names of suspected communists in movies, television, and radio. Faulk's compelling account of fighting back against the blacklist by launching a successful lawsuit against AWARE sold briskly on publication. Eleven years later, a 1975 made-for-TV movie, starring William Devane as Faulk and George C. Scott as his attorney, Louis Nizer, won an Emmy Award.[70]

Fear on Trial exposed the evils of the blacklist and helped pave the way for other similar accounts. In 1976, playwright Lillian Hellman wrote about her own McCarthy-era tribulations in *Scoundrel Time*. The memoir furnished Hellman with a platform to set her sights on the postwar American Red Scare, still fresh in her memory. "If I stick to what I know, what happened to me, and a few others, I have a chance to write my own history of the time," Hellman wrote in *Scoundrel Time*.[71] The book's most riveting moments come when Hellman describes her appearance before HUAC in 1952. Days before she testified, Hellman wrote a letter, which her attorney, Joseph Rauh, delivered to HUAC chairman John S. Wood. "I cannot and will not cut my conscience to fit this year's fashions," she wrote, setting the stage for her refusal to cooperate with HUAC.[72] *Scoundrel Time* conveyed the anxiety Hellman felt during this dark time, when her lover, crime novelist Dashiell Hammett, was broke, hounded by the Internal Revenue Service, and physically ill from his time in prison. She saved her sharpest attacks for the "scoundrels" of her book's title, which, surprisingly, were not Senator McCarthy or HUAC inquisitors but a coterie of anticommunist liberal intellectuals who failed, in her view, to support men and women whose civil liberties were being violated. "I am angrier now than I hope I will ever be again; more disturbed now than when it all took place," she wrote.[73] *Scoundrel Time* was met with almost universal praise among critics and remained on the *New York Times* best seller list for four months. "She was brave because her private code would not allow her to be anything else," noted a review in *Time* magazine.[74]

Cinema, like literature, helped repudiate the McCarthy-era Red Scare and vindicate witch-hunt survivors. The revival of *Salt of the Earth*, a 1954 strike drama with strong feminist themes, shot in New Mexico by blacklisted filmmakers, led to the film gaining a strong cult following on university campuses across the United States in the 1960s and 1970s. Made on a shoestring budget by three blacklistees—producer Paul Jarrico, director Herbert Biberman, and screenwriter Michael Wilson—*Salt of the Earth* told the story of striking New Mexico mine workers and the struggles faced by their supportive wives in making their voices heard during the conflict. The film was shot in documentary-like "neorealism," a technique in Italian movies of the period that emphasized gritty authenticity. Much of the cast consisted of newcomers.[75] Canisters of *Salt of the Earth* collected dust on shelves for years. But changing times led to the film's revival. Youthful audiences turned *Salt of the Earth* into a cult favorite. The movie resonated with a new generation of activists who could relate to its uncompromising verisimilitude, humanization of Latinos, and poignant feminist themes.[76]

While *Salt of the Earth* drew enthusiastic audiences on college campuses in the 1960s and 1970s, formerly blacklisted filmmakers and performers were starting to find employment again in the film industry. Director Martin Ritt and screenwriter Walter Bernstein, both veterans of the blacklist, collaborated on the 1976 comedy-drama *The Front*, about underachieving restaurant cashier Howard Prince (Woody Allen), who becomes a front "writer"—a person willing to put his name on scripts written by blacklisted writers—to help a childhood friend. Howard quickly rises in the world of television to become a renowned writer from putting his name on other people's scripts. The film's humor comes from Allen's character, Howard, pretending to be something he isn't. He fools TV network exec Phil Sussman (Herschel Bernardi) and script

editor Florence Barrett (Andrea Marcovicci) into believing he's a talented
newcomer with deep sensitivity. Howard begins writing for a *Playhouse 90–*
type anthology drama, befriending its host, comedian Hecky Brown (Zero
Mostel). He blossoms into an acclaimed TV writer and expands his "front"
scheme to include other blacklisted writers. After Hecky Brown is blacklisted
for taking part in left-wing causes in his youth, a zealous inquisitor coerces
him to spy on Howard and report back on the writer's activities. Hecky com-
plies but is tortured by having to inform on his friend. The blacklist eventually
drives Hecky to commit suicide, leaving Howard devastated.

After Hecky's death, HUAC subpoenas Howard. In a closed-door session, Howard is pressed by HUAC inquisitors to name the names. Howard
clowns around with the committee, dodging questions with goofy responses.
With HUAC perilously close to finding Howard in contempt, his attorney,
appointed by the network, urges him to name Hecky to appease the congressmen. At this pivotal moment, Howard begins to grasp the depravity of
HUAC, whose only goal is his complete submission. He rises to leave and, on
his way out, faces the committee. "Fellas," he says, "I don't recognize the right
of this committee to ask me these kind of questions. And furthermore, you
can all go fuck yourselves." In the next scene, a federal agent leads Howard in
handcuffs to the penitentiary, to the sounds of Frank Sinatra singing "Young
at Heart." Howard kisses his lover, Florence Barrett, who has quit the network
to become an antiblacklist activist; shakes hands with the blacklisted writers
he helped; and waves goodbye to a crowd of supportive pickets. *The Front's*
end credits poignantly reveal the dates when the director, screenwriter, and
several actors in the film were blacklisted.[77]

The Front inspired other films, including Larry Cohen's critical biopic *The
Private Files of J. Edgar Hoover* (1977); *Tail Gunner Joe* (1977), a made-for-TV
movie that showed Senator Joseph McCarthy (Peter Boyle) as a cunning
demagogue; and the documentary *Hollywood on Trial*, a scathing look at the
careers ruined by the film industry blacklist. *Hollywood on Trial* had a limited
run in theaters in the fall of 1976 and was widely shown on PBS stations the
next year. An Academy Award nomination for best documentary boosted
the film's visibility and cachet. "Who would ever have dreamed, a generation
ago," wrote art critic Hilton Kramer in the *New York Times* that fall, "that the
blacklist and the Hollywood Ten, the sordid proceedings of the House Un-
American Activities Committee and the political vagaries of Joe McCarthy,
would one day re-emerge as a form of cultural chic?"[78] A year after the release
of *Hollywood on Trial*, director Fred Zinnemann helmed the 1977 drama *Julia*,
a film adaptation of another one of Lillian Hellman's memoirs, *Pentimento*.

Jane Fonda played Hellman, and the film received eleven Academy Award nominations, including for best picture. It netted three of the gold statuettes: Vanessa Redgrave for her role as Julia, Jason Robards for his performance as Dashiell Hammett, and best adapted screenplay. More important, it helped bring two blacklisted writers, Hellman and Hammett (who died in 1961), back into the limelight with its sympathetic portrayals of them.[79]

Even as Oscar statuettes were being handed out at the Dorothy Chandler Pavilion in Los Angeles on April 3, 1978, to Robards, Redgrave, and screen-writer Alvin Sargent, the Cold War was returning to dominate American politics, as it had before the Vietnam War. Its resurgence was gradual, almost imperceptible. In the fall of 1976, with the nation healing from the excesses of McCarthyism, Democrat Jimmy Carter defeated his incumbent Republican rival, Gerald Ford, receiving 40.8 million votes to Ford's 39.2 million. Carter was a unique figure in American politics: a Washington outsider, a born-again Baptist southerner who opposed segregation, a former peanut farmer, the ex-governor of Georgia, and a political moderate who championed human rights in the international arena. Early in his presidency, Carter set what he hoped would be the tone for his foreign policy for the next four years. In an address at Notre Dame University on May 22, 1977, Carter boldly condemned what he called the "inordinate fear of communism, which once led us to embrace any dictator who joined us in that fear."[80] For the first time since World War II, an American president was placing top priority—at least in his rhetoric—on a human rights agenda in the realm of foreign policy. The prevailing mood in America nurtured Carter's ambitions on the global stage, but only temporarily.

The Cold War, contrary to what some observers thought at the time, was not dead. America's Cold Warriors were merely waiting in the wings for the opportune moment to reassert their influence in the nation's political affairs. Events around the globe in the late 1970s, beyond Washington's control, would align to deteriorate superpower relations and give new life to the specter of anticommunism. The Cold War would, in time, return to form the basis of the nation's foreign policies. The changes wrought by the eventful Sixties, however, assured that a domestic Red Scare was not in the cards. A different kind Cold War culture lay in store for America—one that would see a newer, freer, more open arena of debate, characterized by widely diverging points of view and strong currents of dissent. In short, a Cold War culture more suited to a healthy democracy.

CHAPTER 2

Nostalgia Wars

> Remembrance of things past is not necessarily the remembrance of things as they were.
>
> —*Marcel Proust*, In Search of Lost Time, *1913*

Nostalgia Tripping 101

Cold War culture in the Reagan era was strikingly different from the Cold War culture that preceded it. The culture of the Second Cold War took shape and gained traction at a time of transition, in the aftermath of the civil rights movement, the counterculture, years of mass protest on multiple fronts, the Watergate scandal, and defeat in Vietnam. The more open atmosphere of the 1980s meant another domestic Red Scare was out of the question. McCarthyism was, for the most part, dead. Yet Cold War sensibilities—particularly the interwoven beliefs of anticommunism and American exceptionalism—continued to exert influence in American society.

Still, changing times demanded new approaches. In the arena of popular culture, nostalgia—at times entwined with a Cold War subtext—found striking vitality in the Reagan era. Nostalgia was nothing new, having existed, in one form or another, for generations. But the type of mass nostalgia consumed in large quantities by Americans in the 1980s was a relatively new variant. Specifically, nostalgia aimed at revisiting, reimagining, and re-creating the Long Fifties, the years from roughly 1947 to 1963, paralleled efforts to restore the shattered Cold War consensus in the Reagan era. Those who championed a return to fifties "values" understood the enduring power of artifacts, symbols, and styles from that bygone period. Reviving "a world we've lost," as well as and the national unity, real or imagined, that went with it, was thought by some to be an essential part of gluing together a shattered sense of shared purpose. Nostalgic longings for the fifties offered, in the minds of enthusiasts, a window into another world that might offer clues about how people in contemporary America could live more virtuous lives. Nostalgia furnished an idealized, gauzy view of an imagined past, but those aching for a return to the 1950s had to contend with the sea changes of the 1960s and 1970s that formed a vast gulf separating the Reagan era from the age of Eisenhower.

Moreover, not everybody wanted to return to the fifties—a time before the civil rights revolution, feminism, and the profound cultural transformations that altered American society. Hence, conflicting versions of the recent past came into conflict in the collective imagination of Americans. Competing forms of nostalgia revealed fissures in public memory, that is, how people remembered or idealized the past. And these fault lines ran parallel in striking ways to the evolution of Cold War culture in the 1980s.

Burying the Sixties, Restoring the Fifties

A group of seven people who knew each other years earlier at the University of Michigan are reunited at the funeral of their friend Alex, who had died by suicide. The friends, all former campus radicals from the 1960s, have since then shunned politics and become prosperous. It is now the early 1980s, although they still listen to music of the 1960s (Marvin Gaye, the Rolling Stones, the Temptations), drink wine, and smoke dope like hippies; a few even have affairs during their brief time together. But all of them—without exception—dismiss the activism of the sixties as a meaningless, juvenile infatuation with righting society's wrongs. Though nostalgic for elements of the bygone era, especially the music, they are now more taken with making money, self-actualization, and embracing things the way they are, instead of fruitlessly resisting injustice, which now seems passé. After all, as the old saying goes: If you can't beat 'em, join 'em. By the end of the movie, having spent a long weekend together getting to know one another again, the friends go their separate ways to make more money, pursue their own gratification, and avoid the lessons of the past.[1]

Such was the plotline of Lawrence Kasdan's comedy-drama *The Big Chill*, which opened in movie theaters in September 1983 to critical and commercial success. *The Big Chill* delighted audiences and won over even the harshest critics. Pauline Kael, known for her caustic movie reviews in the *New Yorker*, called the film an "amiable, slick comedy with some very well-directed repartee and skillful performances" but noted that "it isn't really political."[2] Geoffrey Himes, film critic for the *Baltimore Sun*, lauded the film for its "wit," predicting it was "destined to be the big hit of the fall." Yet he also observed: "*The Big Chill* never asks tough questions about the generation of Sixties students."[3]

A number of film critics, including Himes, noted the similarities between *The Big Chill* and a movie made three years earlier, *Return of the Secaucus 7* (1980), directed by John Sayles. Like *The Big Chill*, Sayles's *Secaucus 7* focuses on a weekend reunion—this one in New Hampshire—involving men and women linked together by friendship and a shared commitment to radicalism. In Sayles's movie, a decade before the reunion, police had arrested the seven antiwar militants in Secaucus, New Jersey, while they were on their way to a protest in Washington, D.C. Now in their late twenties and early thirties, the friends gather to reminisce, sing songs, get closer, and figure out how to stay true to their principles, despite the changing times. Lawrence Kasdan saw *Return of the Secaucus 7* and "loved it" but also felt relieved that it was "very different" from the movie he wanted to make.[4] Sayles's film, like Kasdan's, received instant acclaim. It also attained cult status, enjoying frequent showings in art house theaters around America. Even though *Return of the Secaucus 7* and *The Big Chill* contained essentially the same story line, one key difference was that Sayles's characters discussed their efforts to stay true to their political beliefs, which cannot be said of the former radicals in *The Big Chill*. The striking contrast stemmed from the filmmakers' politics: Sayles was a radical, Kasdan was not. Sayles's film managed to transcend its meager budget of sixty thousand dollars and became a celebrated indie classic.[5] However, when *The Big Chill* opened in 1983, it overshadowed *Return of the Secaucus 7* owing to its enormous popularity and far wider distribution. "No other recent film has been so widely and instantaneously incorporated into the pop cultural mainstream," wrote Janet Maslin in the *New York Times* in 1985.[6]

Given the film's success, a popular stereotype gained traction that viewed sixties radicals as evolving into eighties yuppies, ditching youthful dalliances with radicalism in favor of apolitical materialism. In fact, *The Big Chill* spawned a myth, widely circulated in the Reagan era, that activists from the 1960s and early 1970s had "sold out"—in other words, they abandoned, en masse, their quest for social justice in exchange for wealth and success.[7] Not a single character in *The Big Chill*, in contrast with *Return of the Secaucus 7*, displays a hint of idealism or voices even a slight fondness for the protests they allegedly took part in less than twenty years earlier. Michael Gold (played by

Jeff Goldblum) spoke for all the film's characters when he states: "Everyone does everything just to get laid."[8]

Ironically, some veterans of sixties protest movements helped reinforce *The Big Chill* myth. Most notably, Jerry Rubin, the theatrical Youth International Party (Yippie) radical and partner in crime and publicity with Abbie Hoffman in the 1960s, had by 1980 shorn his curly locks, put away his hippie duds, donned business suits, and transformed into successful, smoothie-drinking, yoga-practicing businessman. His conversion made nationwide headlines. "Jerry Rubin Goes Wall Street, But Still Can't Tie a Tie," proclaimed the front page of the *Baltimore Sun* in 1980. Side-by-side photos of the scruffy Rubin and the clean-cut Rubin in a 1981 *Los Angeles Times* cover story ran with a banner headline: "Another Incarnation: The Transformation of Jerry Rubin." "Jerry Rubin's New Business Is Business," cried a 1983 Bob Greene column in the *Chicago Tribune*. "From Yippie to Yuppie to Daddy," announced a full-page *San Francisco Examiner* profile.[9] Rubin voiced his new philosophy, which eclipsed everything he said in the 1960s: "In America, you've got to follow the dollar, right? And . . . I've always been a sort of mainstream person."[10]

Meantime, Rubin's comrade, Abbie Hoffman, who had gone underground in the early 1970s to avoid legal entanglements, resurfaced in 1980, bearded, thinner, with shorter hair, yet still radical. His return to the spotlight made him a temporary media sensation. He served four months of a one-year sentence in prison and, when he got out, returned to activism. By 1984, Hoffman was taking part in a series of so-called "Yippie vs. Yuppie" debates with Rubin. The traveling "Abbie and Jerry Show," as it was called, was actually a way of making money for the two icons, taking them from city to city across North America. The debates opened at the Stone, a San Francisco nightclub, to a sold-out house.[11] The duo participated in sixty debates over the course of eighteen months. At five thousand dollars per appearance, Hoffman—who was struggling financially—could not afford to say no. But he had misgivings about the whole affair. From his perspective, Jerry Rubin's transformation to Wall Street investor was yet another upsetting reminder of how much America had changed since the 1960s. Still, Abbie tried his best to stay funny. In a move reminiscent of his Yippie days, he made a "Yuppie cocktail" onstage by dropping a Rolex in a blender, adding Perrier, and switching it on. Sure enough, Abbie destroyed the watch, prompting cheers and laughter in the theater. Yet in his debates with Rubin, Hoffman was inadvertently perpetuating *The Big Chill* myth by spending more time insulting his former comrade than promoting radical politics or enlightening audiences about the legacies of sixties protests. "He lost those debates," recalled singer and author Kinky Friedman, Hoffman's close friend. "The audience was cheering for Abbie and they laughed at Abbie and championed him, but they went out and did what Jerry Rubin said."[12]

Sociologist Todd Gitlin, another prominent activist of the 1960s, lent credibility to *The Big Chill* myth, albeit differently from Rubin. Gitlin had been active in Students for a Democratic Society (SDS) throughout the 1960s and went on to become a respected academic. His 1987 book, *The Sixties: Years of Hope, Days of Rage*, a participant-observer history, appeared to glowing reviews, hailed as a pioneering account of the era. Gitlin's kaleidoscopic journey through the turbulent era sheds light on the New Left, the counterculture, and the traumas of the times. However, in his version of events, the period's protest movements were more or less dead by decade's end, done in by excessive militancy, internecine factionalism, and a lack of public support. "The youth culture which had swooped into antiwar action by 1965 found more placid and private ways to strut its generational stuff," Gitlin wrote. By 1970, he claimed, the "riptide of Revolution" went "out with the same force it surged in with."[13] That may have been Gitlin's personal experience, but a number of men and women involved in protest movements stayed active beyond 1970. Later histories of the era—written after Gitlin's book—discovered that mass resistance spilled far into the 1970s. Several movements, in fact, actually flowered more in those years than in the 1960s and contributed to longer arcs of protest, some of which remained robust in the 1980s.[14]

Nevertheless, Gitlin's account—the highest-selling nonfiction book on the 1960s published in the 1980s—gave readers the impression that dissent had faded away long before the 1980s and that the Reagan era was largely free of those divisions. Gitlin was not the only figure on the left to promote this defeatist view. In 1989, a Marxist intellectual bleakly described the Eighties as "the decade when those radicalized in the 1960s and 1970s began to enter middle age. Usually they did so with all the hope of socialist revolution gone—indeed, often having ceased to believe in the desirability of such a revolution."[15]

Reinforcing the Marxist's grim assessment were frequent stories in the press about ex-radicals moving on to greener pastures as they aged. Jerry Rubin was not alone in that regard. Rennie Davis, a militant antiwar leader and defendant in the famous Chicago 8 trial of 1969, later embraced the teachings of Hans Ji Maharaj, an Indian guru with a cult-like following, and by the 1980s he ran a successful management consulting firm in Denver that offered

financial advice to investors. "I'm trying to understand the nature of the econ-
omy and how business works," Davis explained in 1982.[16] In the early 1980s,
Black Panther leader Eldridge Cleaver, whose seminal 1968 memoir *Soul
on Ice* became a dog-eared bible of young radicals, converted to born-again
Christianity, flirted briefly with the Reverend Sun Myung Moon's Unification
Church, and finally made the leap to the Church of Jesus Christ of Latter-day
Saints. He joined the Republican Party, championed conservative values, and
spoke at right-wing events for the rest of his life. "I've made a turnaround,"
he said in 1981. "I don't mind jettisoning a wrong idea. I'm a proud American
now."[17] Like Cleaver, David Horowitz and Peter Collier, two white, former
New Left journalists who backed the Black Panthers, embraced right-wing
politics in the late 1970s. They renounced their old beliefs, voted for Reagan
in 1984, and devoted their careers to vilifying their former comrades and the
Left in general.[18] "Everybody has grown up now," said LSD guru Timothy
Leary in 1981. Once an icon of the counterculture, Leary dismissed recent
protests as "pathetic." "I'm not an extremist. I believe in law and order, police
protection and military defense," he said.[19]

Not everyone radicalized in the 1960s abandoned ship. On the contrary,
a handful of scholarly studies appearing in the late 1980s about the fate of
sixties activism—which served as correctives against prevailing stereotypes—
revealed that most dedicated activists from twenty years earlier had found
ways of staying true to their beliefs in the Reagan era.[20] Moreover, protests
remained a constant fixture of American society. The largest demonstration
in American history, as we will soon see, occurred not in the 1960s but on
June 12, 1982, when a million people gathered in Central Park to protest the
nuclear arms race.[21]

But something had undeniably changed. An opinion prevailed in the
early 1980s that the tumult of the late 1960s and early 1970s had passed into
history, that a page had been turned. Some celebrated its ebbing, while others
mourned the loss. Wherever one stood on the matter, obituaries for sixties
activism became a mainstay early in the Reagan era. "As a movement, the
radical movement of the Sixties is dead," declared neoconservative intellectual
Norman Podhoretz in 1981. "The Sixties are dead and buried, and the eighties
are going to be different," echoed Jeffrey Hart, a right-wing cultural critic
and professor of English at Dartmouth. In 1980, Johns Hopkins University
chaplain and former civil rights and peace activist Dr. Chester Wickwire
looked around and grieved over what he perceived to be the end of an era.
"Where did everybody go?" he asked. "The romanticism of the Sixties is

gone. The pendulum has swung."[22] Or, as Alex P. Keaton (Michael J. Fox), the wisecracking, Nixon-worshipping, Brooks Brothers suit–wearing conservative son of former hippies tells his father, Steven (Michael E. Gross), on the hit eighties sitcom *Family Ties*: "The Sixties are over, dad."[23]

At first glance, *The Big Chill* myth may appear unrelated to Cold War culture. After all, what does a reunion of cynical thirtysomethings who'd once marched against the Vietnam War have to do with souring superpower relations? On closer inspection, however, the film's trope of the ex–sixties activist who had sold out fit neatly into a larger project: rebuilding the Cold War consensus broken apart by the turmoil of the Vietnam era. The extreme societal ruptures of the sixties arose in response to the Cold War turning into a "hot" shooting war in Southeast Asia, one that millions of Americans—including many who fought in it—believed to be immoral and unjustified. An endless succession of antiwar demonstrations and other acts of dissent, the very movement that the *Big Chill* characters claimed to be a part of, brought into question not only the Vietnam War's legitimacy but also American exceptionalism itself.[24]

By the 1980s, a number of influential figures in politics and media sought to navigate the nation away from those divisions, to a calmer place. Their pursuit of domestic tranquility, in many instances, ignored the lessons of the recent past, especially the Vietnam War. These efforts also coincided with President Reagan stepping up his anti-Soviet rhetoric, sharply escalating the nuclear arms race, and formulating an aggressive anticommunist foreign policy. His goals enjoyed strong support in Congress.[25] Therefore, attempts to restore the lost consensus, in part by exorcising the demons of the recent past, harmonized with the Cold War's revival. The close proximity of the early 1980s to the late 1960s—it is worth remembering that *The Big Chill* opened in theaters fifteen years after one of the most explosive years in American history, 1968—meant the United States still teetered perilously close to the rifts that had rocked the nation to its core a short time earlier. Hence, laughing off the commitment of former activists as shallow and insincere, which many moviegoers did in the fall of 1983 when they saw *The Big Chill*, fulfilled the dual purpose of delegitimizing past resistance and isolating present stirrings of dissent.

The quest for societal harmony occurred on multiple fronts in the Reagan era. A first cousin of *The Big Chill* myth that found remarkable traction at the same time was a potent wave of nostalgia for the fifties. Nostalgia was by no means new to American life in the 1980s, nor was there anything uniquely

American about a wistful yearning to return to an imagined golden age. The word "nostalgia" dates back to seventeenth-century Europe and was then used in the medical community to describe extreme homesickness.[26] However, the size and scope of nostalgia, as well as its move from the periphery to the core of American popular culture in the 1980s, was a recent development that owed much to the social fissures, scandal, and loss of prestige abroad in the years leading up to the Reagan era.

"Nostalgia has become an industry," said Bob Garfield, advertising critic for *Advertising Age*, the industry's largest trade magazine.[27] The so-called baby boom demographic—numbering tens of millions—undergirded the modern nostalgia explosion. "The size of the market is big enough to capitalize on it [nostalgia] as a business," said Michael D. Drexler, executive vice president of the Bozell advertising agency, in 1989. Moreover, the changing nature of nostalgia, and the means by which it reached a mass audience, made it more influential and accessible than at any other time in American history. Fred Davis, a sociologist at the University of California at San Diego in the 1980s, differentiated the "new" nostalgia from the old: "Where nostalgia once would have focused on specific places—homes and so forth—the objects of nostalgia are increasingly celebrities of the past, music, films, et cetera. This makes it easier for the media to capitalize on it, because the material is in their archives. Nostalgia today is of the media, by the media and for the media."[28]

The fifties nostalgia wave began years before Reagan's presidency. As early as 1972, with the opening of the Broadway hit musical *Grease* and the publication of fifties-themed cover stories in *Life* and *Newsweek*, celebrations of the Eisenhower era were under way. Ground zero for this national nostalgia trip was George Lucas's *American Graffiti*, a blockbuster released in 1973, set in 1962, about a memorable night in the lives of four young men in Modesto, California, before adulthood's travails snatched them away from youth's innocence. The film glorifies California's youthful custom car culture and was among the first to include a rock 'n' roll soundtrack, with hits by Buddy Holly, Chuck Berry, and the Beach Boys playing in the background. While it does not take place in the actual 1950s—meaning the decade spanning the years 1950 to 1959—*American Graffiti* falls well within the mythic Long Fifties, which lasted from the late 1940s until the Kennedy assassination in November 1963. A sleeper hit, *American Graffiti* inspired similar films, some on a par, others markedly inferior: *Grease* (1978), *The Wanderers* (1979), *The Hollywood Knights* (1980), *Porky's* (1981), *The Flamingo Kid* (1984), *Stand by Me* (1986), and its seventies-infused counterpart, *Dazed and Confused* (1993).[29]

American Graffiti, more than any other pop culture contribution, set off the fifties nostalgia wave. The following year, ABC debuted *Happy Days*, a sitcom set in Milwaukee, Wisconsin, in the mid-1950s. It starred *American Graffiti* alumnus Ron Howard as clean-cut high schooler Richie Cunningham and Henry Winkler as the lovable, thumbs-up, "aaay"-saying greaser Arthur "the Fonz"/"Fonzie" Fonzarelli. *Happy Days* was actually a spin-off of a 1972 episode of *Love, American Style*, an anthology comedy program that featured multiple humorous segments each week. But *Happy Days*, which stayed on television until 1984, owed its high ratings to the success of *American Graffiti*. In fact, some newspapers in 1974 mistakenly identified *Happy Days* as a spin-off of *American Graffiti*.[30]

Nostalgia for the fifties, of the sort found in *American Graffiti* and *Happy Days*, resonated widely during the Reagan years. Media studies scholar Michael D. Dwyer has observed that "both the scale and scope of the Fifties 'nostalgia wave' . . . compel us to pay particular attention to Fifties nostalgia in the 1970s and 1980s. . . . [T]he Fifties was not only important in American popular culture but central to American self-understanding in the Reagan era."[31] One could not escape the fifties wave in the 1980s. Its omnipresence was manifested in a variety of forms. Fifties-style diners abounded from coast to coast, many with checkerboard linoleum floors, counter stools, replica tin Coca-Cola signs, framed pictures of Marilyn Monroe and James Dean, Cherry Cokes on the menu, and booths with Formica tables and sometimes even mini-jukeboxes.[32]

On the nation's airwaves, oldies stations proliferated on the AM and FM dials. The word "oldies" dated back to the nineteenth century to describe a familiar song or book that had been in circulation for a while. In the 1980s, people used "oldies" to describe rock 'n' roll music recorded up to about 1966. The American public loved oldies, and it was not unusual for big cities to have two or three stations in that format. A motorist fiddling with the radio dial in the early eighties was as likely to hear "Cathy's Clown" by the Everly Brothers or Martha and the Vandellas singing "Heat Wave" as any contemporary song. "Several studies have indicated a very high listener preference for oldies. They're seeking that sense of the good old days, which they weren't really, but the music was," explained Alex DeMers, station manager of Philadelphia's oldies station, WIOQ, in 1982.[33]

On television, staples from the 1950s, such as *I Love Lucy*, *Father Knows Best*, and *Adventures of Superman*, further fueled the nostalgia craze. Of all that period's shows, *Leave It to Beaver*, a beloved sitcom about the Cleaver family and the Tom Sawyer–esque adventures of its youngest member, the titular Theodore "Beaver" Cleaver (Jerry Mathers), enjoyed the widest syndication in the Reagan era. "Within the last three, four years it's snowballed like crazy," Mathers said in 1982.[34] During the 1980s, Mathers was a popular speaker across the country, earning four thousand dollars per public talk, and there were over a hundred Beaver Cleaver Fan Clubs nationwide.[35] *Still the Beaver*, an updated sequel with many of the same characters, aired on the Disney Channel, a popular new cable station, in 1983, staying on TV as long as the original. "What we're seeing now in the 1980s is a movement back to the family. *Leave It to Beaver* is the ideal portrayal of the family," explained University of California, Los Angeles, psychology professor Dr. Jeffrey C. Alexander in 1982.[36]

Alongside such recycled pop culture artifacts as *Leave It to Beaver*, audiences in the 1980s consumed reimagined and re-created versions of earlier eras. In certain respects, the popularity of New Wave synth-pop music in the Reagan era, featured so prominently on Music Television (MTV) after its launch on August 1, 1981, represented a desire to return to shorter, catchier pop songs after years of the long, self-indulgent, and complex rock anthems of the 1970s. Some contemporary hits, most notably the music of the Stray Cats, popular in the early 1980s, purposely sought to update 1950s rockabilly for a new generation. Similar sounds could be heard elsewhere on America's airwaves. "Crazy Little Thing Called Love," Queen's Billboard Hot 100 number one hit from 1980, was Freddie Mercury's tribute to Elvis Presley, echoing the King's Sun Records days. Similarly, Billy Joel's 1983 LP *An Innocent Man*—one of his biggest-selling albums—paid homage to soul and doo-wop hits from previous decades with such songs as "Uptown Girl," "The Longest Time," "Tell Her about It," and the title track.

Visual imagery of the fifties also abounded in music videos. The 1982 music video for Donald Fagen's "New Frontier," an ebullient tune about backyard fallout shelters, 1950s fashions, and Cold War anxieties, combined midcentury modern animation with authentic re-creations of the Eisenhower years to tell its story. Madonna's iconic 1985 "Material Girl" music video—on constant MTV rotation—channeled Marilyn Monroe performing "Diamonds Are a Girl's Best Friend" in *Gentlemen Prefer Blondes* (1953). A March 1986 *Esquire* cover showcased a striking Marilyn Monroe close-up and smaller inset photos of Madonna, Jackie Gleason, and Ronald Reagan. It posed the questions, "Why is Madonna pretending she's Marilyn? Why is Ralph Kramden bigger than ever? Why is Ronald Reagan still our matinee idol?" Inside the issue of

Esquire, television critic Tom Shales described the 1980s in his cover story as a decade of "replay, recycle, retrieve, reprocess and rerun."[37]

"Replay, recycle, retrieve, reprocess and rerun" could have been the tagline of *Back to the Future*, the ultimate cinematic romp down memory lane of the 1950s and the highest-grossing film of 1985. In the decades that followed its release, Robert Zemeckis's runaway smash hit earned a reputation as one of the most emblematic movies of its time. The science fiction comedy has Marty McFly's (Michael J. Fox, star of *Family Ties*) traveling back in time thirty years, to 1955, to visit a dramatically different version of his hometown, Hill Valley, California. Aided by eccentric, wild-eyed scientist Dr. Emmett ("Doc") Brown, Marty encounters younger versions of his parents, George (Crispin Glover) and Lorraine (Lea Thompson) and faces the dual challenge of making sure he does not alter history during his trip back in time and figuring out a way to return to 1985.[38] *Back to the Future* has been heavily analyzed in accounts of the Reagan era. For example, journalist and leftist political pundit David Sirota offered the following breathless verdict:

> Robert Zemeckis's film, which ended up grossing more than a quarter billion dollars, features a typically spoiled and cynical suburban teenager escaping America's most hysterical fears (e.g., corrupted youth, family dysfunction, wild-eyed, bazooka-wielding Libyans, etc.) by fleeing to an idyllic 1950s—a time when (supposedly) the kids were all clean-cut, innocent, and optimistic; every home sported a white-picket fence and fluttering American flag; and the only major threats to tranquility were Peeping Toms like George McFly, leather-jacket hoodlums like Biff Tannen, and slacker-loathing high-school principals like Mr. Strickland. Marty flees, in other words, the sixties-soiled present that Alex P. Keaton instructed us to despise and escapes into a 1950s Americana we were being taught to see as one big *Saturday Evening Post* illustration.[39]

Back to the Future represented the apotheosis of fifties nostalgia in the 1980s. It generated two sequels and inspired imitators. The following year's *Peggy Sue Got Married* (1986), directed by Francis Ford Coppola, also featured a character, Peggy Sue Bodell (Kathleen Turner), who goes back in time. Middle-aged and caught in an unhappy marriage in 1985, Bodell awakens to find herself young again in the year 1960. She is given a chance to live her life differently, yet she ends up making many of the same choices she made the first time around. While not as successful as *Back to the Future*, *Peggy Sue Got Married* was Coppola's highest grossing film in the 1980s and enjoyed impressive commercial success.[40]

Flower Power Yearnings: Exhuming the Sixties

At the heart of *Back to the Future* and *Peggy Sue Got Married* was a longing to return to what was thought to be a simpler time. But yearnings to return to the 1950s were not universal. Nostalgia has never been monolithic. A steady diet of only one era did not satisfy American consumers in the 1980s. Before long, competing affections for different moments in the nation's mythic pasts began bumping into one another. The passage of time in the 1980s proved especially kind to the sixties's nostalgia, which experienced a heyday in the popular imagination during the second half of the 1980s. A key example was ABC's successful coming-of-age comedy *The Wonder Years* (1988–93), which presented the late 1960s and early 1970s through a nostalgic lens without concealing the era's traumas. If anything, the show successfully worked social turmoil into several story lines.

Similarly, the "classic rock" radio format, with its heavy doses of post-1965 rock music, including the Beatles, the Rolling Stones, the Doors, Jimi Hendrix, Led Zeppelin, and Santana, to name a few, thrived on the airwaves. "Although the sense of a close connection between 1960s rock and the political and social tumult of the era may have dwindled as the music was recycled into 'classic rock' formats," scholar Daniel Marcus writes, "the residual associations between the music, the counterculture and the 1960s youth politics could still be enjoyed by those who wished to see the sixties as a positive resource for contemporary society."[41] In a closely related example, the cult TV show *The Monkees* returned with a vengeance in February 1986 for a popular twenty-two-hour marathon on MTV. Young viewers—many born during and after the show's two-season run—fell in love with the band's psychedelic and absurdist adventures. That summer, three of the band's members, Davy Jones, Micky Dolenz, and Peter Tork, launched a tour marking their twentieth anniversary as a group (Mike Nesmith, a successful producer by this time, sat out). They played to cheering fans in sold-out venues across North America.[42]

Nowhere was the flower power resurgence of the 1980s more evident than in the spectacular following enjoyed by the legendary Bay Area rock band the Grateful Dead. Armies of so-called Deadheads followed the band from one venue to the next with unwavering loyalty. Many of the band's fans traveled in communal settings, bringing ample supplies of pot, homemade food, and even pets with them on the road. "We feel like we're part of a family," said Deadhead Sara Hudson of Amarillo, Texas, who shadowed the band in 1981. "It's a like a magical party on a huge scale, and the Dead bring the music," an affluent St. Louis attorney remarked in 1986, in the midst of his Deadhead pilgrimage. Grateful Dead chronicler Peter Richardson described the robust community of Deadheads in the Reagan era: "By the early 1980s, Deadheads dominated the Dead's media coverage. Despite its gypsy image, the Deadhead community always included a professional . . . element; the Dead's record company estimated that three-quarters of their audience was college educated, and the band regularly received glowing reviews in elite campus newspapers. Indeed, some Deadheads—including a U.S. vice president and two senators—became downright respectable."[43]

Another account noted that by the "mid-1980s," the Grateful Dead had established a multimillion-dollar "merchandizing empire" that enriched the band's members and promoters alike.[44] In 1987, the Grateful Dead achieved a feat they were never able to pull off in the 1960s and 1970s: a Top 10 hit on the Billboard Hot 100 with "Touch of Grey," a song cowritten by Dead guitarist and vocalist Jerry Garcia and lyricist Robert Hunter. The video, showing the band jamming on stage in the form of marionette skeletons, played often on MTV. The Grateful Dead became a media sensation, and the mobile Haight-Ashbury of Deadheads that kept pace with them captured the nation's attention and stirred imaginations. "By the mid-1980s," writes historian Dennis McNally, "the Deadheads of the late sixties . . . were now in positions of some authority, either in print or television media. They had fond memories of the band, and were quite pleased to offer positive coverage."[45]

The great hippie comeback of the mid- to late 1980s mainly involved young people in their teens and twenties embracing countercultural elements such as classic rock, period fashions (especially tie-dyed shirts and longer hair on men), and drug use, especially pot smoking. It did not necessarily herald a second coming of mass militancy, but it did furnish an alternative to the celebration of all things fifties. It also nurtured an environment of historical inquiry. In 1987, the Public Broadcasting Service aired the successful *Eyes on the Prize* documentary, bringing harrowing footage of the civil rights movement into American living rooms for the first time in years, along with interviews of surviving participants.[46] Other films and books on the civil rights movement, as well as protests of the 1960s in general, followed in the wake of the success of *Eyes on the Prize*. The next year marked the twentieth anniversary of 1968. A series of retrospectives around the country recalled the history of the chaotic year. Assassinations, riots, street clashes between police and protesters, an escalation of the Vietnam War after the bloody Tet

Offensive: all contributed to a loss of faith in institutions and leaders. And that was *just* in the United States. The revolutions of 1968 were global in scope and shook the foundations of modern civilization.

The restoration of order prompted soul searching among some men and women caught in the vortex. One of the veterans of the turbulence, Tom Hayden, founder of Students for a Democratic Society, was still in the media spotlight twenty years later, when the public was ready to reflect on the events of 1968. Once a revolutionary fighting in the streets, Hayden had become a respected figure in Democratic Party and member of the California State Assembly. His new autobiography, *Reunion: A Memoir*, arrived in bookstores in the summer of 1988, and he crisscrossed the country to promote it. Hayden pulled no punches in criticizing his own youthful infatuation with militant resistance while expressing overall pride in the changes wrought by the protests. The outspokenly liberal Hayden of 1988 felt like he was no longer an outsider in the United States, describing himself as "a born-again Middle American, emotionally charged by my re-acceptance in the political mainstream."[47]

Hayden's generation of activists had moved into positions of power and influence in the 1980s, and the more steadfast among them contributed in their own ways to fashioning a counternarrative that promoted more positive impressions of the sixties. The timing was ideal for such revisions. It was not mere happenstance that sixties-themed nostalgia flourished from roughly 1985 onward. Political trends had shifted since the early 1980s, when Reagan seemed invincible, and the rising conservative tide was being felt most acutely. New developments had come into play by mid-decade. President Reagan had begun his dramatic turn toward détente in his pursuit of arms control with Soviet president Mikhail Gorbachev. On the home front, the administration and its backers in Congress had not succeeded in creating a consensus around the arms race and its Central America policies. Dissent, both in the cultural realm and in the form of grassroots resistance—a focus of upcoming chapters in this book—undermined conservative hopes for restoring a new Cold War consensus.

More than any other development, the Iran-Contra scandal cast the darkest shadow over the Reagan administration and undermined the president's popularity. The secretive White House arms deal with Iran included the transfer of missiles to the Islamic Republic, by now a bitter enemy of the United States. Or so it seemed. The story broke in the fall of 1986, revealing that profits from arms sales to Iran were being diverted to fund the Nicaraguan Contras. The White House scheme had been devised to circumvent a congressional amendment banning military aid to the controversial anticommunist rebels waging war in rural Nicaragua against the Sandinista government.[48] In March 1987, Reagan admitted publicly that the scandal occurred: "A few months ago, I told the American people I did not trade arms for hostages. My heart and my best intentions still tell me that's true, but the facts and evidence tell me it is not." The three-member Tower Commission, appointed by Reagan to investigate the affair, cleared him of any wrongdoing. But the president's luster had undeniably faded as a result of the scandal.[49]

The nation's nostalgia trip outlasted the furor caused by the Iran-Contra scandal, but it began to lose its vitality and hold over the nation. Significantly, this reconstituted fifties omitted the more obvious vestiges of the Cold War, in all of its weighty manifestations, especially its recurring threats to civil liberties (in the form of the House Un-American Activities Committee [HUAC], loyalty oaths, blacklists, etc.) and human existence itself. These omissions were not accidental. The threat of atomic war with the Soviet Union that constantly loomed over the United States in the 1950s was hardly the stuff of nostalgia. Not surprisingly, few people in the 1980s wished to revisit the days of atmospheric atom bomb tests or preachy Red Scare movies like *My Son John*, which weren't terribly popular in the 1950s, or purges of dissenters from public life. These darker elements of the Cold War culture's nadir failed to withstand the test of time in the public's selective memory. In the case of the romanticized fifties, the yearning to return to a simpler time offered Americans a series of comforting images to help them adapt to the conservative shift in politics and an uncertain future under a new president committed to Cold War policies and hypermilitarization. Icons of fifties nostalgia—Cape Cod houses surrounded by picket fences, black-and-white family-themed sitcoms with canned laughter soundtracks, rock 'n' roll oldies, and updated versions of clothes and junk food from the era—ignored an actual history fraught with complexities, contradictions, and rebellious undercurrents.

But the demise of McCarthyism was by no means a foregone conclusion in the early 1980s. In the wake of Reagan's electoral triumph, some nervous observers raised concerns about the possibility of a revived Red Scare. Their fears were not unfounded. After all, Reagan had been a dedicated anticommunist since the late 1940s. He had also appeared before HUAC in 1947 as a friendly witness, although his testimony had been more moderate than other cooperative anticommunist Hollywood luminaries, such as director Sam Wood or mogul Jack Warner. Reagan, for instance, told HUAC he opposed making the Communist Party illegal in the United States, stating his belief that communists—only a "small clique" in the film industry, in his words—had no influence over the content of Hollywood movies.[50] Reagan later expressed his concern that "some members of the House Un-American Activities Committee came to Hollywood searching more for personal publicity than for Communists. Many fine people were accused wrongly of being Communists simply because they were liberals." As president of the Screen Actors Guild (SAG), Reagan's anticommunism hardened as he became increasingly determined to rid the union of communists and fellow travelers. His embrace of conservative politics in the 1950s and switch to the Republican Party in 1962 strengthened his anticommunist principles.[51]

It therefore exacerbated Red Scare fears when candidate Reagan, campaigning for president in 1980, made the absurd claim that American blacklists were created by the Soviet Union and enforced through "communist front" organizations in the United States. It was Moscow, not Washington, D.C., Reagan insisted, that "destroyed careers; they were the ones with a blacklist. . . . If you weren't on their side suddenly you found you didn't get a job."[52] It was a bizarre thing for Reagan to say, and he offered no evidence to support his claim. His position on the blacklist, it turns out, had changed little since his days as SAG president in the late 1940s, when he blamed its existence on the Soviet Union. "The communists," he said in 1948, "were among those who reacted in Hollywood by distorting the facts they got, claiming they were victims of the 'blacklist'—when they were actually working members of a conspiracy directed by Soviet Russia against the United States."[53]

In his efforts to revive the Cold War on the 1980 campaign trail, Reagan never condemned the excesses of the pre-détente period. Indeed, he tended to see the congressional hearings, loyalty oaths, and mass firings as necessary evils in a broader campaign against communist infiltration. As recently as 1975, Reagan used his weekly radio show to spotlight the dangers of Soviet espionage inside the United States. He quoted a report from a commission created by Gerald Ford (of which Reagan was a member) to investigate Central Intelligence Agency activities. The report guesstimated that "nearly 2,000" communists were operating within the United States as spies for the Soviet Union. Reagan ended the broadcast with a warning: "The simple truth is Americans are being spied on massively and continually by a dangerous potential enemy."[54]

Not surprisingly, liberals feared the worst after the 1980 election. "There will probably be an effort to revive HUAC," said National Public Radio correspondent Nina Totenberg, referring to an effort in Congress to resurrect the Senate's Internal Security Subcommittee. "The talk of the revival of these committees, along with some of the massive legal changes being planned for our society and constitution, cannot help but evoke memories of the 1950s and the McCarthy era. Let's hope they are just memories," Totenberg said. American Civil Liberties Union attorney John Shattuck echoed Totenberg's fears: "They want to revive the engines of internal security like the House Un-American Activities Committee." Congressman Don Edwards, the California Democrat who chaired the House Judiciary Committee's Subcommittee on Civil and Constitutional Rights, added: "Sadly—alarmingly—momentum appears to be on the side of those who savor the bad old days."[55]

Those who lived through the "bad old days" that Edwards spoke of needed no reminders of the Red Scare juggernaut's power. Dorothy Healey, an ex-Communist prominent in southern California radical circles, told an audience in the fall of 1979 that witch-hunting thirty years earlier had "chilled the atmosphere for those daring to ask questions."[56] Healey and other survivors of the blacklist era spoke of the need to remain vigilant against encroachments on civil liberties. Fears of McCarthyism's return were even more palpable with Reagan about to become president. In a January 1981 op-ed piece headlined "Red Scare, Eighties-Style," Kirk Scharfenberg, a Pulitzer Prize–winning reporter for the *Boston Globe*, wrote in that newspaper's editorial section: "Ronald Reagan, with elements of the far right behind him, is going to Washington. The Senate Judiciary Committee, headed by the doubtable Strom Thurmond, has a new Subcommittee on Security and Terrorism with all the earmarks of a reborn House Un-American Activities Committee. . . . Few on the left want to appear paranoid, to mumble about 'witch-hunts'; but they are worried, and properly so."[57]

Months into Reagan's presidency, a May 1981 *New York Times* editorial posed the question: "Could McCarthyism come back?" Like Scharfenberg's column, *Times* editors pointed to the ominous prospect of the newly formed Senate Subcommittee on Security and Terrorism, headed by right-wing Alabama senator Jeremiah Denton, which had far-reaching HUAC-esque powers to hunt for domestic "terrorist" groups with alleged links to outside powers, especially the Soviet Union. However, the *Times* editorial assured readers that times had changed, that Joe McCarthy had met his downfall due to his own reckless overreach, that J. Edgar Hoover no longer ruled the FBI with an iron fist and a burning obsession with communism, and that President Reagan was still "selling the Soviets grain." The "circumstances have changed," the *Times* concluded, and America of the 1980s was no place for "those who see Reds under beds."[58]

Despite such reassurances, concerns on the left about the prospect of an updated blacklist persisted well into Reagan's presidency. Such fears occasionally had a basis in reality. In 1982, the popular CBS television program *Lou Grant*, which starred Ed Asner as the show's titular crusty newspaper editor (reviving his role from *The Mary Tyler Moore Show*), was suddenly yanked off the air after a five-year run, despite strong ratings. Critics of the decision believed the network canceled the show because of Asner's activism and outspokenness. The actor had repeatedly condemned President Reagan's labor policies and openly sympathized with guerrillas in El Salvador who were resisting a repressive U.S.-backed government. The network's decision to pull the plug on *Lou Grant* sparked controversy, leading many observers to speculate whether the blacklist was rearing its ugly head. The heavily publicized cancellation made it difficult for Asner to find work again. "I wouldn't say I starved," he said, "but we constantly beat the bushes."[59] Executives at CBS never adequately explained the cancellation of *Lou Grant*, and the network's silence prompted skeptics to use words like "blacklist" and "McCarthyism" to describe the decision. Asner himself remained philosophical about the affair. "It's not a blacklist," Asner stated, matter-of-factly, a few years later. "It's a mindset that precludes hiring particularly controversial people."[60]

The cancellation of *Lou Grant* upset leftists, but it did not foreshadow a coming Red Scare. The flames of McCarthyism had been extinguished, although a few embers continued to glow. Handfuls of zealous anticommunists made modest attempts at Red hunting in the 1980s. Some civil libertarians detected echoes of McCarthy in the actions of Reed Irvine, a conservative economist who, since 1969, had used his watchdog organization, Accuracy in Media, to monitor alleged left-wing influences on television and in the press. Irvine actually wielded a fair amount of influence in the Reagan era, and his accusations of bias put a number of media outlets, including the *Washington Post* and CBS, on the defensive. In the mid-1980s, Irvine launched a spinoff, Accuracy in Academia, which recruited "students and local citizens" willing to "audit classes and challenge faculty" who taught leftist ideas.[61] Irvine was not alone in his obsession with keeping an eye on alleged subversives. Days after the presidential election, the Heritage Foundation, a right-wing think tank, issued a lengthy report urging the new president-elect to take the threat of domestic radicalism more seriously and create a list of leftist groups to better monitor their activities. "Clergymen, students, businessmen, entertainers, labor officials, journalists and government workers may engage in subversive activities without being fully aware of the extent, purpose or control of their activities," the foundation warned.[62]

In addition to private groups, some federal agencies also kept lists of alleged subversives and radical organizations in the Reagan era. President Richard Nixon had only recently abolished the infamous Attorney General's List of Subversive Organizations in 1974, which had been started under President Franklin D. Roosevelt in the 1940s to monitor radical groups.[63] Other agencies in Washington possessed similar lists. A lawsuit filed by attorneys for the Socialist Workers Party uncovered a list kept by the Immigration and Naturalization Service (INS) of "proscribed" and "questionable" subversive organizations. The INS used that information to arrest, detain, and deport aliens who were allegedly tied to those organizations.[64] In 1984, the United States Information Agency (USIA) admitted it maintained "a list of people banned from Government-sponsored overseas speaking engagements." The USIA's list contained 84 names, mostly left-leaning luminaries, including Coretta Scott King, poet Allen Ginsberg, consumer rights advocate Ralph Nader, *Washington Post* editor Ben Bradlee, newscasters Walter Cronkite and David Brinkley, author James Baldwin, and international relations scholar and former Carter administration official Madeleine Albright.[65]

Hence, blacklists were not entirely dead. But the modest, poorly organized efforts to maintain them into the 1970s and 1980s were a far cry from the heyday of the postwar inquisition. Despite occasional echoes of what British historian David Caute called "the Great Fear"—the mass anticommunist anxieties of the 1940s and 1950s—the post-détente Cold War never experienced a meaningful relapse of the domestic Red Scare.[66]

CHAPTER 3

In the Shadow of Vietnam

But this too is true: stories can save us.

—*Tim O'Brien*, The Things They Carried, *1990*

Noble Cause?

"It is time we recognized that ours was, in truth, a noble cause," said Ronald Reagan on the campaign trail in August 1980. His reference to the Vietnam War won the applause of the forty-five hundred delegates at the Veterans of Foreign Wars Convention in Chicago. When the clapping subsided, Reagan gazed out confidently at the audience. "We dishonor the memory of 50,000 young Americans who died in that cause," he went on, "when we give way to feelings of guilt as if we were doing something shameful."[1] The speech Reagan delivered that day popularized the term "Vietnam Syndrome," which until then had been used only among small circles of neoconservatives and Washington insiders since 1975.[2] By Vietnam Syndrome, Reagan meant the extreme reluctance of elected officials and the public to support military interventions overseas, especially those involving large numbers of young American soldiers.

With defeat in Vietnam so recent, the prospect of another foreign war had little appeal for most Americans. Still, in his campaign for the presidency, Reagan challenged negative perceptions of the war. He viewed the Vietnam War as a valiant fight against the forces of international communism. The soldiers who fought in it, Reagan believed, served bravely and won nearly every direct military engagement against a determined enemy. In speech after speech, Reagan used the words "noble" and "honorable" to describe the men and women who served in Vietnam. Reagan reiterated these sentiments in 1984 while running for a second term. "I think there's a new feeling of patriotism in our land, a recognition that by any standard America is a decent and generous place, a force for good in the world. And I don't know about you, but I'm a little tired of hearing people run her down," Reagan told a cheering crowd in New Jersey in September 1984.[3]

Rehabilitating the Vietnam War in the public's collective memory mattered a great deal to Reagan. He hoped most Americans would, in time, come to regard the war as just and see the nation's defeat as the result of poor political leadership in Washington, D.C. "Let us tell those who fought in [Vietnam] that we will never again ask young men to fight and possibly die in a war our government is afraid to win," Reagan said in 1976.[4] In his speeches, Reagan repeatedly perpetuated the myth of timid bureaucrats betraying American soldiers by forcing them to show excessive restraint on the battlefields of Vietnam. Reagan knew defeat in Vietnam had hurt the nation's morale and undermined public trust in the White House and Congress. By invoking Vietnam repeatedly, he was not merely trying to repair people's shattered faith in government but also attempting to convince them that he was uniquely qualified to lead the country into another war should it become necessary.

For Reagan, this was no abstract exercise. He and his advisers were eyeing strife-torn Central America, where the Sandinistas had recently toppled the U.S.-backed Somoza dictatorship, and El Salvador, scene of a deadly civil war between a military dictatorship backed by Washington and Marxist guerrillas. "The Vietnam War had left one indisputable legacy: massive press, public, and congressional anxiety that the United States—at all costs—avoid getting mired in 'another Vietnam,'" wrote George P. Shultz, who would later serve as Reagan's secretary of state. Looking back on Reagan's attempts to elevate the Vietnam War in the nation's popular memory, Edwin Meese, a member of the president's inner circle and later his attorney general, reflected: "Reagan's building up and restoring the morale of the military, and the patriotic feelings—getting the military back into wearing their uniforms, putting marine guards visibly at the White House—were all part of overcoming the Vietnam syndrome. It was a conscious effort."[5]

That effort soon collided with resistance. The long shadow of the Vietnam War, the most divisive event in American history since the Civil War, darkened the United States in the age of Reagan. The president calling it a "noble cause" did not necessarily make it so in the minds of millions of wary Americans.

Polls taken between 1978 and 1982 revealed that that anywhere from half to three-quarters of American adults believed the war to be either "wrong" or "wrong and immoral."[6] With the war still fresh in people's minds, Reagan was taking a risk by bringing it up so often. American intervention in Vietnam had been devastating, both overseas and at home. In addition to leaving giant swaths of Southeast Asia in bomb-cratered, herbicide-wilted ruins, at the cost of approximately fifty-eight thousand American and three million Vietnamese lives and tens of billions of dollars, the war ripped an immense chasm into American society, turning a nation against itself in a protracted, often fierce debate about the country's proper role in the world.[7]

Those who served in Vietnam, like the general public, were divided in their opinions on the war. Many vets sought to put it behind them and move on with their lives. They shifted their attention to family, careers, and communities and tried to avoid revisiting painful memories of Vietnam. "I buried my Vietnam experience. My way of not letting it interfere with my life was burying it. I really denied that I was a Vietnam veteran," said Milt Evans, a Marine combat veteran from Eau Claire, Wisconsin, in 1983. Other veterans agreed with President Reagan's description of the war as a "noble cause" and supported his efforts to ennoble it. "I still have the belief in my God, my country, myself as a man and my Marine corps," proclaimed a conservative Vietnam veteran in 1983.[8]

Finally, some veterans adopted a critical perspective and looked back on the Vietnam War as a catastrophic event that should never have happened and must not ever be repeated. Vietnam veteran and poet W. D. Ehrhart, from Perkasie, Pennsylvania, served as a Marine sergeant during the war. After experiencing bloody combat in the burned-out rubble of Huế during the Tet Offensive in 1968, he returned home to dedicate his life to writing poetry and prose about the Vietnam War and taking part in peace activism. "I'm almost always at odds with the policies of my government and my fellow country people, because of the way most people unthinkingly accept what the government tells them," Ehrhart told an interviewer in 1983. "We allow our country to behave in ways that I consider to be grossly irresponsible and appalling."[9]

The Wall and Its Discontents

Debates about the meaning and legacies of the Vietnam War spotlighted widely divergent points of view. The first major national controversy over the

war took place during the planning stages of the Vietnam Veterans Memorial
or "the Wall," as it would come to be known. The most revered war memorial
in the United States had contentious beginnings and owed its existence to
the tireless work of Vietnam veteran Jan Scruggs. During the war, Maryland
native Scruggs volunteered for two tours of combat duty as a mortarman in
the U.S. Army's 199th Light Infantry Brigade. In January 1970, he was almost
killed and lost twelve men in his unit after an accidental explosion of three
mortar rounds occurred as they were being removed from a truck. Honorably
discharged with numerous medals and a severe case of post-traumatic stress
disorder (PTSD), Scruggs drifted from job to job, later earning a bachelor
of arts and master's degree in psychology at American University.[10] In 1979,
he founded the Vietnam Veterans Memorial Fund, a nonprofit organization
dedicated to raising the money necessary to build a memorial in the nation's
capital to the Americans who died in the Vietnam War. Scruggs worked
around the clock, writing letters, calling people, visiting potential supporters,
and pleading for donations wherever he went. Months into his undertaking,
the press widely reported that he had raised only $144. Undeterred, Scruggs
pressed on with his one-man mission, telling whomever would listen that if
one-tenth of the people who served in Vietnam would contribute five dollars,
he would have the money he needed to build a memorial. "I'm not shy about
asking anyone to do anything to reunify the country and to remember the
Americans who gave their lives in Vietnam," Scruggs said.[11]

After CBS television news anchor Roger Mudd mentioned the meager
amount raised by the Vietnam Veterans Memorial Fund in a June 1979 segment, donations began to pour into Scruggs's office.[12] Contributors across
the country sent whatever they could—most donations ranged from five to
ten dollars—and the fund's bank account steadily grew. Congress authorized three acres in the National Mall in Washington, D.C., to be used as
the memorial site. This was an important milestone, as cultural historian
Kristin Hass notes: "Whereas previously all the memorials on the Mall had
commemorated great men and their ideas, Scruggs changed that . . . with
the Vietnam Veterans Memorial." Texas billionaire businessman Ross Perot
provided a huge boost with a $160,000 donation, which helped finance a
nationwide design competition. The call went out for entries, and by the
March 31, 1981, deadline, 1,421 design proposals had been submitted from
across the country.[13]

After lengthy deliberations, a jury of professionals selected a design by
Maya Ying Lin, a twenty-one-year-old architecture major at Yale University.

Lin, the daughter of Chinese-born academics who taught at Ohio University in Athens, Ohio, where she was raised, was surprised her design won. "I knew it was never going to be chosen. It was too strong," she said. But chosen it was, and nobody was more pleased than Jan Scruggs, who revered Lin's design. Asked to weigh in on the winning entry on its announcement in May 1981, Scruggs told reporters: "I am so glad to see a David beating the Goliaths of the architecture world. Maybe it required someone who was detached, who did not have the direct experience to come up with the way to design the memorial."[14]

The black granite chevron Lin designed, with its east wall facing the Washington Monument, its west wall aimed at the Lincoln Memorial, measuring roughly five hundred feet long and ten feet high at its tallest point, broke dramatically with traditional war memorial designs in its complete rejection of conventional norms and traditions. The monument was not even readily visible from afar. Only when visitors drew closer did they realize its grand sweep, and by then it overwhelmed the onlooker, like a tidal wave. From one end to the other, the 57,692 names carved into the Wall (additional names would be added over time, reaching 58,390 by 2019) conveyed the overwhelming totality of the loss of lives on the American side. The polished black granite shifts in the observer's line of vision between the names of the dead and the visitor's reflection. Judges on the selection jury applauded the memorial's "contemplative and reflective" design, calling it "superbly harmonious with the site. . . . This is very much a memorial to our times, one that could not be achieved in another time or place." In the fall of 1982, *Washington Post* columnist Richard Cohen perceptively observed: "The monument starts like the war itself, small and unseen. It grows larger, as the war did, by degrees, until it is higher than a man's head, and then, also like the war, it slowly fades until it is gone. It has almost no beginning and no end. The war was like that."[15]

Lin's winning design famously sparked intense disapproval. Detractors were more than vehement in their objections—they were downright vitriolic. Ross Perot promptly voiced his dislike of the Wall and encouraged Scruggs to pick a different design.[16] Perot adamantly stated he "did not want to see a 'flower power' memorial," and he referred to Lin as "egg roll," a pejorative reference to her Chinese ancestry.[17] Two of the Wall's most outspoken critics were Vietnam veterans Tom Carhart, an early supporter of Scruggs who turned on the Wall when it was not to his liking, and Jim Webb, a member of the National Sponsoring Committee of the Memorial Fund. Webb would go on to serve as President Reagan's Secretary of the Navy, then later be elected to the United

States Senate from Virginia.[18] Carhart referred to Lin's design as a "black gash of shame and sorrow" and "an open urinal."[19] He suggested an inscription for the memorial: "Designed by a gook."[20] Webb despised the design so strongly he resigned from the National Sponsoring Committee in protest and urged the luminaries serving on the fund's Sponsoring Committee—including Gerald Ford, Rosalynn Carter, Nancy Reagan, Bob Hope, and Jimmy Stewart—to do likewise. Thankfully for Scruggs, none of them followed Webb's advice. Webb called the memorial "nihilistic" and a "mockery" of service, predicting it would become a "wailing wall for anti-draft and antinuclear demonstrators."[21] He also derided the memorial as a "black ditch," which prompted Army Brigadier General George Price—an African American—to respond: "Black is not a color of shame. I am tired of hearing it called such. . . . Color meant nothing on the battlefields of Korea and Vietnam."[22]

Despite the memorial's defenders standing their ground, the attack from the right went on for months unabated. "That trench would be a permanent political statement endorsing the view of the American Left: that the Vietnam veterans fought and died in a worthless cause," wrote Patrick Buchanan, a former adviser to President Richard Nixon. Novelist Tom Wolfe reserved his razor-sharpest words for the memorial, calling it a "monument to Jane Fonda," inflicted on the American people by the "Mullahs of Modernism." "Shouldn't public sculpture delight the public or inspire the public or at least remind the public of cherished traditions? Nonsense. Why reinforce the bourgeoisie's pathetic illusions?" Wolfe wrote.[23]

From the revealing of Lin's design in May 1981 until the dedication of the Wall in November 1982, a steady stream of polemical newspaper editorials and public denunciations took aim at the memorial. "Clouds of Doubt Engulf Viet Nam War Memorial," said a *Chicago Tribune* headline. At the heart of the protests was the insistence that Lin did not sufficiently glorify the Vietnam War or those who fought in it. The main quality Scruggs wished to see in the Wall—the absence of a "statement about the war or the way it was conducted"—was the very thing that angered its right-wing opposition. In May 1981, Charles Krauthammer articulated this viewpoint in the *New Republic* when he wrote: "This memorial says one thing: only the dead, nothing besides, remain. Its purpose is to impress upon the visitor the sheer human waste, the utter meaningless of it all." Representative Henry Hyde, a conservative Republican from Illinois, added his voice to the chorus, calling Lin's design "a political statement of shame and dishonor, rather than an expression of our national pride at the courage, patriotism and nobility of all who served."[24]

To appease critics, the Memorial Fund commissioned sculptor Frederick Hart, a member of the team that submitted the third-place design in the competition, to create a figurative bronze statue of three American soldiers in uniform, to be placed near the memorial on completion. Hart accepted the challenge, yet he poured gasoline on the flames when he assailed Lin's design as "intentionally not meaningful" and "art that is contemptuous of life."[25] He called Lin an "ingénue" and a "little girl" and lamented that the media had "turned her into a Cinderella."[26]

Behind the scenes, the memorial's opponents—led by Ross Perot and a group of conservative congressmen—lobbied Reagan's interior secretary, James Watt, to stall construction on the Mall. Watt, one of the most notoriously regressive reactionaries in the president's cabinet, needed little persuading. He controlled the Mall in his official capacity, and his delaying tactics slowed the building of the memorial considerably. Throughout the bombardment of criticism, Jan Scruggs remained philosophical in public. He knew he enjoyed widespread support among Vietnam veterans. "I was not going to back down," Scruggs recalled.[27] Meantime, the memorial's backers mobilized to counter the opposition. They testified before Congress, wrote op-ed page editorials, and lobbied politicians, veteran's organizations, and military brass to firm up support. Watt eventually relented, approving the construction permit after months of holding it up. "Construction of the controversial Vietnam Veterans Memorial officially began March 26 when 120 veterans and dignitaries each turned a shovelful of dirt on Washington's Mall," reported U.S. News & World Report.[28]

Dedication ceremonies for the memorial began Wednesday, November 10, 1982. During the next several days, tens of thousands people streamed into the Mall to lay wreaths, read names of the dead, hold candlelight vigils, and reunite with old friends. At one point, President Reagan and First Lady Nancy Reagan visited the site to light candles. The formal dedication of the Vietnam Veterans Memorial happened on a chilly, overcast Saturday, November 13. It began with a march of Vietnam veterans down Constitution Avenue, followed by a gathering of 150,000 people at the Wall as jets flew overhead.[29] For those who made the journey there, it was a day of remembering and catharsis. Visitors wept, hugged, ran their fingertips over the names of the dead, and took in the pathos of it all. "It is a reminder of the cost of war. It is a bill of sale," explained Vietnam veteran William Broyles Jr.[30] A new tradition was born at the opening ceremony: visitors left letters and other offerings at the Wall for the dead.[31] A letter left behind at the dedication read: "Larry Lee

Baxter: It was pure fate that we ever met on 5-12-69. You needed a shotgun rider. It was not until 11-11-82 that I learned your first name. . . . Larry, I wonder why two people could ride in the same truck together and one survive an ambush and the other die. I will probably ask that question for the rest of my life. You are the reason I traveled from East Texas to Washington, D.C. this Veterans' Day. . . . You will be remembered as long as I am capable of remembering. . . . Philip Watson."[32]

Divided They Stand: Vietnam Veterans

The opening of the memorial ended all opposition to Maya Lin's design. It was as if the clamor had never occurred in the first place. The Wall became the most famous and instantly recognizable war memorial in the United States. "The Wall," said Jan Scruggs, "gave people the license to mourn publicly."[33] The success of the Vietnam Veterans Memorial signified the changing times. Societal upheavals in the late 1960s and early 1970s had the paradoxical effect of making the Vietnam War more unpopular while also empowering an array of previously neglected or marginalized constituencies, including veterans. Earlier generations of veterans—particularly those who had served in World War II—had been famous for their reluctance to talk about their wartime experiences. Documentary filmmaker Ken Burns referred to veterans of the Second World War as "this extraordinarily and admirably reticent generation."[34] Historian Michael D. Gambone echoed Burns's observation: "The reticence of World War II veterans to talk about their personal experiences would take decades to breach. In many cases, the deaths of old soldiers in their seventies and eighties circumvented their inclination to talk."[35]

By contrast, Vietnam veterans were generally more willing to discuss their time as soldiers, in part owing to the greater frankness of post–Vietnam War culture. The origins of that openness dated back to the war years. On the home front, antiwar activism helped create a space for Vietnam veterans to be more outspoken than their forebears in previous wars. In the early 1970s, the organization Vietnam Veterans Against the War (VVAW) helped birth a renaissance of self-expression among Vietnam vets. Members of the VVAW formed "rap groups" to encourage vets to open up about their experiences, with the help of psychiatrists and psychologists who attended the meetings. At these group therapy sessions, participants, in the words of Vietnam vet and psychologist Arthur Egendorf, "talked, argued, made up, hugged, got confused, told stories, asked for advice, gave advice, complained, cried, and occasionally laughed. We followed no special formula or set procedure."[36] Additionally, VVAW members published books of poetry and short stories, reenacted shocking war scenes from Vietnam in public guerrilla theater, and testified at war crimes hearings about atrocities in Southeast Asia. In the late 1970s, VVAW activists helped launch Vietnam Veterans of America (VVA), an advocacy group based in Washington, D.C., that demanded increased funding for the Veterans Administration, comprehensive counseling for veterans, and drug treatment programs to help struggling addicts.

Emboldened by mass dissent, a sizable segment of Vietnam veterans became outspoken in debates about the meaning and legacies of the war. Regardless of their political leanings—right, center, or left—most held anti-authoritarian sensibilities, views they came by honestly. Their distrust of authority reflected the divisive nature of the Vietnam War. One could backdate their skepticism to release of the Pentagon Papers in 1971. The Pentagon Papers comprised documents from an extensive, secret study of U.S. intervention in Vietnam commissioned by Secretary of Defense Robert McNamara in 1967. Thanks to Daniel Ellsberg, a disillusioned economist and military analyst, the study was leaked, raising public awareness about decades of systematic deceit at the highest levels of government.[37] The report's thousands of pages of classified documents revealed that several presidential administrations had misled the American public about Washington's Vietnam policies since the 1940s. Among the deceived were the young men who fought in Vietnam in their nation's time of need. The Pentagon Papers helped disillusion an entire generation. Repairing that broken trust—and the schisms it caused—would take time and effort. When Jan Scruggs turned over ownership of the Vietnam Veterans Memorial to the National Park Service in November 1984, President Reagan appeared at the Wall to thank Vietnam veterans for their service. Reagan admitted to a crowd of 150,000 on November 12 that divisions over the war still ran deep. "The war in Vietnam threatened to tear our society apart," he said, "and the political and philosophical disagreements that separated each side continue, to some extent."[38]

Thanks to this legacy of deception, Vietnam veterans inhabited the trenches of the Cold War culture wars in disproportionately large numbers. Disagreements about the war—often heated—erupted in the 1980s, as Americans, still historically close to the conflict, sought to make sense of it. Vietnam veterans were particularly eager to weigh in, having participated the most directly in the conflict. They wrote memoirs, books, poetry, and plays about the war. Tens of thousands joined Vietnam Veterans of America, founding local chapters and stepping up lobbying efforts for improved benefits.[39] In nearly every community in the United States, veterans spoke at high schools and civic groups about their experiences in Southeast Asia. Some of them became counselors and drew attention to the high rates of PTSD, suicide, drug abuse, and homelessness among their fellow Vietnam vets. They also attacked negative stereotypes in popular culture and the media depicting Vietnam vets as troubled and violent.[40] Veterans suffering from health problems as a result of exposure to Agent Orange—a toxic defoliant that was among the twelve million gallons of herbicides sprayed by U.S. airplanes over Southeast Asia in the 1960s and 1970s—filed class action lawsuits against such chemical giants as Dow and Monsanto with the help of activist lawyers.[41]

Of all the contentious debates about the Vietnam War in the Reagan era, none was more emotionally charged than the myth of prisoner of war/missing in action (POW/MIA) service members still being held captive in Vietnam. The families and friends of men listed as MIAs by the Department of Defense clung desperately to any shred of evidence they could find that might explain the fate of their missing loved ones. "You Are Not Forgotten," was the slogan of the haunting black-and-white POW/MIA flag, which featured the silhouette of a POW with his head titled forward. These somber flags could be seen at parades and picnics, and the POW/MIA symbol was plastered in bumper sticker form to the rears of vehicles nationwide. As a sign of the movement's clout, White House staff flew the POW/MIA flag with the American flag over the White House in the 1980s, and it was displayed in the Capitol Rotunda.[42]

But the POW/MIA crusade had a sinister side. The movement became a magnet for conspiracy theorists, fanatics, and mercenaries. Desperate relatives and loved ones of MIAs invested so much emotional energy into hopes that American servicemen would be found alive in Vietnam that they ignored ample evidence to the contrary. Worse yet, the movement attracted con artists who profited unscrupulously from the families of MIAs. A lucrative business of scams involved doctored photographs, bogus tape recordings, forged letters, and other pieces of fraudulent "evidence" designed to raise the hopes of families of MIAs.[43] Moreover, the POW/MIA lobby effectively dictated America's Vietnam policies throughout the Reagan years, although the end of the Cold War in the late 1980s and early 1990s weakened its size and influence. Communism's collapse naturally reduced the potency of anticommunism and the conspiracies it nurtured. Moreover, a series of famous hoaxes in the early 1990s tarnished the POW/MIA movement's reputation.

Finally, Senate hearings in 1991 and 1992 confirmed there were no living American prisoners of war in Southeast Asia.[44] For dedicated POW/MIA activists, that was a bitter pill to swallow.

Despite sparse evidence that POWs were still alive in Vietnam, popular culture in the 1980s repeatedly reinforced the myth with POW-themed box office hits, such as *Uncommon Valor* (1983), *Missing in Action* (1984) and its sequels, and one of the decade's highest grossing movies, *Rambo: First Blood Part II* (1985). In *Uncommon Valor*, Gene Hackman played a Marine colonel who organizes a ragtag team to fly into communist Laos to rescue his son and other American captives. The film celebrates male bonding and is populated by characters with distinct personalities who are shown training, becoming friends, and traveling to Southeast Asia together. *Uncommon Valor* was a commercially successful movie with dramatic pretensions that portrayed its subject matter with a mix of realism and humanity. Chuck Norris's *Missing in Action* films, on the other hand, were drive-in schlock, marred by wooden acting, bad dialogue and B-movie production values. In them, Colonel Braddock (Norris) returns to Vietnam to hunt for missing POWs and obliterates hordes of evil Vietnamese and other commie stooges. *Missing in Action* spawned two sequels, *Missing in Action 2: The Beginning* and *Braddock: Missing in Action III*, each bloodier than its predecessor.[45]

However, it was John Rambo (Sylvester Stallone), from *Rambo: First Blood Part II*, who became a household name and a cultural icon symbolizing the times. The film was a sequel to *First Blood* (1982), an action-drama that pitted the main character against a sadistic sheriff (Brian Dennehy) and his deputies in rural Washington state. The original *First Blood* not only lacked the jingoism of its sequels but also contained themes that all viewers across the political spectrum could appreciate. Moviegoers on the right were treated to a disgruntled veteran who did not get the respect that society owed to him and his brothers who served in Vietnam, while those on the left could root for a long-haired, antiauthoritarian protagonist fighting against a "redneck" sheriff and his deputies.[46]

First Blood's sequel, however, was an unabashedly right-wing comic book fantasy. In *Rambo: First Blood Part II* (1985), Rambo, a superhuman Vietnam veteran, former Green Beret, and expert in guerrilla warfare, is recruited to return to Vietnam to collect intelligence information on American POWs. Murdock, the heartless, lantern-jawed bureaucrat who organizes the mission, issues strict orders: "Now if there's any of our men in this POW target camp, you confirm their presence by taking photographs." "Photographs?" asks a shocked Rambo. "Just photographs," snaps Murdock. "Under no circumstances are you to engage the enemy!" Rambo stares angrily at his supervisor and asks, "I'm supposed to leave 'em there?" "I repeat," Murdock commands, "don't engage the enemy!"[47] Rambo returns to Vietnam and locates the POW camp with the help of a female Vietnamese guide, but the communists and their evil Soviet adviser kill her and capture and torture Rambo. He escapes and single-handedly obliterates his enemies. Returning to base with gaunt American POWs in tow, Rambo almost kills Murdock, who symbolizes the callous Washington establishment that forced Americans to fight "with one hand tied behind their backs." But Rambo allows Murdock to live. As the movie draws to a close, Rambo's mentor, Colonel Trautman, asks the anguished Rambo what he wants. "For our country to love us as much as we love it! That's what I want!" Trautman appears reflective and asks, "How will you live, John?" "Day by day," Rambo replies, facing an uncertain future as the credits roll.[48]

More than any film made in the 1980s, *Rambo: First Blood Part II* tapped into popular resentments still lingering ten years after the fall of Saigon. When Rambo asked Trautman at the beginning of the film whether "we get to win this time" in Vietnam, he expressed a widely shared belief of the Reagan era that American policymakers of the 1960s and 1970s did not possess the will to win in Vietnam. Rambo offered movie audiences—which consisted primarily of young men and boys who missed the chance to serve in Southeast Asia— another opportunity to fight the Vietnam War and to win it this time. Not surprisingly, President Reagan loved the movie, and a popular poster featured his face superimposed over Rambo's brawny body under the words "Ronbo." Referring to the recent hijacking of a TWA airplane by Lebanese terrorists in the summer of 1985, the president remarked: "Boy, after seeing Rambo last night, I know what to do next time this happens."[49] Reagan was not alone. *Rambo*'s success at the box office—it was the second-highest-grossing film of 1985—helped push the POW/MIA issue from the fringes to the mainstream.

The spate of POW/MIA movies in the 1980s were the first major Vietnam-related films to come out of Hollywood since Francis Ford Coppola's surreal 1979 *Heart of Darkness*–inspired epic *Apocalypse Now*. But unlike Coppola's magnum opus, a finely crafted work of cinema filled with dark Conradian themes, the Reagan-era POW/MIA movies reduced the Vietnam War to the stuff of comic books. By allowing the heroes to refight the war and defeat fiendish Vietnamese adversaries, *Uncommon Valor*, the *Missing in Action* movies, and *Rambo: First Blood Part II* all appealed to audiences that shared

Reagan's view of the Vietnam War as a noble cause. Hollywood's alternate right-wing universe had stripped Vietnam of its complex history, reducing it to a jungle where invincible Americans spray bullets into remorseless, insect-like Vietnamese by the dozens and liberate their fellow compatriots, as if it had been the United States—not Vietnam—that was invaded and subjected to wholesale devastation. Rambo, writes sociologist James William Gibson, was "the emblem of a movement that at the very least wanted to reverse the previous twenty years of American history and take back all the symbolic territory that had been lost."[50]

But the film was also reviled. Vietnam veterans, in particular, frequently expressed contempt for *Rambo: First Blood Part II*. Chet McLeod of Detroit, once a Marine in Vietnam, disliked John Rambo and the triumphalism he embodied: "There's real damage in the way Rambo tried to rewrite the ending of the war. Here he is, bow and arrow, rescuing everyone. It does a lot of disservice to combat vets who get to watch this guy raking in all the money for something he eluded. I mean Stallone wasn't there when I was there." At a February 1987 reunion of Vietnam War infantrymen in New York City to attend a screening of *Platoon*, the topic of conversation turned to *Rambo*: "'I hope this movie blows *Rambo* right out of the water,' said one. 'Yeah,' said another, 'because Rambo was nothing but one hero that never went there.'" Paraplegic Vietnam veteran and antiwar activist Ron Kovic echoed McLeod's criticisms: "I want people to remember that war is not John Wayne and Rambo movies. John Wayne glamorized war in my generation. I was fooled. Rambo is romanticizing war in this generation. War is a painful, terrifying ordeal."[51]

In the end, Rambo answered his own self-pitying question—"Do we get to win this time?"—by effortlessly defeating his communist foes and securing a victory that had eluded Americans in Vietnam years earlier. Rambo wins. Evil loses. But Rambo did not have the last word on Vietnam's divisive legacy. A war that had been so polarizing in its duration could not be tucked away so easily. During the Reagan era, the president's "noble cause" statement—and the movies it inspired—faced constant challenges. In this case, the most persuasive critics of the war were the veterans themselves. Those who served in Vietnam, and who later concluded the war was wrong and should not be rehabilitated in the public's memory, faced an arduous task. Whereas opinion polls indicated widespread doubts about the nobility of the Vietnam War, that skepticism did not translate to a willingness to come to terms with the war's shocking destructiveness or the flawed reasoning that led to the catastrophe. Moreover, the war's apologists were often caustic and fierce in their criticisms, as they demonstrated during the fight over designs for the Vietnam Veterans Memorial.

That vitriol was on full display after four Vietnam veterans made a historic journey back to Vietnam in December 1981. The travelers—Robert "Bobby" Muller, Tom Bird, Michael Harbert, and John Terzano, all affiliated with Vietnam Veterans of America—flew to Hanoi days before Christmas to meet with Vietnamese government officials. On the flight over, the vets felt tense, not knowing what to expect. The trip's organizer, Bobby Muller, the founder and executive director of VVA, had been a combat Marine in Vietnam and was the most well known of the group. Over a decade earlier, Muller had returned from the war a paraplegic after being shot in combat. He immersed himself in antiwar activism, joining Vietnam Veterans against the War, attending protests, and taking part in veterans' advocacy. His fellow travelers in 1981 shared his antiwar views. Tom Bird, an infantryman in the war, had been captured by the enemy and tortured. Former Air Force sergeant Michael Harbert claimed he'd flown bombing missions over North Vietnam in the 1960s. Returning to the country years later, Harbert echoed the feelings of his comrades when he admitted, "I was nervous as hell."[52]

Three items topped their agenda: requesting help from the government in locating missing-in-action servicemen; coordinating visits by U.S. scientists to assess the impact of Agent Orange use in the war; and facilitating cultural exchanges in the arts between Vietnam and the United States. During their six-day visit, the vets adhered to a hectic schedule, holding long meetings with government ministers, touring Hanoi, and seeing the countryside. They visited a war museum, a bomb shelter, Ho Chi Minh's tiny wooden house on stilts, a care facility for wounded Vietnamese veterans, and the huge granite mausoleum that entombed Ho's mummified body, on display under a glass sarcophagus. At Ho's mausoleum, the veterans, at the insistence of their hosts, laid a wreath to honor the revolutionary. The men expected to encounter hostility in Vietnam, but all they found was warmth and laughter. "The veterans are so cheerful and friendly. We know the American people are like that," said a Vietnamese official.[53] "Throughout all our travels, we did not receive one hostile glance. They said they wanted our friendship," explained Bobby Muller. Tom Bird was not expecting such a kind reception, but the trip was an important healing experience for him. "The war finally stopped in my mind," he later said.[54]

Back in the United States, a furious homecoming awaited the veterans. At their press conference in New York City on December 28, 1981, right-wing opponents showed up to shout and jeer. Al Santoli, a former rifleman for the 25th Infantry Division in Vietnam, called the men "a total disgrace."[55] Frank McCarthy, head of Agent Orange Victims International, declared, "These gentlemen are a fraud."[56] In the months that followed, the veterans were inundated with hate mail and death threats and called "traitors" in the press and in public. A veterans' association consisting of pilots who flew in the Vietnam War disputed Michael Harbert's claims that he had taken part in bombing operations over North Vietnam in F105s.[57] But the worst sin committed by the travelers, according to their foes, was laying a wreath at Ho Chi Minh's mausoleum. Muller was unrepentant in his response: "Ho Chi Minh is the founding father of their country. His mausoleum is their greatest shrine. We asked to visit it. We were told that the proper protocol for visiting foreign delegations requires that a wreath be laid. Having asked to go, we agreed to their custom."[58]

In the aftermath of the Hanoi trip, VVA likewise endured a drubbing. Detractors said it was poorly managed and questioned Muller's leadership skills and sincerity. Vietnam Veterans of America was criticized for being too wrapped up in celebrity culture as a result of taking money from concert fundraisers featuring performances by Bruce Springsteen and Pat Benatar and for allowing *Penthouse* magazine to pay for the trip to Hanoi. A handful of former VVA supporters wrote letters to the Internal Revenue Service encouraging the agency to investigate VVA's finances, resulting in an audit of the organization. "They're just in it to raise money and promote themselves," charged Cooper Holt, executive director of Veterans of Foreign Wars.[59]

Revising the Narrative

Like the barrage of negativity directed at Maya Lin's memorial design, the attacks against the VVA delegation's Hanoi trip revealed the raw anger aimed at anyone who contradicted the narrative of the war's apologists. With the passage of time, however, dissenters grew emboldened. Leading the charge from the left flank were Vietnam veteran writers who had been penning poetry, novels and memoirs since the 1970s. In 1972, the antiwar organization Vietnam Veterans Against the War broke new ground by publishing a book of Vietnam veteran poetry titled *Winning Hearts and Minds*.[60] The first collection of Vietnam War soldier poetry ever published, the book was an instant hit, selling so briskly that the Brooklyn-based press that published it sought the help of book giant McGraw-Hill to print an additional run to meet the enormous demand. The following year, VVAW published a book of short stories by Vietnam veterans titled *Free Fire Zone*, once again relying on the printing and distribution muscle of McGraw-Hill, which amounted to another milestone in the infant genre of Vietnam War literature.[61]

The foray by VVAW into publishing was one of its most successful ventures, raising the organization's exposure and revealing a demand for realistic stories and verse about the Vietnam War. In the second half of the 1970s, a vanguard of veteran memoirists wrote important nonfiction books about their war experiences. Leading the way was the combat memoir of Minnesota-born U.S. Army vet Tim O'Brien, *If I Die in a Combat Zone, Box Me Up and Ship Me Home* (1973), which told a gritty "day-in-the-life" story of a soldier's experience in Vietnam.[62] In 1976, Ron Kovic's emotional *Born on the Fourth of July* recounted the author's transformation from an all-American young patriot who volunteered to fight in Vietnam to an embittered paraplegic in a filthy Veterans Affairs hospital and, finally, to an impassioned antiwar activist.[63] The following year saw *A Rumor of War* by author and journalist Philip Caputo, a chronicle of his time as an infantry lieutenant in South Vietnam, and Michael Herr's *Dispatches*, an account of the two years he spent in Vietnam as a journalist, from 1967 to 1969, covering the war for *Esquire* magazine.[64]

Critics at the time hailed all four books as instant masterpieces. *Dispatches*, in particular, won acclaim for its vivid descriptions of combat in Vietnam. Born in Lexington, Kentucky, in 1940, raised in Syracuse, New York, Herr joined in the U.S. Army Reserve while still in his teens and worked as a free-lance journalist for years before becoming a regular contributor to *Esquire* in the 1960s. The magazine sent him to Vietnam to cover the war, where he reported on such dramatic events as the siege at Khe Sanh and the savage Tet Offensive in Huế. The combination of the relentless pace, the deaths of several friends, and being in the middle of dangerous combat operations drove Herr to the breaking point. "I experienced a massive physical and psychological collapse. I crashed. I wasn't high anymore," he later recounted. Herr returned to the United States in 1969 and spent years writing what would become *Dispatches*, which British novelist John le Carré called "the best book I have ever read on men and war in our time."[65]

The publication of *Dispatches* in 1977, acclaimed as a masterpiece of "new journalism" in the tradition of Truman Capote's *In Cold Blood* (1965), transformed Herr into a literary giant overnight. "It is as if Dante had gone to hell with a cassette recording of Jimi Hendrix and a pocketful of pills: our first rock-and-roll war, stoned murder," gushed *New York Times* literary critic

John Leonard.[66] Far from depicting the war as a Reaganesque noble cause, *Dispatches* captured the stark brutality and absurdity of the Vietnam War. "You could be in the most protected space in Vietnam and still know that your safety was provisional," Herr wrote, "that early death, blindness, loss of legs, arms or balls, major and lasting disfigurement—the whole rotten deal— could come in on the freakyfluky as easily as in the so-called expected ways, you heard so many of these stories it was a wonder anyone was left alive to die in firefights and mortar-rocket attacks."[67]

Like *Dispatches*, the postwar literary contributions of Vietnam veterans— whether memoirs, novels, or poetry—tackled themes of disillusionment, violence, despair, absurdity, and fleeting moments of humor. Vietnam veteran authors such as Tim O'Brien, Larry Heinemann, Robert Olen Butler, Tobias Wolff, W. D. Ehrhart, and Bruce Weigl wrote prose and verse containing deeply antiwar themes. Their approach to storytelling influenced other Vietnam War accounts. Even James Webb, one of the war's most famous supporters, an opponent of Maya Lin's memorial design, and a member of the Reagan administration, struck a dark tone in his 1978 Vietnam War novel *Fields of Fire*. As one character in the novel tells another: "That's the game out here. That's what we're here for. To kill gooks. . . . Kill gooks and make it home alive."[68] Indeed, there is not a glimmer of nobility to be found in most Vietnam War novels of the Reagan era. Quite the opposite, as Tim O'Brien wrote in the most famous of his essays, "How to Tell a True War Story": "If at the end of a war story you feel uplifted, or if you feel that some small bit of rectitude has been salvaged from the larger waste, then you have been made the victim of a very old and terrible lie."[69] The net effect of this style of writing was the rise of a Vietnam War narrative devoid of sentimentality and jingoism. Historian Robert D. Schulzinger found "several consistent themes" evident in contemporary Vietnam War literature: "War is hell, but the Vietnam experience seemed worse than earlier passages of arms. Characters in Vietnam fiction are almost inexpressibly alone, cut off from the rest of American society, from the Vietnamese, from their superior officers, and from each other. Others, fortunate not to have endured the trauma of combat, reject, misunderstand, or betray them. Veterans long to escape the horrors of war. . . . But try as they might, the war overpowers them. Their thoughts and their emotions in one way or another remain fixed in the alien and unpredictable landscape of Vietnam."[70]

The dark prose of such Vietnam War novelists as Robert Stone (*Dog Soldiers*, 1974); Tim O'Brien (*Going After Cacciato*, 1978); Gustav Hasford

(*The Short-Timers*, 1979); Larry Heinemann (*Close Quarters*, 1974; *Paco's Story*, 1986); Robert Olen Butler (*The Alleys of Eden*, 1981); and others—along with the contributions of celebrated memoirists—reflected the violence, trauma, fear, confusion, randomness, elusiveness of the enemy, and absence of clear goals so rife in the war. The nature of the war left an indelible stamp on the content and style of postwar Vietnam War novels. Reinforcing these books were volumes of Vietnam War veteran oral histories published in the Reagan era, among them Al Santoli's *Everything We Had* (1981) and its follow-up, *To Bear Any Burden* (1985); Mark Baker's *Nam* (1983); Wallace Terry's *Bloods* (1984); Keith Walker's *A Piece of My Heart* (1985); and Charley Trujillo's *Soldados* (1990).[71]

Oral history books represented a relatively new approach to understanding the past. Their sudden appearance in book form, along with their rising popularity, grew out of recent methodological shifts in the profession, with greater attention being paid to previously neglected peoples. The Chicago raconteur, historian, and broadcaster Studs Terkel bore greater responsibility than anybody for the oral history craze. His first major success came in 1970 with his best seller *Hard Times*, which he followed with the equally successful *Working* in 1974, in which Terkel asked people to discuss their jobs. His book *"The Good War,"* a collection of interviews with Americans from all walks of life who lived through World War II, spent weeks on the *New York Times* best seller list in 1985 and won the Pulitzer Prize.[72] As in Vietnam War literature, oral histories overflowed with themes of disillusionment, loneliness, and alienation, as well as vivid accounts of the horrors of combat.

Vietnam War books—fiction and nonfiction alike—often challenged President Reagan's mantra that the Vietnam War was a noble cause. Ultimately, however, movies were a more effective medium at reaching—and influencing—large segments of the American public. Until 1986, the war's defenders enjoyed an advantage on that cultural front. A game-changer was the release of Oliver Stone's *Platoon*, days before Christmas in 1986. *Platoon* was a landmark achievement in antiwar cinema and an authentic refutation of the "noble cause" school. *Platoon* was not only a critical success, earning almost universally glowing reviews, but also the third-highest-grossing film in the United States in 1986. It went on to receive multiple Academy Award nominations and netted two of the coveted gold statues for best picture and best director. Nobody was more surprised by its triumph than Stone, who spent a decade struggling to bring the film to the big screen.

Born in 1946, Stone had a middle-class upbringing in New York City, son of a conservative stockbroker who met Oliver's Parisian mother while a soldier in France during World War II. Oliver attended prep schools in his youth, stayed in France often with his maternal grandparents, and developed a case of wanderlust as a teenager. In 1962, his parents divorced, and his mother ended up being an uneven presence in his life, although he remained close to his father. While visiting Vietnam to teach and work as a merchant marine in the mid-1960s, Stone volunteered for the army, serving combat duty at his request in the 2nd Platoon, B Company, 3rd Battalion, 25th Infantry Division. Wounded twice, heavily decorated, Stone returned to the United States disillusioned with the war. He was arrested in San Diego ten days after his discharge in 1968 for marijuana possession. He drove cabs and had a short-lived failed marriage. He abused drugs and booze and developed a reputation for reckless behavior. He eventually enrolled in New York University's prestigious film program, where he studied under Martin Scorsese. "I thought he was a real filmmaker. He'd been through a lot more than other students and had something to say," recalled Scorsese.[73] Obtaining a Bachelor of Fine Arts in film at NYU in 1971, Stone became a screenwriter, winning his first Oscar in 1979 for his screenplay to the previous year's *Midnight Express*, Alan Parker's Turkish prison drama.[74]

As a screenwriter, Stone never had trouble finding work. He wrote scripts to the Arnold Schwarzenegger action film *Conan the Barbarian* (1982), Brian De Palma's gangster epic *Scarface* (1983), and Hal Ashby's crime drama *8 Million Ways to Die* (1986). His first stab at directing came in 1974 with *Seizure*, an unsuccessful horror film with a limited drive-in run. A second horror film, *The Hand* (1981), about a comic book artist (Michael Caine) who loses his hand in a traffic accident, only to have the severed body part return to wreak havoc, flopped. His 1986 drama *Salvador*, about a gonzo journalist covering the horrific civil war in El Salvador, fared better among critics but not at the box office. Yet it secured Stone a reputation as an up-and-coming director, helping him obtain funding to make *Platoon*. He traveled with his crew and actors to the Philippines in early 1986 to begin shooting his Vietnam War film.[75]

Working with a paltry $6 million budget, Stone filmed *Platoon* in nine weeks in sweltering jungles, all the while convinced his film was wholly unique: a bottom-up view of the ordinary grunt's experience, not like any of the other Vietnam War movie made up to that point. He told an interviewer at the time: "*Apocalypse Now* was a powerful film, but it was not about the everyday war. I liked it, and I liked *The Deer Hunter*, but the first was about Joseph Conrad, and the second was about Pennsylvania. It was about Meryl Streep."[76] Stone's film was semiautobiographical, but also partly based on stories he heard about other infantrymen during and after the war. In a tense moment, Chris Taylor (Charlie Sheen)—the film's main character, loosely modeled on Stone—enters a Vietnamese village with his fellow soldiers of the 25th Infantry Division. He finds an elderly woman and a young man hiding in a hut and in a fit of rage begins firing his machine gun at the man's feet, yelling, "Dance, you one-legged motherfucker!"[77] The scene was based on one of Stone's experiences, in which he fired at the feet of an elderly man in a sweep through a small rural hamlet. "I told him to get out of the hole. He wouldn't get out. I just wanted to scare him to the verge of dying. I wanted to kill him, but I couldn't quite cross the barrier."[78]

The theatrical release of *Platoon* was a major event. Word of mouth was feverish. Screenings routinely sold out for the first month. Lines wrapped around city blocks. *Platoon* introduced audiences to a young infantryman torn between the competing influences of two sergeants: Elias (Willem Dafoe), an idealistic, Christlike figure with strong antiwar sentiments, and Barnes (Tom Berenger), a battle-hardened, merciless killer with a face covered in scars, willing to kill as many innocent Vietnamese as it takes to win the war. To the sound of Samuel Barber's heart-wrenchingly sad *Adagio for Strings*, effectively evoking the pathos of the conflict, the platoon cuts through the jungles of Vietnam, variously fighting the North Vietnamese Army, fatigue, insects, and each other.

For Stone, the real war was not between the Americans and the Vietnamese—although plenty of combat is shown—but rather infantryman against infantryman. The platoon is a microcosm of American society in the late 1960s, with tensions rising between pot-smoking, antiauthoritarian GIs and macho, booze-drinking, anticommunist warriors. Vietnamese villagers, caught in the cross fire, pay the ultimate price in *Platoon*, losing loved ones to violence and witnessing their homes and way of life burned to the ground by American soldiers trying to separate them from a determined foe. At one point, Taylor asks Elias if he believes in the war. "In '65, yeah. Now, no," says Elias. "What happened today is just the beginning. We're going to lose this war." Chris cannot believe his ears. "Come on! You really think so? Us?" Elias tells Chris, "We've been kicking other people's asses for so long I figure it's about time we got ours kicked."[79] By the film's final frames, Vietnam is revealed to be a smoldering, bomb-cratered landscape, with bodies being bulldozed into mass graves—hardly the stuff of John Wayne flag-wavers.

Platoon set the stage for other antiwar films. The following year, 1987, saw the release of Stanley Kubrick's *Full Metal Jacket*, based on Vietnam veteran

Gustav Hasford's 1979 episodic autobiographical novel *The Short-Timers*, which focused on the author's training for the United States Marine Corps and his time in Vietnam as a military journalist. Kubrick, renowned for being methodical, cast R. Lee Ermey, who'd been a Marine Corps drill instructor at the San Diego Recruit Depot from 1965 to 1967, as Gunnery Sergeant Hartman, whose creative foul mouth was the result of Ermey's direct input into the script. The making of *Full Metal Jacket* overlapped with the filming of *Platoon*, but Kubrick took longer to make his film, shooting much of it at studios in England between August 1985 and August 1986. The film opened in theaters in June 1987 to universal acclaim, praised for its horrifying reenactment of the Tet Offensive and the Marines defending the battered, rubble-choked imperial capital Huế. Subsequent anti–Vietnam War films included *Gardens of Stone* (1987); *Good Morning, Vietnam* (1987); *Casualties of War* (1989); *84 Charlie MoPic* (1989); and *Born on the Fourth of July* (1989), Oliver Stone's biopic of paraplegic antiwar veteran Ron Kovic (played by Tom Cruise).

By the late 1980s, debates about the Vietnam War had shifted in striking ways. After *Platoon*, only one POW/MIA film, *Braddock: Missing in Action III* (1989), made it to theaters, faring poorly at the box office. A disgusted Chuck Norris said of Stone's unexpected blockbuster: "If I was a Vietnam vet who'd put my life on the line over there, and then went to see *Platoon*— with those scenes of GIs tormenting villagers and raping young girls—I'd be furious."[80] By the middle of the following decade, the POW/MIA movement was largely spent, except for a few lone holdouts. As for the Rambo franchise, a third film in the series came out in 1988, this time pitting the muscle-bound killing machine against Soviet soldiers in Afghanistan. It was a commercial disappointment compared with the second installment, barely making it into the top twenty highest-grossing films of 1988. Not until 2008—twenty years later—would Stallone repeat the infamous role, this time taking on noncommunist foes in Myanmar. In one of his more reflective moods after the release of *Rambo: First Blood Part II*, Stallone confessed to having a "love-hate thing from Rambo," admitting "the heat I catch from it is very exasperating."[81]

Meantime, the chorus of war apologists, so outspoken in the early 1980s when Maya Lin's memorial design was under construction, had largely fallen silent. When the nation celebrated the tenth anniversary of the Wall in November 1992, the public had forgotten the controversy it sparked prior to being built. At the ceremonies marking the anniversary, a quarter of a million people flooded the Mall to pay their respects to the beloved monument. One of those in attendance, Vietnam veteran John Vickers, who served with the

1074th Assault Helicopter Company, summed up the widely held views of his fellow vets and the rest of the country when he said, "There's a spirit here, and when you get close to it you can feel it. I really believe it's a healing place."[82]

Likewise, traveling to Vietnam stopped being taboo. As the decade drew to a close, contingents of veterans returned to Vietnam on a regular basis to revisit the ruins of military bases now swallowed up by foliage and to walk through areas that had once been battlefields. American visitors to Vietnam found it a scarred land, pockmarked by bomb craters in the countryside, racked with grinding poverty in its cities. Along the way, vets typically encountered Vietnamese who were welcoming and kind, wishing to put the war behind them. Many trips doubled as humanitarian missions, with veterans bearing gifts: hospital equipment, medicine, physicians, technical experts, and monetary contributions to help build schools and clinics in rural areas. A group of Vietnam veterans in Massachusetts, for example, raised funds to supply a hospital in rural Vietnam in 1989 with new medical equipment.[83] That year, Vietnam vet Michael Castellano, who ran a company called Indochina Communication Service, which specialized in organizing trips for veterans to return to Vietnam, commented: "It's not for everybody—maybe half the vets are ready to go back—but it can be a real healing experience."[84]

William Broyles Jr., a journalist who served in Vietnam from 1969 to 1971 as a Marine infantry platoon commander, returned to the country in 1984 with other veterans. Moved by what he witnessed, he returned to the United States to cocreate (with writer John Sacret Young) *China Beach*, a weekly television show about Vietnam that aired on ABC in April 1988. Imbued with strong pacifist themes, *China Beach* told the story of nurse Colleen McMurphy (Dana Delany) and her many friendships and ordeals during the war. Broyles and Young based the show on *Home before Morning*, the 1983 memoir of Lynda Van Devanter (1947–2002), a nurse assigned to the 71st Evacuation Hospital in Pleiku. During her time as an army nurse, Van Devanter developed antiwar beliefs and returned home to advocate for other women who served in Vietnam. She died at age 55 of collagen vascular disease, which she believed was due to Agent Orange exposure.[85] *China Beach*, with echoes of Van Devanter's experiences, was a major critical success. It drew a small yet dedicated audience and won several Emmy Awards.

For Broyles, a milestone in his personal healing experience came during his 1984 trip to Vietnam. He was so moved by the dignity and generosity of the Vietnamese people he met that he sought out the grave of a former enemy soldier to honor his fallen former foe. Returning to America, Broyles had concluded "that I had more in common with my old enemies than with anyone except the men who had fought at my side. My enemies and I had something almost beyond words."[86]

Rebuilding and rehabilitating Vietnam would take decades of hard work, trial and error, and patience. But it could be done. By contrast, rehabilitating the war's legitimacy in the public's memory—recasting it as a noble cause, as Reagan sought to do—was an impossible task. Neither Reagan nor the war's defenders could salvage the war's reputation. Making their job impossible were the veterans who came home from Vietnam and refused to allow the war to be glorified and turned into something it wasn't. These men and women could have surrendered to despair, but instead they told the truth as they remembered it and, in doing so, served an extended tour of duty for the country they loved so deeply.

CHAPTER 4

Seeing Reds

Most of them don't know what communism is, could not pick
it out of a lineup. They only know what anticommunism is.
The two are practically unrelated.

—*Barbara Kingsolver,* The Lacuna, *2009*

I don't want no commies in my car!

—*Bud (Harry Dean Stanton),* Repo Man, *1984*

Reds in Reagan's America

In 1979, a major Hollywood studio took a bold step, unprecedented in the history of American cinema: it green-lit a major motion picture that was openly and unabashedly sympathetic to a communist. The studio was Paramount. The film was Warren Beatty's *Reds*, a biopic about revolutionary journalist John Reed (1887–1920). Beatty embraced the project as a labor of love. He planned to direct and star in *Reds*, based on a screenplay he cowrote with British socialist playwright Trevor Griffiths, with uncredited help from writer, actress, and comedian Elaine May, his close friend. It took some convincing to win the backing of jittery Paramount execs. But if anybody could pull it off, it was Beatty, who'd starred in a string of successful films, most recently in the fantasy-comedy *Heaven Can Wait*, one of the highest-grossing movies of 1978. Still, a favorable portrayal of a communist was a tough sell, even in liberal Hollywood. "We're not making a picture about communists. We're not glorifying them," studio chairman Barry Diller told Beatty.[1] Unwilling to take no for an answer, Beatty pleaded his case to the studio's Austrian-born president, Charles Bluhdorn. "A picture about a Communist who dies?" Bluhdorn thought it over. "What's it going to cost?" Beatty gave the Paramount president a figure of $30 million, to which Bluhdorn begged, "Please, don't make this picture."[2]

In the end, however, Beatty won and received the financing to make Reds.[3] From August 1979 to December 1980, Beatty filmed on locations in London, in New York City, and in parts of Finland and Spain, working with a budget somewhere in the ballpark of $20 million. To introduce documentary-style realism to the film, Beatty interviewed a number of aging historical witnesses who either knew Reed or were his contemporaries. By the time Reds was made, most of them were in their nineties. Authors Rebecca West and Henry Miller, American Civil Liberties Union founder Roger Baldwin, radical activist and scholar Scott Nearing, former Republican congressman Hamilton Fish III, entertainer George Jessel, and journalists Adela Rogers St. Johns and George Seldes all appeared, along with many others, as real-life commentators. Post-production on Reds involved months of painstaking work, including an army of sixty-five editors working with millions of feet of footage. The finished product opened December 4, 1981, in hundreds of theaters across North America to positive reviews. Reds depicted the relationship between radical journalist John Reed (Warren Beatty) and writer and feminist Louise Bryant (Diane Keaton), which unfolded against the sprawling backdrops of Greenwich Village bohemian activism, labor strikes, the reelection of Woodrow Wilson in 1916, the founding of the Communist Labor Party, and the Bolshevik Revolution in Russia. The film's most famous sequence shows Reed and Bryant in Moscow for the storming of the Winter Palace, along with massive crowds rushing through the streets to a rousing chorus of the "Internationale."[4]

The real John Reed, born and raised in Portland, Oregon, lived an eventful life, traveling around the world after graduating from Harvard in 1910 and leaping headlong into radical journalism in his early twenties. A prolific writer, he documented labor unrest, the Mexican Revolution, and World War I, but his most famous book was Ten Days that Shook the World, an engrossing account of the Russian Revolution, published by New York City–based Boni & Liveright in 1919.[5] Reed was only thirty-two when he died of typhus in Moscow in 1920. Beatty was in his forties when he played Reed; critics lauded his performance, and the Academy of Motion Picture Arts and Sciences rewarded him with a best actor nomination at the 54th Academy Awards in 1982. Reds scored more nominations than any other film that year—twelve in total—and was the odds-on favorite to win best picture. It lost to the British historical drama *Chariots of Fire*, about a pair of runners in the 1924 Olympics, but Beatty won an Academy Award for Best Director, and Maureen Stapleton received an Oscar for her spirited portrayal of anarchist Emma Goldman.

Beatty felt disappointed his film did not win best picture. Yet the fact that *Reds*—with its positive portrayal of a man committed to radical left politics— even got made, not to mention financed and released by a major Hollywood studio, and nominated in so many categories at the Academy Awards, only thirty years after people in the entertainment industry were blacklisted for voicing mildly left-leaning beliefs, was itself a miracle. Author Kurt Vonnegut hailed the film as "one of the most audacious and unexpected political acts in my lifetime." Vonnegut never thought he'd live to see a mainstream Hollywood film celebrating communists or the Soviet revolution. Beatty "might as well have gone over Niagara Falls in nothing but his Jockey shorts and a football helmet," Vonnegut said.[6] Even more astonishing, *Reds* failed to generate much controversy upon its release. Denunciations of the movie were few. One came from *Barron's*, the weekly newspaper of Dow Jones & Company, which ran a scathing critique under the headline, "Paramount Has Made a Communist Propaganda Epic."[7]

Other than that, *Reds* did not elicit much criticism from the Right. In fact, William F. Buckley Jr., syndicated columnist and editor of *National Review*, praised the film for showing John Reed's disillusionment "with a despotic and impenetrable Soviet bureaucracy," advising conservatives to see it.[8] President Reagan, who loved watching movies more than had any other commander in chief, invited Beatty and Keaton to a special screening of the film in the White House. After the credits ended and the lights went up in the room, the president and the first lady praised the film and congratulated Beatty. At this point, Reagan told Beatty, "I was kind of hoping for a happy ending."[9]

Reactions to *Reds* are telling and shed light on the times. Anticommunism in the United States—though still vibrant in certain circles—had lost much of its potency by the early 1980s. The steadily shrinking size of the Communist Party of the United States of America (CPUSA) partially accounts for diminished anxieties. Once an organization of one hundred thousand members in the depths of the Great Depression (by its own claims), with a cultural prestige that extended far beyond those numbers, the CPUSA in the Reagan era was a fragment of its former self, boasting only ten to twenty thousand members on its rolls, and had virtually no influence.[10] Much of its membership consisted of aging radicals, still dedicated to the cause. The face of the party was CPUSA's tireless chairman, Gus Hall, a lifelong party member and labor organizer, now in his seventies—balding, crinkly eyed, always smiling. Hall dedicated his boundless energy to campaigning for the presidency of the United States in 1980 and 1984, alongside his vice presidential candidate, activist and scholar Dr. Angela Davis. Hall told tiny crowds of supporters wherever he went that a revolution was around the corner. "We want to overthrow the capitalist system. But the means that we have chosen are ones of mass education and propaganda. We have our newspaper, and we appear on talk shows and we will take part in elections," Hall explained.[11] Only a handful of dedicated communists took Hall seriously. Even by his own self-deprecating admission, he was a product of a bygone era, a steadfast keeper of the flame.

In a country that had turned decisively against the excesses of McCarthyism—and where the infamous senator from Wisconsin had become widely reviled—it was not surprising that communism, once a taboo subject, was no longer widely viewed as an existential threat to America. The relaxing of fears allowed people to take a second look at communism in the United States, as moviegoers did in *Reds*. The acclaimed documentary *Seeing Red*, released in 1983, offered an even bolder reevaluation of American communists than had *Reds*. While *Reds* celebrated a real-life communist from the past, it focused on John Reed's volatile relationship with Louise Bryant, without exploring the reasons behind his radicalization or his views on capitalism in any meaningful way. *Reds*, for all of its radical flourishes, was essentially a love story. In a different vein, *Seeing Red* profiled ordinary, rank-and-file women and men—fifteen in total—who had been active in the Communist Party during its heyday in the 1930s and 1940s and had endured the wrath of McCarthyism after World War II. *Seeing Red* examined, in depth, the reasons why these people joined the party and the injustices they sought to redress.

Filmmakers Jim Klein and Julia Reichert, married left-wing activists who cofounded the radical film collective New Day Films in 1971, codirected *Seeing Red*. They met at Antioch College in the 1960s and went on to make several shoestring-budget documentaries, including *Union Maids* (1976), about a trio of female union organizers in the Great Depression, which was nominated for a Best Documentary Feature Academy Award. Thanks to a $160,000 grant from the National Endowment for the Humanities, Klein and Reichert were able to conduct numerous interviews for *Seeing Red*, and to select choice historical footage to mix with the talking heads (by comparison, *Union Maids* was made for a measly ten thousand dollars and more limited in scope).[12] Klein and Reichert were not communists. In fact, Reichert grew up in a conservative Republican household and supported Barry Goldwater in her youth. A leftist roommate in college, the daughter of Communist Party members, introduced her to communist ideas. Klein admitted they "were fairly ignorant of the subject when we started out."[13]

Seeing Red featured a diverse group of writers, academics, labor organizers, political activists, and at least one entertainer, singer Pete Seeger, who performs in the film. The lively interviewees tell vivid stories about their involvement in labor strikes, protests against tenant evictions, and organizing sharecroppers in the Deep South. One of the film's "stars," Bill Bailey, a colorful, Popeye-like longshoreman from San Francisco, traveled to Spain with other American volunteers in 1937 to defend the left-wing republic by taking up arms against the fascists.[14] Many of the people profiled in *Seeing Red* had left the Communist Party by the time the movie was made. California labor organizer Dorothy Healey quit in 1968 to protest the Soviet invasion of Czechoslovakia. Revelations of Joseph Stalin's crimes in 1956 by Soviet leader Nikita Khrushchev's led to huge membership losses for the CPUSA. Yet, unlike the ex-communists who wrote about their disillusionment in the influential 1949 book *The God That Failed*, the former party members in *Seeing Red* remained unrepentant. "I have only an enormous amount of pride in what our generation did," Healey tells Reichert toward the end of the film.[15]

While *Seeing Red* was not uncritical of American communism, its message was that in spite of the party's flaws, the members shown in the film were decent men and women who dedicated their lives to fighting social ills and should not be demonized. Such a sympathetic portrayal of communists— akin to that of John Reed in *Reds*—was unheard of in American cinema before the 1980s. *Seeing Red* won acclaim and an Oscar nomination for best documentary feature film at the 56th Academy Awards in 1984.[16] It lost, but the fact that it was even nominated revealed how far the film industry had evolved since the blacklist period. *Seeing Red* reached smaller audiences than *Reds*, mostly through screenings at university campuses, where one or both of the filmmakers provided a verbal introduction.[17] *Seeing Red* was successful as documentaries went, making a profit for Klein and Reichert, who resisted the pull of Hollywood in the wake of its success.[18]

Anticommunism in the Reagan Era

The absence of a backlash against *Reds* and *Seeing Red* demonstrated the waning influence of anticommunism. Times had changed. The political and cultural landscapes had been altered dramatically. By the time Reagan occupied the White House, anticommunism had been retreating from public life for years. But embers of anticommunism still glowed. Opposition to communism had always been a big tent in American society, attracting diverse constituencies. Far from monolithic, it assumed different forms, depending on its adherents, which included socialists, anarchists, liberals, centrists, conservatives, libertarians, and right-wing extremists. Anticommunism also came in secular and religious flavors. In the modern American conservative movement, which helped mobilize voters to elect Reagan in 1980, anticommunism functioned as cement that held together disparate elements: libertarians, the Religious Right, and social conservatives. Indeed, several groups whose purpose was opposing communism flourished in the 1980s, including CAUSA International, the secular anticommunist educational wing of the Reverend Sun Myung Moon's Unification Church, and the World Anti-Communist League (WACL), a global body of anticommunist organizations and politicians based in Taipei, Taiwan.[19]

For decades, the most controversial anticommunist group in America was the John Birch Society (JBS). Founded in 1958, the JBS instantly gained attention owing to the outlandish conspiracy theories of its members. The organization's heyday was in the early 1960s, peaking with one hundred thousand card carriers, as well as chapters across the country.[20] Anticommunism had always been the JBS's raison d'être. The society's books, films, and other promotional materials propagated the belief that the United States had fallen under the control of a sinister, global communist plot. By the 1980s, the JBS was headquartered in Belmont, Massachusetts, with around fifty thousand members, according to its leaders. It published a newspaper, *American Opinion*, and ran summer youth camps where courses were offered on the "duties of citizenship" and the perils of communism.[21]

For "Birchers," the communist conspiracy involved a nefarious combination of the federal government, the Trilateral Commission, the Council on Foreign Relations, presidents such as Dwight D. Eisenhower and John F. Kennedy, and an influential cabal of wealthy millionaires, all working closely together to usurp the liberties of freedom-loving peoples. Martin Ohlson, a JBS coordinator from Appleton, Wisconsin, explained the complexity of the "master plan" in 1985: "Trying to understand the conspiracy in a day is like trying to understand calculus in an hour. If you don't present it in an educational way, you turn people off. People need to be spoon-fed the information so they can put the puzzle together."[22]

A severe blow to the JBS came on September 1, 1983, when Soviet jets shot down Korean Air Lines Flight 007, a Boeing 747 passenger plane that strayed off course over Soviet territory during a flight from Anchorage, Alaska, to Seoul, South Korea. The incident escalated Cold War tensions to ominous levels, at a moment when Soviet-American relations had virtually bottomed out. The far-reaching consequences of this incident are explored later in this book. However, one of the 269 passengers and crew on board was Representative Larry McDonald, a conservative Democratic congressman from Georgia and member of the John Birch Society. Not surprisingly, many in the JBS—an organization named after an American Baptist missionary and U.S. Army intelligence officer killed in China by Mao's communist forces in 1945—thought the Soviets had targeted McDonald specifically when they shot down KAL 007. Televangelist Jerry Falwell gave voice to such suspicions when he said: "There is a real question in my mind that the Soviets may have actually murdered 269 passengers, including sixty-one Americans and crew on the KAL Flight 007, in order to kill Larry McDonald."[23]

The next major loss in leadership occurred over a year later with the death of JBS founder and businessman Robert W. Welch on January 6, 1985, at age eighty-five. Welch had been instrumental in building the JBS from a tiny fringe group to an influential national organization. Yet his stark belief that communists effectively controlled the United States, including his insistence that President Eisenhower was a "conscious, dedicated agent of the Communist Conspiracy," kept the Birchers outside the mainstream. Despite these difficult losses, JBS spokesman John F. McManus remained philosophical. "There is a huge battle between the forces of good versus the forces of evil. There will be no change in the Society. We will continue to wake the town and tell the people."[24]

A reputation for being fringe extremists still haunted the JBS in the Reagan era. Since the 1960s, moderate conservatives had sought to distance themselves from the organization. William F. Buckley denounced the JBS in the pages of *National Review* magazine, and mainstream Republicans regarded the society's endorsement as a kiss of death. Such fears persisted into the 1980s and were evident around election time. When Rob Scribner ran as a Republican in California's Twenty-Seventh Congressional District in 1984, his campaign ran an advertisement accusing his Democratic opponent, Mel Levine, of being a member of the New Left organization Students for a Democratic Society in the 1960s.[25] Levine fired back by informing the press that JBS members in Scribner's church were campaigning for him.

Scribner issued a panicky statement denouncing and disavowing the JBS: "I have never associated nor wish to associate with the John Birch Society. I do not approve of their extreme positions politically and ideologically. I openly request no support from the Birch Society whatsoever, and criticize their extreme prejudices."[26] For much of the rest of the campaign, Scribner nervously denied direct ties to the JBS.

A similar imbroglio erupted in the United States Senate race in Massachusetts. A hard-fought campaign in 1984 between Democrat John Kerry, a Vietnam veteran, antiwar activist, and the state lieutenant governor, and Republican Ray Shamie, a wealthy businessman, took an ugly turn when Shamie's supporters in the John Birch Society, along with Major General George S. Patton Jr., son of the renowned World War II general, accused Kerry of being "soft on communism" and giving "aid and comfort to the enemy" during the Vietnam War. The ugly allegation stemmed from Kerry's leadership role in Vietnam Veterans Against the War thirteen years earlier.[27] Retired lieutenant general James M. Gavin, who lived in Massachusetts, fired back at Patton and the JBS by supporting Kerry. "There are all types of courage," Gavin said, "but two in particular are battlefield courage and moral courage. And moral courage is a lot harder to come by. It took great moral courage for John Kerry to oppose that war after having served in it."[28]

The Kerry campaign retaliated by revealing Shamie's ties to the John Birch Society. Investigative reporting by the *Boston Globe* unearthed a 1975 political action meeting held at his office in which Shamie had asked JBS leader John McManus to speak. Shamie also selected nine "friends and business associates" to invite to the gathering and gave them copies of *The Naked Capitalist*, by former Salt Lake City police chief W. Cleon Skousen. The book—a right-wing anticommunist polemic—described the role that corporations, financial institutions, and wealthy individuals played in the global communist conspiracy, with an emphasis on the activities of "prominent Jewish families."[29] Shamie confirmed the allegations that he had invited McManus to his office to speak but insisted that JBS members were "sincere, patriotic Americans." In the November elections, Kerry defeated Shamie, who later insisted that "personal attacks"—a reference to his connections to the John Birch Society—influenced the outcome. Meantime, in California, Rob Scribner's rejection of the John Birch Society did not help his campaign for the House of Representatives: he lost to Mel Levine.[30]

Like the Birchers, the Religious Right embraced right-wing anticommunism, but a less conspiratorial variety. The Religious Right was a loose-knit coalition of conservative activists representing Roman Catholics, evangelical Protestants, Mormons, and Jews. Since the early 1970s, the movement had grown thanks to energetic grassroots support around such highly charged issues as abortion, school prayer, homosexuality, pornography, sex education, and the waning influence of religion in public life. Prominent figures in the Religious Right included Jerry Falwell, Pat Robertson, Francis Schaeffer, Tim LaHaye, Charles Stanley, D. James Kennedy, Jimmy Swaggart, and Jim Bakker. Several of the movement's titans had built multimedia empires that utilized television, radio, and publications to give them a broad national reach and staggering fortunes.[31]

Communism—and anticommunism—assumed a prominent place in the Religious Right's agenda. With the return of the Cold War, conservative religious figures cited communism as a dire threat to religious liberties. As a general rule, they embraced a Manichaean worldview, which regarded communism, atheism, and secular humanism as a triple threat to faithful, God-fearing believers. "Satan has mobilized his own forces to destroy America," proclaimed the Reverend Jerry Falwell, doyen of the movement.[32] The Satanic "forces" Falwell warned of encompassed an array of enemies, of which communism was but one—albeit a powerful and relentless one. Falwell believed nuclear war with the Soviet Union was imminent, a view he stressed in interviews, articles, and in his 1980 booklet *Armageddon and the Coming War with Russia*.[33] He predicted Soviet aggression over oil in the Middle East would trigger a massive confrontation, which would lead to global nuclear war. He viewed the total destruction of the Soviet Union and everybody who lived there as inevitable. "All of history is reaching a climax and I do not think . . . we have 50 years left. I don't think my children will live their full lives out, as I probably will," Falwell said in 1981.[34] His views on this matter resembled those of President Reagan. "The president had fairly strong views about the parable of Armageddon," explained Robert McFarlane, Reagan's national security adviser. Reagan addressed the issue in a 1985 interview with the *Wall Street Journal*: "I don't know whether you know, but a great many theologians over a number of years . . . have been struck with the fact that in recent years, as in no other time in history, most of the prophecies have been coming together."[35] Despite his stark forecasts, Falwell assured the public that he and his allies in the Religious Right were "mobilizing a potential army numbering in the tens of millions. The fight was on."[36]

In 1982, the "fight" Falwell spoke of was momentarily directed against the most famous evangelist minister in the United States, Billy Graham. On

May 13, Graham returned from a heavily publicized trip to the Soviet Union. Once upon a time, Graham had been a hardened Cold Warrior, preaching anticommunism from the pulpit. Addressing a massive crowd in Los Angeles in 1949, he sounded the alarm about the "Red threat" to thunderous applause. He told his captive audience there were "1,100 social-sounding organizations that are communist or communist operated in this country," which "control the minds of a great segment" of America, including educators, entertainers, politicians, and other important cultural figures. In the early 1950s, Graham encouraged his followers to "pray that . . . some day the Iron Curtain will be cracked for Christ and that materialistic communism will be destroyed by the love, grace, and truth of the risen Christ." He famously wrote in 1954, "Either Communism must die, or Christianity must die."[37]

The passage of time softened Graham's positions. He eventually assumed the role of spiritual adviser to several presidents and moved to the center politically. He addressed the need for reconciliation between communist and noncommunist nations and supported President Nixon's détente policies. During Reagan's presidency, with Cold War tensions resuming, Graham decided to go the Soviet Union because he believed "it is time . . . for religious leaders to meet and make whatever contribution we can to peace on our earth."[38] During his whirlwind five-day trip in May 1982, Graham visited churches, attended a wreath-laying ceremony for Soviets killed in World War II, and took part at a world religions conference focused on the threat of nuclear war. Graham also met with Pentecostals who sought refuge in the U.S. embassy in Moscow, hoping to emigrate to the West. The high point of the trip, Graham thought, was a sermon he delivered to a packed house at Moscow's Church of Evangelical Christian-Baptists. The fiery minister used the talk as an opportunity to condemn the nuclear arms race, which he said was putting the human race "at the gate of hell."[39]

The journey left Graham "exhausted," yet he praised Soviet leaders for giving churches in the country what he believed to be a surprising amount of autonomy. There were, Graham told reporters, "hundreds or even thousands of churches in this country" operating relatively freely, a stark contrast to other countries he had visited where "preaching the gospel is forbidden by law."[40] In an interview with Soviet journalist Vladimir Markov, Graham condemned the nuclear arms race in stronger terms than most disarmament activists in America, calling it "irrational, insane and criminal." He also spoke frankly about the need for closer relations between the superpowers: "The citizens of the United States and the Soviet Union are, above all, people made in the image of God. We are not different, but we have strange stereotypes of each other, and that must be eliminated. And we must get to know each other. I would like to see more exchanges in the sphere of culture, education, trade and tourism. Extended cultural exchanges, student exchanges, educational exchanges, trade relations, tourist travel—all of these can help us get to know one another as people and lead to greater understanding and trust. This is what our religious contacts are serving, too."[41]

On his return to the United States, it surprised Graham to discover his comments had ignited a firestorm of controversy. "I am more than a little perplexed. His statement that he has not seen any evidence of religious persecution is just not believable," said Graham's friend, Dr. Edmund Robb, a Methodist clergyman.[42] Abraham Foxman, national director of the Anti-Defamation League of B'nai B'rith, condemned Graham's remarks about religious freedom in the Soviet Union. "When a respected American theologian makes a statement the Soviets in their wildest dreams could not hope for, then everyone suffering inside the Soviet Union—be it a Soviet Christian or Jew—has even less of a chance ever to gain religious freedom."[43] Presbyterian minister and human rights advocate Rev. Blahoslav S. Hruby called Graham "a very poor witness," adding: "He did a great disservice to the cause of religious liberty."[44] As part of his public rebuke of Graham, William F. Buckley Jr. telephoned Joseph Stalin's daughter, Svetlana Alliluyeva, now a naturalized U.S. citizen, to ask about the state of religious freedom in the Soviet Union. He promptly announced her response in his syndicated weekly column. "It is forbidden to buy a copy of the Bible" in the Soviet Union, Alliluyeva told Buckley. That "edict," Buckley reminded readers, came directly from Alliluyeva's father.[45]

On the opposite end of the political spectrum, Graham's trip to the Soviet Union earned the applause of liberal clergy and peace activists, who welcomed his about-face.[46] Their statements of support, however, were drowned out by the outrage of his critics, whose disapproval did not prevent Graham from turning his energies toward advocating arms control and improved relations between the United States and Soviet Union.[47] Meanwhile, key figures in the Religious Right warned of menacing developments closer to home. Pastor Charles Stanley, who served as president of the Southern Baptist Convention from 1984 to 1986, cautioned that the communist threat lurked inside of the United States. "For the last half century, the Marxists in this country have influenced and penetrated every single area of our society." Pat Robertson, host of the popular television program *The 700 Club*, furnished a more specific assessment of the origin of the threat within, laying it at the door of institutions of higher learning. "In the United States of America," he said, "key universities . . . have been taken over by people who are sympathetic with Marxism. . . . While only a few label themselves Marxists, almost all identify themselves as 'secular humanists.'"[48]

Nailing Jell-O to a Tree

Since the 1960s, the term "secular humanism" had wormed its way into the parlance of the times. Precise definitions were elusive, but it was typically used to describe a worldview that emphasized the importance of knowledge, human reason, and scientific methods in day-to-day human affairs, while downplaying the role of divine intervention. It "snuck into" the United States from Europe, claimed Rev. Tim LaHaye, a founder of the Moral Majority, and became one of "the most dangerous religions in the world." Fundamentalist preachers in the Reagan era used the term as a catchall buzzword for everything they hated. Secular humanism, said Jerry Falwell, "challenges every principle on which America was founded. It advocates abortion-on-demand, recognition of homosexuals, free use of pornography, legalizing of prostitution and gambling, and free use of drugs, among other things."[49] Many in the Religious Right associated secular humanism with communism. Televangelist Jimmy Swaggart drove home this point in a fiery June 1985 speech at Toronto's Maple Leaf Gardens, a huge hockey arena where fifty thousand followers showed up to hear him. "I'm sick of fellow traveling communist liberals who constantly praise Russia and kick the United States of America," Swaggart told the cheering audience. "I'm sick of evolution, secular humanism, materialism and communism!"[50]

To Swaggart, Falwell, Robertson, and others, secular humanists were dupes of communism, carrying out the communist agenda on American soil, much like the "fellow travelers" of yesteryear. According to fundamentalist reasoning, because the Communist Party had lost its credibility, the minions of darkness were forced to subvert American freedoms under the cloak of secular humanism. Schools turned into the front lines of a modern struggle pitting the Religious Right against secular humanist foes and their American Civil Liberties Union attorneys. The most famous legal battle in this conflict took place in 1987, when U.S. District Judge William Brevard Hand of the United States District Court for the Southern District of Alabama ruled in favor of hundreds of plaintiffs suing the state of Alabama for making students read textbooks with "secular humanist" content. In total, Hand banned forty-four textbooks—thirty-nine in history and social studies, five in home economics—for promoting "secular humanism," which he called "a religious belief system," and for not sufficiently discussing religion. "It is common knowledge that miscellaneous doctrines such as evolution, social-ism, communism, humanism and other concepts are advanced in public schools," Hand declared. Within months, the Eleventh U.S. Circuit Court of Appeals overturned Judge Hand's ruling.[51]

Judge Hand's ruling was part of a larger crusade aimed at containing the perceived threat of secular humanism creeping into the education system. School districts across the country faced similar legal challenges, and univer-sities also weathered the assault. In the fall of 1984, Senator Orrin Hatch, a Republican from Utah and chair of the Senate Labor and Human Resources Committee, inserted a paragraph into an education bill prohibiting govern-ment grants from going to "courses of instruction" at universities "the subject of which is secular humanism." When asked to define "secular humanism," Hatch's spokesman, Ed Darrell, replied, "There are a lot of different definitions of it, just as there are a lot of different definitions of religion."[52] Although secular humanism's denouncers had a hard time explaining what it meant, they claimed it was inextricably tied to the communist threat. Thanks to "secular humanism," said Jesse Helms, the archconservative senator from North Carolina, "communism has made substantial inroads into the thinking of our people." Jimmy Swaggart put it more bluntly: "The result of secular humanism is communism."[53]

Ultimately, efforts to stem the specter of secular humanism were inef-fectual, largely because no two people could agree on what the term meant. "Trying to define secular humanism," said a spokesperson for Norman Lear's liberal advocacy group People for the American Way, "is like trying to nail Jell-O to a tree."[54] Linking secular humanism to communism did little to turn public opinion against it, and efforts to combat it in schools by legal means generally went nowhere. In 1985, Fred Edwords, executive director of the American Humanist Association, argued that fear of change on the part of fundamentalists was what drove the war against secular humanism: "What are they going to do? They can't say, 'This is the devil's work.' That's too corny. They can't say, 'This is godless communism.' That went out in the 1950s, in the McCarthy era, and people spot it immediately for what it is. They had to come up with something else."[55]

But that "something else" failed to convince a large segment of the American public that their freedoms were in peril. The inability of the

Religious Right to mount an effective opposition to secular humanism revealed the movement's limitations. By decade's end, fundamentalism—once seemingly invincible—was on the retreat. A series of sexual and financial scandals led to the downfall of several televangelists, including Jim Bakker and Jimmy Swaggart, in the second half of the 1980s.[56] Pat Robertson's 1988 presidential campaign—initially a source of high hopes for many in the Religious Right—ended abruptly after his poor showing in the primaries. "Between 1985 and 1988 Pat Robertson lost 52 percent of his audience. The televangelism scandals almost certainly had an impact on Robertson's audience ratings, as they negatively affected his bid to challenge George Bush for the Republican nomination for the presidency," wrote religion scholar Jeffrey K. Hadden. In 1989, Jerry Falwell disbanded the Moral Majority, the controversial Christian Right organization at the forefront of so many of the battles against secular humanism, claiming it had largely accomplished its mission.[57]

The American education system had been at the heart of the short-lived battles over secular humanism, but with fundamentalism retreating, the controversy withered. In the culture wars of the Reagan era, public schools repeatedly provided the turf on which conservatives and liberals fought over curriculum matters. Such conflicts derived significance from the symbolic weight placed on children and teens as the future of the country. Ideological contests around education often lacked a Cold War subtext, as was the case when President Reagan pushed unsuccessfully for the passage of a school prayer amendment in 1984. But the conflation of secular humanism with communism by fundamentalists gave that controversy a Cold War flavor.

An even more overtly Cold War showdown in the public school system occurred in Florida in the spring of 1983. At stake was a mandatory course taught in the state's high schools called "Americanism vs. Communism." Since 1961, Florida high school students were required by state law to take the class, and by the 1980s, a growing number of educators and parents were troubled by its political content. Florida had long been a bastion of right-wing anticommunist politics throughout the 1950s, becoming even more so after Fidel Castro swept into power following the Cuban Revolution at the start of 1959. Situated roughly ninety miles from Key West's southernmost point and with its new communist government, Cuba made Floridians uneasy, especially during the tense Missile Crisis in October 1962.

A year before that terrifying event, the Florida legislature had voted to create the new mandatory high school course, Americanism vs. Communism.

The wording of the state law spelled out the reasoning behind the class: "The course shall lay particular emphasis upon the dangers of communism, the ways to fight communism, the evils of communism, the fallacies of communism and the false doctrines of communism. No teacher or textual material assigned to the course shall present communism as preferable to the system of constitutional government and the free-enterprise competitive economy indigenous to the United States."[58] Students taking the course learned about the horrors of life in the Soviet Union, Cuba, and "Red" China through films, lectures, and a textbook called *The Masks of Communism*, featuring the squinting eyes of V. I. Lenin peering out over oversized block letters spelling out "Communism." "Today, the United States is threatened by an enemy dedicated to its destruction," read the book's opening sentence. *Orlando Sentinel* columnist Bob Morris took the class when he was a high school student in 1969. "Unfortunately," he wrote, "our teacher was a borderline John Bircher who instructed us in the 'Seven Warning Signs of Communist Infiltration,' as if they were the warning signs for cancer."[59]

The course made sense in 1961, given the tenor of the times and the state's close proximity to Cuba. "Of course, the intent of the legislature in the 1960s was to persuade us that all communists were evil monsters, the absolute antithesis of American capitalists," recalled David Lee McMullen, who took the class in high school right after it was introduced.[60] But in 1983, a growing number of Floridians, including some Republicans in the legislature, found it hopelessly out of date. It was, after all, one of the last remaining mandatory high school–level courses of its kind left in the United States (the other being in Louisiana), and critics argued it was time that Florida joined the rest of the country. On April 25, 1983, the House Education Committee voted eleven to four to recommend that the required Americanism vs. Communism class be abolished by the Florida legislature and replaced by a more modern comparative political systems class. "The kids are too bright to accept anticommunism as prescribed by the statute," insisted Representative Walt Young, a member of the Education Committee.[61]

As a result of the committee's vote, the future of the mandatory course now rested in the hands of the state's House of Representatives. Advocates of scrapping the class faced resistance from anti-Castro Cuban émigrés determined to keep it. "People should know about communism. If we had school lessons about communism, Castro wouldn't be here today," said Cuban-born legislator Rep. Roberto Casas, who encouraged his fellow representatives to vote to preserve the course. Rep. Humberto Cortino, wounded at the Bay of Pigs in 1961 and a prisoner for two years under Castro, concurred: "I have felt in my flesh what communism is. I want my children to know what communism is." In the weeks leading up to the vote, Florida's large Cuban-American community lobbied against repeal. On May 31, the Florida House of Representatives voted eighty-nine to twenty-six to keep the course. "It's difficult to even talk about changing Americanism vs. Communism because somebody will get the idea that you've gone soft on communism," lamented Zollie Maynard, a veteran education lobbyist.[62] A Republican legislator who voted to keep the course speculated that "some members" feared the consequences of voting against it.[63]

The fight to keep Florida's mandatory anticommunism course ended well for Cold Warriors. A combination of clear goals, support from the Cuban-American population, and a primary focus on communism abroad gave the course's advocates advantages missing in the fight against secular humanism. And yet, even in victory, the course's days were numbered. In 1991, it died a quiet death in the legislature, a casualty of the Cold War's abrupt end.[64] Despite that, two key aspects of Reagan-era Cold War culture were strikingly apparent in this case: Cuban-Americans living in Florida, who virtually dictated Washington's policies toward Havana for decades, played a vital role in sustaining the Cold War revival in the 1980s; and focusing on perceived threats of communism abroad, as well as human rights violations under those regimes, was a more effective strategy than trying to spook the public with warnings of alleged subversion at home.

Left and Right, Communism and Anticommunism

Few Americans needed to be persuaded of President Reagan's belief, shared by many members of Congress and government officials, that communist countries were totalitarian and brought misery to their inhabitants. Cold Warriors were united in their loathing of communism, even if they didn't always see eye to eye on how best to transform that perspective into policy. Their views mirrored the opinions of a majority of the American public. The Cold War's critics, therefore, confronted a dilemma in the Reagan era: criticizing the last vestiges of McCarthyism posed no risks, but showing the mildest understanding of communist regimes overseas—even arguing for a more nuanced perspective—could potentially discredit dissenters and be used against them by anticommunists.

The Cold War's leftist critics grappled with anticommunism. One camp of resisters—sometimes called "anti-anticommunists"—believed that criticizing communism should be done cautiously, lest it legitimize the assumptions and policies of Cold Warriors. Human rights activist and civil libertarian Aryeh Neier, founder of Human Rights Watch, adopted this approach. A tireless opponent of authoritarianism, Neier nonetheless considered anticommunism a driving force behind a number of destructive policies in Washington, particularly the Vietnam War, and he did not wish to endorse it. "There have been many times since the 1950s," Neier wrote, "when I have been angry at friends and colleagues on the left who have seemed willfully to ignore or to try to explain away Communist tyranny. That anger has been tempered, however, by the awareness that mainstream American anticommunists have given anticommunism a terrible name."[65] Sharing Neier's view were a number of prominent writers on the left, including E. L. Doctorow, Barbara Ehrenreich, Kurt Vonnegut, Gore Vidal, Arthur Miller, Elizabeth Hardwick, Norman Mailer, James Baldwin, and William Styron.[66]

A small subset of anti-anticommunists steered clear of criticizing the Soviet Union and its allies altogether, either because they preferred communism over capitalism or they wished to avoid fanning the flames of Russophobia. Journalist and political commentator Vladimir Pozner, for example, built a career on trying to help Americans understand Soviet politics, rarely uttering a negative word about the Kremlin. Born in Paris in 1934 to a Russian Jewish father and a French Catholic mother, Pozner grew up in France, the United States, and the Soviet Union. His father, also named Vladimir Pozner, worked for years for the U.S. government and quietly spied for Soviet intelligence.[67] The younger Pozner experienced frequent moves between the three countries he called home until the family settled in Moscow in the early 1950s. Graduating with a degree from Moscow State University in physiology in 1958, young Pozner entered the world of journalism, first writing for *Soviet Life* magazine, then hosting his own program on Radio Moscow, which beamed into North America on shortwave signals. He moved back to the United States, where he worked for radio station KABC in Los Angeles and wrote op-ed pieces in newspapers about the Soviet Union. By the 1980s, Pozner had become a respected journalist and was a frequent guest on Ted Koppel's *Nightline* and the *Phil Donahue Show*. His special talent was helping Americans understand their chief Cold War adversary, and he achieved a unique status as a reputable Kremlin supporter.[68] He summed up his role in 1981: "I think the most important thing I do is serve as a small bridge between two countries and two cultures that are very dear to me, that are part of me. . . . It is true that on most issues I share what I believe to be the view of Soviet government, especially on international affairs. But I've also made it clear that certain things I do not share, and I say so."[69]

Parting ways with anti-anticommunists, a sizable portion of the Left had no qualms about championing anticommunism. They felt in no way beholden to communism and pulled no punches. Socialist writers Michael Harrington and Irving Howe, for example, routinely criticized the Soviet government's policies. As founders of Democratic Socialists of America in 1982, the nation's largest social democratic organization, the two veteran radicals often took strong anticommunist stands to distinguish their socialism from more authoritarian versions and challenged their comrades in the democratic left to do likewise. In June 1984, the *New York Times Magazine* published a long dialogue between the two men about the contemporary state of the American left. During the conversation, Howe mentioned the "terrible problem" of communism being "a major force . . . within the American left" and expressed relief that "the democratic left did win the intellectual battle against Stalinism." "It was an obligation of moral hygiene," Howe declared. For his part, Harrington acknowledged his own "visceral anticommunism," which he thought might have made some people on the left "feel a little uncomfortable."[70]

The critique of Stalinism by Howe and Harrington in the *New York Times Magazine* was downright genteel compared with a scathing attack against communism from an unlikely source: radical filmmaker, social critic, and novelist Susan Sontag. One of twenty speakers at a packed town hall gathering on West 143rd Street in Manhattan on February 6, 1982, Sontag addressed her comments to "the so-called democratic left—which includes many people here tonight." A number of prominent figures were in the audience, including authors Gore Vidal, Kurt Vonnegut, and E. L. Doctorow; poet Allen Ginsberg; and musician Pete Seeger. Sontag spoke about the labor movement in Poland known as Solidarity, which had been banned by General Wojciech Jaruzelski, head of the communist government. Jaruzelski also declared martial law and was busily cracking down on antigovernment dissidents while the gathering in Manhattan was happening. At first, Sontag lashed out at Reagan for his "utter hypocrisy" in supporting Poland's Solidarity movement while being a "union buster" at home, a reference to the president firing members of the air traffic controllers union when it went on strike. While she was at it, Sontag attacked Reagan's role as "puppet master of the butchers in El Salvador." But Sontag reserved her harshest condemnation for American leftists. She pointedly criticized "people on the left" who "have willingly or unwittingly told a lot of lies. We were unwilling to identify ourselves as anti-Communists because that was the slogan of the right, the ideology of the cold war and, in particular, the justification of America's support of fascist dictatorships in Latin America and of the American war on Vietnam." Leftists abandoned the moral high ground, she argued, by not siding with oppressed people in communist countries. Sontag called communism "Fascism with a human face," triggering boos and hisses and catcalls in the audience. She questioned the Left's commitment to justice given what she thought was its unwillingness to support persecuted dissidents in communist nations. "We thought we loved justice; many of us did. But we did not love the truth enough. Which is to say that our priorities were wrong. The result was that many of us, and I include myself, did not understand the nature of the Communist tyranny. We tried to distinguish among Communisms—for example, treating 'Stalinism,' which we disavowed, as if it were an aberration, and praising other regimes, outside of Europe, which had and have essentially the same character."[71]

Sontag, once a supporter of revolutionaries in Cuba and Vietnam, admitted afterward that she'd hoped to "make a little trouble that night" by saying something "a little different." Perhaps sensing trouble, she ducked out of the building immediately after speaking, but her remarks triggered months of responses. The leftist *Nation* magazine, which Sontag trashed as a less reliable source of information on communism than *Reader's Digest*, dedicated an entire issue to her speech, reprinting it along with multiple responses from writers, activists, and academics. Critics assailed Sontag from all directions: some argued the Left was already sufficiently critical of communism and didn't need Sontag's policing; others felt her remarks were accusatory, self-righteous, and not helpful; and a few said her talk smacked of McCarthyism. British-born author and activist Jessica Mitford felt that Sontag was "out to get the liberals along with the communists," and "she is not the first one."[72] A handful of leftists praised Sontag for her speech, most notably *Nation* columnist Christopher Hitchens. "Susan Sontag," he wrote, "is still a paid-up member of the 'better red than dead' party. She has not really abandoned her old allegiances."[73] Yet Sontag had little support on the democratic left. Novelist E. L. Doctorow, one of the organizers of the event, took a dim view of Sontag's speech. He thought she presented "old news," nothing new or revelatory. As the town hall had been organized by Doctorow's group, American Workers and Artists for Solidarity, as a show of "support of the Polish workers' movement," Sontag's attack on those in attendance for not being sufficiently anticommunist struck Doctorow as misguided, given the event's purpose. "Nobody substantially under 75 really needs to be taught" about oppression under the Soviet government, Doctorow argued.[74]

Predictably, conservatives applauded Sontag's talk, despite her disdain for them. William F. Buckley Jr. wrote in his syndicated column that if her speech had "been delivered in Poland, by a Pole," it "would have got her not boos, but in prison. She is welcome, and one honors her courage." "Welcome aboard," echoed right-wing cultural critic and Buckley associate on the *National Review* staff, Jeffrey Hart, who could not conceal his excitement at the news. "It was almost as if Angela Davis had applied for membership in the American Legion," Hart exclaimed. John Chamberlain, an ex-communist New York journalist who defected to the far right, posed a series of questions about Sontag in the conservative newspaper *Human Events*: "Where are the thousands of students who should be rallying to Ms. Sontag's newly unfurled banner? Why aren't they clamoring to send help to beleaguered anti-Castroites in Angola, Guatemala and El Salvador? Where [are] the deputations that might be calling on Ronald Reagan to reinstitute the grain embargo against the Soviets?"[75]

The kind of debate that Susan Sontag touched off with her speech—introspective, heated, and, at times, emotional—rarely consumed Cold Warriors on the right in a similar fashion. Conservatives tended to be more confident in their beliefs, less prone to self-analysis, crippling self-doubt, and bitter infighting, than were people on the left. As a general rule, they had the advantage of being more unified in their opinions, and their anticommunism was seldom nuanced. There was also the weight of history to contend with. The ideological forebears of men and women on the right, that is, those who paved the way for modern conservatism, lacked the complex history of the American left, which faced the dual challenges of persecution under McCarthyism and the dilemma of whether to support, reject, or remain neutral about communist regimes abroad. These were not simple or straightforward issues facing the Left, and their opponents on the right had the fortune of being able to avoid this thorny briar patch.

The Right faced a different set of challenges in the Cold War culture wars. Conservatives prioritized restoring the Cold War consensus, a daunting prospect after détente. As inhospitable as American society was to radical ideas, most people were also apathetic about anticommunism. For the majority of Americans who avoided the arcane specifics of right and left politics, debates about the Cold War in the 1980s had little bearing on their day-to-day lives. Cold War culture exercised less influence and was less visible in the Reagan era than it had been during the Truman, Eisenhower, and Kennedy presidencies. Indeed, millions of Americans who lived through the 1980s were able to ignore much of the Cold War.

Wolverines of the World Unite

Winning hearts and minds in the Cold War cultural conflicts of the Reagan era was no easy feat. An effective way to reach a broad swath of the general public was through film. Movie theaters, like schools, were arenas where ideological clashes sometimes played out. While leftist filmmakers had mastered emotionally engaging dramas with deep humanist themes—*Reds* and *Platoon*, for example—right-wing Cold Warriors proved more adept at making action-packed summer blockbusters. The megahit *Rocky IV* (1985), for example, pitted the title character (Sylvester Stallone) against superhuman Soviet boxer Ivan Drago (Dolph Lundgren), a towering blonde, muscular fighting machine. This Cold War–infused Rocky outing was one of two anticommunist Stallone films among the top-five-highest-grossing films of 1985, the other being *Rambo: First Blood Part II*.[76]

Some Hollywood feature films contained less overbearing anticommunist themes. Movies about Soviet defectors, for instance, addressed an inherently tense subject matter. Paul Mazursky's comedy-drama *Moscow on the Hudson* (1984) told the story of a Soviet musician, Vladimir Ivanoff (Robin Williams), who plays saxophone for a traveling circus and defects to New York City, where he encounters a variety of offbeat characters. The following year's *White Nights*, directed by Taylor Hackford, spun a more dramatic tale of two dancers, one a Russian (Mikhail Baryshnikov), the other an American who defected years earlier to the USSR to escape racism in Vietnam (Gregory Hines), and the unlikely friendship that forms between them in the Soviet Union. The two men end up plotting a harrowing escape to the West in search of a better life. Other films sought to depict daily life under communism, usually emphasizing grim conditions. The 1983 mystery-thriller *Gorky Park* starred William Hurt as a Soviet police investigator and Brian Dennehy as a New York detective pursuing a ruthless killer in Moscow. Directed by British filmmaker Michael Apted, the movie walked a fine line between portraying Soviet characters sympathetically and showing the harsh relentlessness of the Kremlin bureaucracy in trying to apprehend a murderer.

The Soviet Union was not the only setting of films about communism. A harrowing portrayal of the Khmer Rouge's rise to power in Cambodia is shown in Roland Joffé's *The Killing Fields* (1984), a film that emphasizes the friendship between *New York Times* correspondent Sydney Schanberg (Sam Waterston) and his interpreter, Cambodian photojournalist Dith Pran (played by Dr. Haing S. Ngor, a newcomer and survivor of Khmer Rouge prison camps in this Oscar-winning role). *The Killing Fields* depicts, with frankness, the horrors unleashed by the American war in Cambodia before the fall of Phnom Penh in 1975, but it is even more unflinching in depicting the nightmarish conditions under the Pol Pot's reign of terror. In 1987, Italian Marxist Bernardo Bertolucci directed and cowrote *The Last Emperor*, a biopic of Puyi, the final emperor of the Qing dynasty before Mao's communists seized power in 1949. The film, which won the Academy Award for Best Picture, featured scenes of authoritarian communist reeducation camps in Beijing in the early 1950s and the excesses of the Cultural Revolution in 1960s.

The directors who made these films—except *Rocky IV*—either leaned to the left (Hackford) or were committed leftists (Apted, Bertolucci). Despite taking a dim view of communist rule, they refused to let kitschy anticommunism mar their movies. Such was not the case with the most notorious anticommunist film of the Reagan era, *Red Dawn*. Released in August 1984, *Red Dawn* showed a Soviet invasion and takeover of the United States and a guerrilla movement formed by Colorado high school students to resist the communists. *Red Dawn*'s director, John Milius, had a reputation for being a right-wing iconoclast in Hollywood. Earlier in his career, he cowrote the screenplay for *Apocalypse Now* (1979) and directed the B-gangster picture *Dillinger* (1973) starring Warren Oates, as well as the fantasy action movie *Conan the Barbarian* (1982), with Arnold Schwarzenegger in the lead role, based on a screenplay collaboration between Milius and Oliver Stone.

For *Red Dawn*, Milius rewrote the original script by Kevin Reynolds. The revisions were so drastic that Reynolds, after seeing the film, said he "hated it" and called *Red Dawn* "propaganda." Reynolds claimed Milius had "changed the whole thrust of the picture," away from a *Lord of the Flies*–type tragedy to a straight-up action film.[77] To strengthen the film's verisimilitude, Milius sought the input of Alexander M. Haig Jr., President Nixon's former chief of staff and President Reagan's former secretary of state, as an adviser. Haig eagerly pitched in and loved the movie. Thanks to the *Red Dawn*'s "unusual degree of realism," said Haig, "I think it's going to make a major impression on the political and social thinking of viewers."[78] In a poster for the film, Soviet troops parachute into a small, snow-blanketed American town early in the morning, under the grim tagline, "No foreign army has ever occupied American soil. Until now."[79]

In *Red Dawn*, the Soviets, with the support of Cuban and Nicaraguan allies, invade and occupy the United States. A wordy title sequence explains how this implausible feat happened, reinforced later in the film by a heavy dose of expository dialogue by a weary Air Force pilot (played by Powers Boothe). A guerrilla resistance movement forms in Colorado to fight the Soviets. Known as the "Wolverines," the resisters consist of high school students who are fearless in combat and skilled with automatic weapons. The film stars Brat Pack–era actors Lea Thompson, Jennifer Grey, C. Thomas Howell, Charlie Sheen, and Patrick Swayze as Jed, older than the others and senior member of the Wolverines. The fate of the republic rests in the hands of adolescents because the invaders have rounded up all of the adults and forced them into reeducation camps. *Red Dawn* is unrelentingly dark—only two of the Wolverines survive and make it to the so-called Free America zone by the film's end. The movie is full of far-right stereotypes, such as Nicaraguans sneaking into America to sabotage the country to pave the way for their Soviet masters, thus exploiting long-held fears of illegal aliens. Predictably, Russophobia abounds in the movie, with the conquering Soviets portrayed as barbaric and crude. Finally, *Red Dawn* showcased popular right-wing tropes from the time, such as fears of a weakened military and the importance of a thriving gun culture.

Panned by critics, *Red Dawn* did respectable box office business in August 1984. Its release date, timed to coincide with the Los Angeles Olympics, which the Soviets boycotted, placed *Red Dawn* squarely in the summer blockbuster season. Even before it opened, *Red Dawn* caused controversy by being the first film to earn a PG-13, a new rating introduced in July, which meant kids under thirteen needed an adult chaperone to see the movie. Adding to the buzz surrounding the film, a watchdog group called the National Coalition on Television Violence issued a detailed report calling *Red Dawn* the "most violent movie" ever made, averaging 134 acts of violence per hour. "Movies like *Red Dawn* are rapidly preparing America for World War III," proclaimed Dr. Thomas Radecki, the group's chair, who warned that parents "should be very careful" about allowing their children to see it.[80]

After an impressive opening weekend, *Red Dawn* was regarded as a box office disappointment. Commercially, the film did not approach the overwhelming success of the following year's Cold War–themed *Rambo: First Blood Part II* and *Rocky IV*. In fact, *Red Dawn* ranked nineteenth for gross domestic box office in 1984, making less money at the box office than had *Reds* three years earlier.[81] Still, *Red Dawn*'s modest success demonstrated that despite anticommunism's waning influence, there was still an appetite for action films with communist bad guys and Russophobic themes. At some showings, excited young viewers cheered or shouted "Wolverines!" in movie theaters.[82] *Red Dawn* also inspired such imitators as *Invasion U.S.A.* (1985), in which an former CIA agent played by Chuck Norris defends America against hordes of Soviet-led Cuban invaders, and the ABC miniseries *Amerika* (1987), a big-budget drama with Kris Kristofferson and Mariel Hemingway dramatizing American life under Soviet rule.

Decades after its release, *Red Dawn* has assumed a significance beyond its initial importance in 1984. The film has come to be regarded as emblematic of Reagan-era Cold War culture. Right-wing fans revisited it and embraced it in the first two decades of the twenty-first century for its uncompromising anticommunism, whereas devotees of schlock cinema laughed it off as *Reefer Madness*–like camp. A 2012 remake of *Red Dawn* portrayed an even more implausible invasion of the United States by North Koreans, backed by Russian ultranationalists, leading to resistance from a new generation of machine gun–toting millennial Wolverines.

The original *Red Dawn* was a cultural milestone. Released three years after Warren Beatty's *Reds*, *Red Dawn* represented a bookend, of sorts, on the far right side of the spectrum, of what was possible in American cinema. Its very existence, like that of *Reds*, illustrates the dramatic differences in how communism was portrayed in popular culture in the 1980s. When viewed as an artifact of its era, *Red Dawn* remains remarkable in the way it expanded cultural expression to make room for mainstream movies full of John Birch Society–style paranoia. Cold War films had evolved in striking ways since the 1950s, when the range of storytelling was more limited. By comparison, the restraints were off in the 1980s, and anything seemed possible in this age of greater openness and free expression, even such polar cinematic opposites as *Reds* and *Red Dawn*.

CHAPTER 5

No Nukes

We have heard the rationales offered by the nuclear superpowers. We know who speaks for the nations. But who speaks
for the human species? Who speaks for Earth?

—*Carl Sagan,* Cosmos, *1980*

A Million People in the Street

On June 12, 1982, a million people converged on Central Park in New York
City to protest the nuclear arms race in what turned out to be the largest single demonstration in U.S. history. "The entire parking lot at Yankee Stadium
and lots at the World's Fair grounds and smaller sites throughout the city
have been commandeered to handle the influx of vehicles," observed the
New York Daily News the day of the event.[1] Hours before the 9:30 a.m. start
time, untold numbers of protesters had gathered outside the United Nations
headquarters to march to Central Park. Five thousand officers of the New
York Police Department appeared in full force—by car, by foot, by horseback,
in helicopters—to monitor the march. Months in the planning, organized
by the June 12 Rally Committee, a coalition of two dozen organizations, the
protest had been timed to coincide with the United Nations' Special Session
on Disarmament. That morning, New York radio stations warned listeners
to take the subway owing to multiple street closures.[2]

The protesters, by all accounts, were a diverse mix of people from all walks
of life. "They represented a rainbow spectrum of religions, ethnic groups,
trades, professions, unions, cultural and educational institutions, political
organizations and other interests," observed *New York Times* correspondent
Robert D. McFadden. For a number of participants, this was their first act

of public protest. "We all want to be here in ten years," said twelve-year-old Billy McGrath, who came from Evanston, Illinois, with his father.[3] The demonstrators in this case aimed for respectability, and there were no arrests or incidents of violence. Thousands of marchers packed into the streets, moving forward at a brisk pace, impressed Charles Leven, general manager of Saks Fifth Avenue. He found the passersby to be "orderly and pleasant. It's been a delight to watch. There have been no security problems at all."[4]

The sprawling throng flooded into Central Park's Great Lawn, where a sound stage had been installed with towering loudspeakers. The march was so long that even though the rally in the park started at 1:00 p.m., the last of the marchers arrived around 3:40.[5] Peace activist Rev. William Sloane Coffin delivered an impassioned speech, as did Coretta Scott King and film director Orson Welles, who told a friend "this was the first political issue worth fighting for in decades."[6] Welles strode up to the microphone with the help of a cane, and his voice projected long and far through the powerful sound system: "We have two choices—life or death. Do you hear that, Mr. Reagan?"[7] The audience listened to performances by Linda Ronstadt, Jackson Browne, Bruce Springsteen, James Taylor, and Joan Baez. "It was a celebration of life. But it also was a battle cry, you could say, against any force that would threaten to wipe it out," wrote Linda Case, a writer from Hartford, Connecticut.[8]

The June 12 disarmament march marked the apotheosis of the antinuclear movement. Nothing on this scale had ever been witnessed before in the annals of American dissent. On the same day, smaller disarmament rallies occurred in a dozen other cities, but the giant New York protest overshadowed all others. Predictably, media coverage brought out naysayers who sought to downplay the event. It did not help matters when, on the day as the march, Soviet authorities cracked down on a gathering of eleven men and women who had worked up the courage to appear at an antinuclear protest in Moscow. Officers in the KGB rounded up the dissidents and took them to police headquarters to issue stern warnings against engaging in "anti-Soviet" activities.[9] Thus, when Soviet authorities lauded the New York protest, their praise rang hollow. In the United States, the march's critics argued it was Moscow, not Washington, that was blocking the advance to peace, and no protest, no matter how big, could change that or reduce Cold War tensions. "As far as whether or not a rally of that kind will make everybody suddenly change policies or not, I think clearly the answer is no," said Secretary of Defense Caspar "Cap" Weinberger on the day of the march.[10] Popular radio host Paul Harvey warned that the Soviets could not be trusted, claiming the

Kremlin had violated every major treaty it had ever signed since the 1920s. "God knows nobody wants a nuclear war. But what in the world is the purpose of demonstrations against it?" he asked. William F. Buckley Jr. similarly attacked the Soviets' trustworthiness. "Better a cold war than a hot war," he wrote, days after the protest, "and better no illusions than disillusions."[11]

"The Most Heartening Development"

Skeptics did not hinder the antinuclear campaign's momentum. What began as a fringe movement in the 1940s, based mainly in New York City, had grown into a national coalition—an alphabet soup of acronyms—working in tandem to end the arms race. During the Vietnam War, peace activists put aside their ban-the-bomb signs and turned to antiwar organizing, but when the war ended, many kept their marching shoes on. Years of organizing and hard work, along with the accumulation of public protests, moved the struggle into the mainstream. In September 1979, the antinuclear movement flexed its muscle by holding a series of well-publicized, well-attended "No Nukes" concerts in New York's Madison Square Garden. Musicians John Hall, Bonnie Raitt, Jackson Browne, and Graham Nash were the main creative forces behind the concert. They persuaded such prominent friends as Bruce Springsteen and the E Street Band, Tom Petty and the Heartbreakers, and Carly Simon to perform.[12]

At the time of the No Nukes Concert, scholar and peace activist Dr. Randall Forsberg published her influential *Call to Halt the Arms Race*, which became the manifesto for the nuclear freeze movement. Forsberg, born and raised in Alabama, had been active in antinuclear organizing since the 1960s, getting her start as a typist for the Stockholm International Peace Research Institute in Sweden. By the late 1970s, she'd earned a reputation as one of the most effective antinuclear organizers in the United States. Her landmark *Call to Halt the Arms Race* challenged Washington, D.C., and Moscow to "adopt a mutual freeze on the testing, production and deployment of nuclear weapons and missiles and new aircraft designed primarily to deliver nuclear weapons."[13] Forsberg's eloquent and accessible statement was widely circulated and instantly gained endorsements from many members of Congress, as well as an impressive list of prominent establishment figures, including former undersecretary of state George Ball, former secretary of state Clark Clifford, former CIA director William Colby, diplomat and Cold War strategist George Kennan, famed astronomer Dr. Carl Sagan, and Nobel laureate

Dr. Linus Pauling.[14] More important, it helped spawn a grassroots nuclear freeze movement that spread rapidly across America. "In 1982 freeze resolutions were introduced in nine states and passed in eight; later, freeze resolutions, though in watered-down form, passed the House and the Senate," wrote author and peace activist Jonathan Schell. As a further show of strength, freeze movement activists went door to door nationwide with petitions, collecting more than 2,300,000 signatures supporting a nuclear freeze, which they presented to the U.S. and Soviet missions in the United Nations.[15]

The antinuclear coalition attracted an array of groups, with different agendas and tactics. Movement moderates hoped to win the hearts and minds of ordinary Americans living in the heartland, whereas radicals favored militant methods of direct action designed to jolt people into greater awareness. In general, however, the Nuclear Weapons Freeze Campaign steered clear of controversial statements and protest methods, sticking closely to the middle of the road. Steve Ladd, a San Francisco activist in California Nuclear Freeze Campaign, voiced the moderate position: "If we are to turn around the arms race and move toward disarmament, our most basic priority must be to build a massive movement that has the active and tacit support of large segments of this society."[16]

Radical peace advocates, by contrast, backed civil disobedience, obstructing military operations, and other forms of confrontational direct action. Ed Hedemann of the New York City–based War Resisters League, a revolutionary pacifist organization founded in 1914, favored more militant tactics. "The basic Freeze strategy," he wrote, "seeks to create change primarily through the educational means of petitions, referendums, resolutions, letters to the editor, visiting Congresspeople, and ads—while discouraging direct action. This is a strategy programmed to fail. Simply persuading the general public is not enough to alter government policy."[17] In spite of varied approaches, antinuclear activists cast aside their differences, at least publicly, hoping to avoid the kind of nasty infighting that had undermined other protest movements.

The urgency of their cause mitigated sectarianism. The election of Ronald Reagan in 1980, in particular, galvanized the movement. Global thermonuclear war posed an ever-present danger during Reagan's presidency. How close was America to the brink? Decades earlier, in 1945, Dr. Eugene Rabinowitch, a Russian-born biophysicist based at the University of Chicago's Metallurgical Laboratory, founded the Bulletin of the Atomic Scientists, which functioned as both a nonprofit organization and the title of its publication. The bulletin's most significant and lasting contribution was the creation of a Doomsday

Clock in 1947, to measure the threat of an atomic war. The closer the clock hands got to midnight, the closer the world was to that horrifying fate. Thanks to the organization, the clock became a stark symbol of time running out on the human race. The hands were set at seven minutes to midnight in 1947. By 1953, amid the deep freeze of the Cold War, the clock had reached 11:58. Détente brought the clock back to twelve minutes to midnight in 1972. In 1980, the bulletin moved the hands to seven minutes to midnight, bringing it back to its pre-détente point.

The hands crept forward to four minutes to midnight in 1981, then three at the beginning of 1984.[18] "The accelerating nuclear arms race and the almost complete breakdown of communication between the superpowers have combined to create a situation of extreme and immediate danger," the *Bulletin* warned in its explanation for the Doomsday Clock's setting in January 1984.[19] All was not lost, however, according to the *Bulletin*, thanks to the groundswell of peace activism. Thus, what began as a dire warning ended on a hopeful note: "The most heartening development of the last few years has been the great upsurge of public concern about the nuclear arms race. Millions throughout the world have become aroused, have undertaken to educate themselves, and sustained by a belief in the power of argument and moral witness, have sought to engage the issue politically. It would be tragic if they were now to lose heart."[20]

In light of the gravity of the threat facing humanity, solidarity within the antinuclear movement assumed a top priority. Activists knew that petty political squabbles had to take a backseat to the danger at hand. Their united front was reinforced by a culture of resistance that nurtured varied forms of expression, including books, music, and film. The weighty topic of nuclear war attracted the attention of an array of academic and cultural figures, including authors, scientists, musicians, and filmmakers, who regarded the arms race as the most pressing issue of the time.

"Historians of the Future"

Resistance took on many forms. Among the book-buying public, there was a spike in demand for nonfiction books about nuclear weapons and nuclear war. Historian William Knoblauch notes that "between 1979 and 1983, more than 130 antinuclear books entered the literary marketplace."[21] Of the many new titles arriving at bookstores, the most influential was Jonathan Schell's *The Fate of Earth*. Schell, a staff writer at the *New Yorker* from 1967 to 1987, expanded a series of articles he wrote for that magazine about nuclear war into a book. Published by Knopf in 1982, *The Fate of the Earth* described, in vivid and carefully researched detail, the sheer destructive capacity of nuclear weapons to wipe out life on earth. Most disturbing, Schell imagines in the book's darkest passages what the planet would look like after nuclear war and the ordeal survivors would face. "Usually people wait for things to occur before trying to describe them," Schell writes, setting the stage for the desolate narrative to follow. "But since we cannot afford under any circumstances to let a nuclear holocaust occur, we are forced in this one case to become the historians of the future—to chronicle and commit to memory an event that we have never experienced and must never experience."[22] Schell's book soared high on the *New York Times* bestseller list. The decision by Knopf to hurriedly publish a lower-cost paperback edition, as well as its selection by the popular Book of the Month Club, undoubtedly boosted sales. Moreover, the book enjoyed extensive promotion in the press and on network news.[23]

The Fate of the Earth hit a raw nerve with the public, and its impressive sales demonstrated a demand for antinuclear nonfiction books in the United States. Like Jonathan Schell, Dr. Helen Caldicott rose to prominence on the strength of her prolific writing. Born and raised in Melbourne, Australia, Caldicott trained to be a pediatrician, specializing in cystic fibrosis, and by the late 1970s she worked on the staff of the Children's Hospital Medical Center in Boston, Massachusetts, and taught at Harvard Medical School. In 1978, she became president of Physicians for Social Responsibility, an organization of physician activists concerned about the looming threat of nuclear war. At this pivotal time, Caldicott wrote two important books, *Nuclear Madness: What You Can Do!*, published in 1978 by W. W. Norton, and *Missile Envy: The Arms Race and Nuclear War*, published in 1984 by William Morrow. She also starred in two documentaries routinely shown at antinuclear events: *Eight Minutes to Midnight: A Portrait of Helen Caldicott* in 1981 and *If You Love This Planet*, an Academy Award–winning short made in 1982 by the National Film Board of Canada.

Caldicott wrote and spoke in a trenchant, uncompromising style that conveyed urgency. In her best-selling *Nuclear Madness*, she likened the "terminally ill planet" to a "terminally ill patient," arguing the nuclear arms race was bringing the earth closer to death. "They're building more weapons," she wrote, "they're metastasizing the cancer." In *Missile Envy*, Caldicott linked the arms race to a sexualized male obsession with weapons of mass destruction. She implored all people—women, in particular—to resist the manufacturing and proliferation of nuclear weapons. "If you love this planet, and I'm deeply in love with it, . . . you will realize that you're going to have to change the priorities of your life—if you love this planet."[24] In addition to books, Caldicott wrote her own speeches, which were printed and disseminated by antinuclear activists and published in anthologies. "We are at a crossroads of time," Caldicott told an audience in 1981. "Only emotional maturity, evoked by extreme danger combined with personal responsibility and total commitment, will save our planet for our descendants."[25]

A third author, Robert Scheer, wrote *With Enough Shovels: Reagan, Bush, and Nuclear War*, an influential 1983 exposé of the Reagan administration's nuclear policies.[26] A longtime left-wing journalist, Scheer first worked for the New Left muckraking magazine *Ramparts* from 1962 to 1975, then he relocated to the *Los Angeles Times* in 1976. During his thirty years at the *Times*, Scheer built a reputation as a thorough investigative reporter and a leftist columnist who took strong stands on a variety of matters.

In *With Enough Shovels*, Scheer explored "how our leaders during the time of Ronald Reagan have come to plan for waging and winning a nuclear war with the Soviet Union, and how they are obsessed with a strategy of confrontation—including nuclear brinksmanship—which aims to force the Soviets to shrink their empire and fundamentally restructure their society."[27] Relying on interviews with high-level government officials, including President Reagan and Vice President George Bush, and extensive research, Scheer painted a Strangelovian portrait of the Reagan White House engaged in a feverish arms escalation, under the guiding belief that a nuclear war with the Soviet Union was winnable.

The author's interviewing style provoked his subjects to offer candid replies, to the point of occasionally sounding outrageous. For example, when Scheer asked Vice President Bush if he thought the administration's escalation of nuclear arms was excessive, Bush replied, "Yes, if you believe there is no such thing as a winner in a nuclear exchange, that argument makes sense. I don't believe that." When Scheer asked Bush if he guessed that at least 5 percent of the population would survive a nuclear war, Bush responded: *"If everybody fired everything he had,* you'd have more than that survive." Scheer bluntly asked Reagan if he thought a nuclear war was survivable. "It would be a survival of some of your people and some of your facilities that you could start again. It would not be anything that I think in our society you would consider acceptable, but then, we have a different regard for human life than those monsters [in Moscow] do," Reagan told Scheer. Other members of the Reagan administration echoed the Reagan-Bush view of a nuclear war being survivable, a position consistent with a statement by the Federal Emergency Management Agency: "With reasonable protective measures, the United States could survive nuclear attack and go on to recovery within a relatively few years."[28]

With Enough Shovels made it clear that while nobody in the Reagan White House wanted a nuclear war, administration officials were sanguine about the human race's prospect for survival in the aftermath of one. There is evidence that Scheer's book had a significant impact on how Reagan and the men around him discussed nuclear weapons in public. Testifying in the U.S. Senate in the wake of the controversy caused by Jones's comments, Reagan's cabinet members, including Jones himself and Assistant Secretary of Defense Richard Perle, began walking back statements about the ability to win a nuclear war.[29] Before the publication of *With Enough Shovels*, Bush was asked to clarify his position on whether a nuclear war was even survivable, much less winnable. "Well, if—ah—I hope we won't ever have one."[30]

The Cold War's apologists were unable to respond in kind to the spate of antinuclear books, and a counterweight literature never materialized. What was there to argue? Not even the most hardened Cold Warriors wished for a nuclear war or thought it would improve the state of world affairs. Nor was there anything to be gained by trying to downplay the potential devastation wrought by a World War III. The closest thing to an opposing point of view to antinuclear tomes was a handful of books published early in the decade informing readers how they could survive a nuclear war. With titles such as *Nuclear War Survival Skills* (1979); *The Nuclear Survival Handbook: Living through and after a Nuclear Attack* (1980); *Life after Doomsday: A Survivalist Guide to Nuclear War and Other Major Disasters* (1980); and *Survive the Coming Nuclear War: How to Do It* (1982); these books fit into a larger literature on self-help, popular in the 1970s and 1980s, and contained a mix of medical advice, food and water preparation tips, checklists of essential shelter items, and information about two-way radio communications.[31] These books had much in common with civil defense booklets and pamphlets churned out by government agencies and private groups during the First Cold War. Historian Gaddis Smith offered a decisive verdict on the nuclear survival manuals: "Is the behavior advocated by these books dangerous? Yes. It is behavior bereft of any sense of the meaning of life. There are no values. No morality, except that of shooting those who would invade your shelter."[32]

By 1983, the postapocalypse survivalist literature had dried up, thanks to pervasive skepticism about the likelihood of a nuclear war being survivable. Poll after poll indicated that Reagan's "peace through strength" doctrine was losing public support. Antinuclear campaigns—especially the nuclear freeze movement—were having the desired effect, undermining the nation's confidence in Reagan's nuclear policies. A nationwide survey conducted in 1983 found that "70 percent of all Americans wanted a negotiated freeze on nuclear weapons."[33] Years later, Reagan's national security adviser Robert MacFarlane admitted the nuclear freeze movement influenced the administration. "We took it as a serious movement that could undermine congressional support for the [nuclear] modernization program, and potentially . . . a serious partisan political threat that could affect the election in '84," he said. David Gergen, Reagan's White House communications director, echoed MacFarlane: "There was a widespread view in the administration that the freeze was a dagger pointed at the heart of the administration's defense program."[34]

World War III in Pop Culture

Books critiquing the arms race and nuclear war were but one visible manifestation of a powerful antinuclear ethos in the Reagan era. Themes of nuclear war abounded in other areas of popular culture as well. In video gaming, *Missile Command*, introduced in 1980, instantly emerged as one of the most beloved coin-op arcade games in the country. In malls, movie theater lobbies, pizza parlors, and convenience stores, kids plunked down quarters to fire away at incoming nuclear missiles raining down from the sky, threatening towns at the bottom of the screen. A cartridge version of the game for the Atari 2600 arrived in stores in the fall of 1981, in time for Christmas season. "Big time push button war! And you're in command of an ABM missile silo with 6 cities to protect from attacking ICBMs!" announced a newspaper ad for the game.[35] Yet *Missile Command*, one of the biggest selling games for the Atari 2600, contained a blatant antinuclear message. It was an unwinnable game, and once all six cities were flattened into rubble—an inevitable ending every time one played it—"THE END" flashed grimly across the screen. "That was the point, to show if there was a nuclear war, you couldn't win," said the game's creator and programmer, Dave Theurer.[36]

Antinuclear themes resonated more widely in the era's music. The 1979 No Nukes concert spotlighted a commitment among top figures in the music industry to the antinuclear cause, which was shared by musicians in different rock subgenres. Heavy metal and hard rock, for example, spawned several songs about nuclear war. In the 1980 tune "Crazy Train," Ozzy Osbourne, former vocalist of Black Sabbath, sang of a world leaping "off the rails" as a result of "millions of people living as foes," and he references the Cold War in the song's lyrics.[37] British heavy metal band Iron Maiden performed "2 Minutes to Midnight," a direct reference to the Doomsday Clock. Featured on Maiden's 1984 *Powerslave* album, "2 Minutes to Midnight" is possibly the darkest song about nuclear war, filled with bleak verses about the "war machine" devouring children and delivering "doom" to the human race.[38]

The same year, hard rock band Queen recorded "Hammer to Fall," which mentions "the shadow of the mushroom cloud" and asks, "What the hell are we fighting for?" Queen performed the song at the giant outdoor Live Aid concert at London's Wembley Stadium in July 1985, and plenty of critics reached the same conclusion as record reviewer Pete Bishop of the *Pittsburg Press*, who called it "a musical slam-banger . . . with pointed antiwar lyrics."[39] But it was the Canadian band Rush that had the distinction of recording the most songs with lyrics about nuclear war and the arms race of any major commercial band in the 1980s. The power trio racked up four in total: "Between the Wheels" (1984); "Distant Early Warning" (1984); "Manhattan Project" (1985); and "Lock and Key" (1987). A fifth Rush song, "Heresy," filled with Cold War imagery, was released in 1991, as the U.S.-Soviet rivalry drew to a close. Each song contained drummer Neil Peart's cerebral songwriting, which deliberately lacked a preachy feel.

More than hard rock, punk music combined the political and rebellious. Critiques of the Cold War were ubiquitous in punk songs of the 1970s and 1980s. Renowned British punk group The Clash, the so-called "band that mattered," led the way with "London Calling" on their landmark album of the same name, released late in 1979. Raw-voiced Joe Strummer in "London Calling" sang postapocalyptic visions of a "nuclear error," warned an "ice age is coming," and predicted a "meltdown" is "expected" and all of this destruction would unleash the "zombies of death."[40] The record *London Calling*—a double-album blend of punk, ska, reggae, jazz, rockabilly, hard rock, and rhythm and blues—would go on to achieve platinum sales in the United States and top "best of" lists for decades after its release.

Within a few years, the themes of destruction in "London Calling" assumed an edgier sound in America's hard-core punk music scene, with President Reagan serving as a frequent target of youthful musical insurgents. The Crucifucks, a band from Lansing, Michigan, initiated the first of many

"Rock against Reagan" concerts in March 1983.[41] Crude photocopied posters advertised the events with pictures of Reagan, dressed like a cowboy or playing a gangster in the movie *The Killers* (1964), cut and pasted alongside mushroom clouds, fallout shelter signs, cemeteries, and scenes of chaos in the streets. The concerts, featuring underground punk bands and political speakers, drew thousands of fans, mainly disaffected middle-class youths. Before long, "Rock against Reagan" concerts were happening across the country. Not all young punks embraced radical leftist politics, but quite a few did, and politicized punks tended to be vocal about their beliefs and a visible presence at protests. Rock against Reagan concerts featured anti-nuclear and Central America solidarity activists staffing literature tables at venues. Regular performers included the Dead Kennedys, the Crucifucks, Corrosion of Conformity, MDC (Millions of Dead Cops), Agnostic Front, the Dicks, and the Minutemen. At San Francisco's Dolores Park, comedian Whoopi Goldberg emceed the event.[42] Rock against Reagan organizer Nick Victor of Phoenix, Arizona, described the political purpose of the concerts: "We're trying to integrate music and energy and use it as a positive political force. It's a way of expressing our fear and anger at the threat the Reagan administration and the Soviet government are posing to our safety."[43]

While hard-core bands blasted furious instrumental rants at Reagan and the Cold War, John Lydon, also known as Johnny Rotten, former lead singer of the Sex Pistols, collaborated with hip-hop pioneer Afrika Bambaataa on a project called Time Zone, resulting in a single titled "World Destruction." Released in the fall of 1984. "World Destruction" was overtly political and featured elements of punk, electronic music, and hip-hop. In duet form, Lydon and Bambaataa lamented global leaders—both secular and religious—rushing headlong in a frenzied race to destroy the earth and wipe out all life. The song was also a call to action, exhorting listeners to "start to look for a better life." Lydon's piercing, nasally voice infused a punk sound into "World Destruction," and the song became a favorite at dance clubs and on alternative radio stations across the country, including the trend-setting KROQ in Pasadena, California.[44]

New Wave, punk's morose first cousin, generated a host of antinuclear songs. Dating back to David Bowie's "Bombers" in 1971, a promotional single about "sirens" wailing and "sunshine on the wasteland," red lights flashing and "A-bombs and H-bombs" falling, lyrics about nuclear war turned up in many New Wave songs.[45] The introduction of MTV (Music Television) on August 1, 1981, ushered in the golden age of music videos and popularized

New Wave. The refreshing new network, aimed at a demographic of viewers in their teens and twenties, devoted abundant air time to synth-pop bands like Squeeze, A Flock of Seagulls, The Human League, and Gary Numan. By the late 1970s, thanks to outspoken bands like The Clash and The Police, topical songs with hard-hitting political content were more numerous than they had been a decade earlier. The heyday of antinuke New Wave songs arrived in 1980, when British singer, songwriter, and keyboardist Peter Gabriel, formerly of Genesis, recorded "Games without Frontiers," a soulful song that compared children's games to the calculating coldness of global realpolitik championed by world leaders.[46] Kate Bush, another British singer-songwriter and keyboardist, who sang background vocals on "Games without Frontiers," recorded an antinuclear track the same year, "Breathing," about a woman giving birth during a nuclear war.[47]

A slew of New Wave songs about nuclear war and the Cold War followed.[48] The most famous was "99 Luftballons" by the West German band Nena. In late February 1984, the song seemed to soar out of nowhere to the number two spot on the Billboard Hot 100 in the United States. Its popularity surprised German vocalist Gabriele Susanne Kerner, who went by the stage name "Nena," her childhood nickname and the band's namesake. Often described as a Cold War "protest" ballad in the *Neue Deutsche Welle* (New German Wave) genre, "99 Luftballons" was written by the band's guitarist, Carlo Karges. "He had gone to see the Rolling Stones concert in Berlin and a lot of balloons were let go at the end of the show and Carlo thought of what might happen if these balloons went over the border into East Germany," Nena explained in 1984.[49]

The tune opens with Nena's contemplative vocals, asking in German if the listener has time to hear a song about ninety-nine balloons drifting off to the horizon. Then comes a burst of futuristic synthesizer-driven music, heavy on the percussion, with a beat/tempo alternating between slow (97 beats per minute) and fast (picking up to 194 beats per minute). The titular 99 balloons rise into the heavens in the lyrics, drifting across the skies, panicking leaders who aren't sure what they are, and setting off a Third World War. Near the end of "99 Luftballons," when the frenzied synth-rock dies down, the narrator tells of walking through the ruins, finding a balloon, and releasing it into the heavens in her mind.[50]

Pressured by their label, Nena recorded an English-language version of "99 Luftballons," called "99 Red Balloons," which made the song's antinuclear lyrics clear to millions of listeners who couldn't understand the original.

But it was the German version that received more airplay on U.S. radio stations and climbed the charts. For months, Nena was ubiquitous in North America—on the radio and MTV, in newspapers and magazines—and there was brief talk of a "German invasion."[51] But the band's fame proved fleeting. A one-star review of Nena's self-titled debut album in *Rolling Stone* in April, along with the band's failure to produce a chart-topping follow-up, meant Nena would be remembered as a "one-hit wonder." However, unlike most bands in that category, Nena's sole U.S. hit assumed historical importance as the quintessential antinuclear protest song of the Reagan era, a synth-pop hit—catchy, compelling, haunting—that left a lasting impression.

While there is no evidence that songs like "99 Luftballons" or "2 Minutes to Midnight" mobilized millions of citizens to attend antinuclear rallies, the sheer number of these types of songs—spanning many genres—exerted the subtler effect of giving millions of people who listened to popular music the impression that opposition to the Cold War was robust in American pop culture. Music videos drove this point home forcefully by pairing the visual with the audio. Videos full of doomsday scenarios and nuked landscapes made the rounds frequently on MTV. An early example was the 1982 music video for "You Got Lucky," by Tom Petty and the Heartbreakers, showing Petty and bandmates driving dusty, futuristic vehicles across a blighted wasteland, reminiscent of George Miller's postapocalyptic action film *The Road Warrior* (1981).

Music videos filled with nuclear war imagery appeared often on MTV.[52] The British rock band Genesis made the most buzzworthy Cold War–themed music video of the decade for their hit "Land of Confusion." The video stars grotesque puppet caricatures of the three band members—vocalist-drummer Phil Collins, guitarist Mike Rutherford, and keyboardist Tony Banks—as well as a host of celebrities and world leaders. Debuting on MTV and NBC's hit show *Friday Night Videos* in the fall of 1986, "Land of Confusion" makes a heartfelt plea for peace and making the world a more humane place, yet it delivers this somber message in a hilarious, over-the-top style. The weightiness of the lyrics—which address global conflicts, reckless leaders whose actions are imperiling the planet, and a world lacking love—are at odds with the absurd mayhem happening onscreen.

The video's most prominent puppet is Ronald Reagan, who nods off to sleep and sweats profusely as he plunges into a surreal nightmare about the world being threatened by Muammar al-Gaddafi, the Ayatollah Khomeini, Mikhail Gorbachev, and Benito Mussolini. Genesis insisted on hiring British caricaturists Peter Fluck and Roger Law to design the puppets used in *Land of*

Confusion. Fluck and Law had created similar puppets for the hit Independent Television (ITV) comedy *Spitting Image* in Great Britain. The duo designed an all-star cast for *Land of Confusion*, including hilarious likenesses of Bob Hope, Madonna, Prince, Michael Jackson, Richard Nixon, David Bowie, Leonard Nimoy (as Spock), Princess Diana, Margaret Thatcher, Bob Dylan, Nancy Reagan, and plethora of assorted dinosaurs. Ronald Reagan enjoys the most screen time in the video, alternating between his pajamas, a cowboy getup, and a Superman outfit. Like a comic book superhero, he rushes in to save an imperiled world, riding atop a stampeding dinosaur to face villains. Ultimately, Reagan awakens from his dream dripping sweat, greets Nancy, and reaches over to push the "nurse" button to request a glass of water. In an ending inspired by *Dr. Strangelove*, Reagan accidentally pushes "nuke" instead of "nurse" and sets off a nuclear explosion. "That's one heck of a nurse!" he quips, prompting Nancy to knock him upside the head with her snorkel.[53]

In its day, *Land of Confusion* was celebrated as groundbreaking. Genesis won the 1987 Grammy Award for Best Concept Music Video for "Land of Confusion," and the essayist and music journalist Robert Christgau, who had a reputation for being a harsh critic, picked it as his choice for best video of the year. "Land of Confusion" was "not supposed to be a particularly anti-Reagan thing," insisted Genesis keyboardist Tony Banks. The song was intended to be "a general attack on world political figures," he explained in 1987, but "because *Spitting Image* do Reagan so well, it ended up being Reagan."[54] Heavy MTV rotation cemented the video's iconic status, and it arrived at a moment in time when irreverent portrayals of Ronald Reagan as bumbling and erratic were still relatively uncommon in popular culture. Ultimately, *Land of Confusion*, in all of its madcap zaniness, perfectly captured the zeitgeist of 1980s antinuclear anxieties.

The Road to *The Day After*

None of the above cultural contributions—music videos, video games, or books—came close to matching the seismic, paradigm-shifting impact of one made-for-television movie. In the anti–Cold War culture of the Reagan era, all roads lead to and away from *The Day After*, shown on the American Broadcasting Company (ABC) four days before Thanksgiving, on November 20, 1983. It is impossible to overstate, or exaggerate, the influence and significance of *The Day After*. In terms of its profound effect on American society, the film has few equals in the history of television. Brandon Stoddard, head of ABC Entertainment, said it best when he referred to *The Day After* as "the most important movie we or anyone else ever made."[55]

Company executives picked a perilous moment to show *The Day After*.[56] Superpower relations had reached a deep freeze by the fall of 1983, with each development more ominous than the last. The chill began with President Reagan's infamous "evil empire" speech, which he delivered on March 8, 1983, to the National Association of Evangelicals in Orlando, Florida. Referring to communism as the "focus of evil in the modern world," Reagan summoned Americans to "pray for the salvation of all of those who live in that totalitarian darkness—pray they will discover the joy of knowing God," but warned against "the aggressive impulses of an evil empire."[57] Reagan's speech set the tone for a year full of blows to U.S.-Soviet relations. Two weeks later, on March 25, Reagan announced plans to utilize new technology to intercept incoming Soviet nuclear missiles. Reagan used the televised address to unveil his so-called Strategic Defense Initiative (SDI). "I call upon the scientific community who gave us nuclear weapons to turn their great talents to the cause of mankind and world peace: to give us the means of rendering these nuclear weapons impotent and obsolete," Reagan said into the television camera.[58] The president revealed plans to move the nation's defense in a more advanced direction, utilizing space-based weaponry, lasers, and particle beams to protect the country from Soviet nuclear missile attacks. "This could pave the way," Reagan told the American people, "for arms-control measures to eliminate the weapons themselves. We seek neither military superiority nor political advantage. Our only purpose . . . is to search for ways to reduce the danger of nuclear war."[59]

The Strategic Defense Initiative specifically, and more generally the nuclear weapons buildup under Reagan, alarmed the Soviets. Their fears had foundation in reality. Long before he ran for president in 1980, Reagan made no secret of his belief that the Washington political establishment had let the military down by failing to sufficiently fund it or his view that defense spending needed to be steeply increased. Once in the White House, he moved quickly to correct these perceived ills. Defense outlays during Reagan's two terms in office increased 93 percent, from $157.5 billion in 1981 to $303.6 billion in 1989. As a percentage of the gross national product, defense spending under Reagan rapidly climbed from 5.7 percent to 7.4 percent. The military-industrial complex, which President Dwight D. Eisenhower presciently warned of in his 1961 farewell address, experienced halcyon years under Reagan. In this age of General Dynamics charging the Air Force $9,609 for a forty-five-cent Allen wrench, the arms race accelerated at a staggering rate, with few restraints.[60] The strongest support for the escalation came from the Oval Office. President Reagan, as the old quip went, never met a weapons system he didn't like.[61] The president backed the MX "Peacekeeper" missile, eventually costing taxpayers $30 billion, as well as the building of one hundred B-1 bombers for $28 billion, which had so many design problems that the Air Force continued to rely on its aging fleet of B-52s. A host of other land-, air-, and sea-based weapons systems—including the Trident submarine, the F-14 fighter plane, and the neutron bomb—won the strong backing of the Reagan administration and led to Pentagon spending of $28 million per hour by the middle of the decade.[62]

The Soviets monitored developments under Reagan, especially SDI, with apprehension. Most Kremlin officials found Reagan to be hawkish and erratic. Anatoly Dobrynin, Soviet ambassador to the United States, thought the anti-Soviet atmosphere in Washington, D.C., had become "difficult and unpleasant" by the 1980s. "We had practically no room for really constructive diplomatic work. The useful and direct contacts I had long established with the White House were broken," he recalled. Soviet general secretary Yuri Andropov counseled Dobrynin and other high-level Kremlin officials to watch Reagan carefully. "We should be vigilant, because he is unpredictable. At the same time, we ought not to ignore any signs of readiness to improve our relations," said Andropov.[63] The president's hyperbolic rhetoric—especially calling the Soviet Union the "evil empire"—only ratcheted up tensions in Moscow in 1983. For its part, the Kremlin struggled to keep up with the Americans in the arms race. Still, hard-liners put on their best stone faces as they waved from high balconies on May Day while columns of troops and weapons of war paraded past them below.

These were uneasy times for the Soviets. Red Army troops were spread thin in Afghanistan, fighting what one State Department analyst aptly described as "a war with the vast majority of the Afghan people in support of an unpopular government."[64] Moreover, the Reagan administration had made clear its intention—in adherence with a decision made by the North Atlantic Treaty Organization (NATO) while President Jimmy Carter was still in the White House in 1979—to deploy 565 cruise missiles and 385 Pershing II missiles to five Western European countries.[65] The Pershing II and cruise missile deployments came in response to Moscow placing SS-20s, intermediate-range ballistic missiles, at locations across the Soviet Union. Plans to deploy the Pershing II and cruise missiles led to huge protests across Europe in 1983, with the strongest resistance in Great Britain and West Germany. The decision by NATO placed the deadly Pershing IIs within a twelve-minute striking distance of targets in and around Moscow.

Dire setbacks continued in the fall of 1983. If one had to pinpoint a nadir in superpower relations in the Reagan era, it would have to be when a Soviet jet shot down Korean Air Lines Flight 007 on September 1, 1983. The flight from New York to Seoul, with a stop in Anchorage, Alaska, strayed into Soviet airspace, resulting in a Soviet Su-15 interceptor firing a pair of air-to-air missiles at it, striking it in the wing and tail. "It took twelve minutes for Flight 007 to spiral its way to the waters north of Moneron Island and crash. When hit, the airliner was 365 nautical miles off course," wrote investigative journalist Seymour M. Hersh in the *New York Times*.[66] Flight 007 broke up over the Sea of Japan and plunged into the water, killing all 269 people on board.

The downing of KAL 007 sparked near-universal outrage and a chorus of condemnations around the world. Protests erupted in major world cities, calls for sanctions and boycotts of Soviet products abounded, traveling delegations canceled trips to the country, and various institutions rescinded invitations to prominent Soviet figures. "Murder in the Air," said a September 12 *Newsweek* cover story with a 747 in the middle of a bullseye over a map of the Soviet Union. Not to be outdone, *Time*, its chief competitor, had as its cover, on the same day, a vivid painting of a Soviet fighter jet and an exploding 747, with the words, "Shooting to Kill" and below that, "The Soviets Destroy an Airliner." "Words can scarcely express our revulsion at this horrifying act of violence," said President Reagan, upon learning of the incident. Three days later, Reagan went on television to tell Americans about "the Korean airline massacre, the attack by the Soviet Union against 269 innocent men, women, and children aboard an unarmed Korean passenger plane. The crime against humanity must never be forgotten, here or throughout the world."[67] Advocating harsh reprisals, Secretary of Defense Casper Weinberger "wanted to expel all suspected spies, freeze Soviet assets, and walk out of arms control negotiations," writes Marc Ambinder.[68]

The Kremlin's vacillating response to the incident only made matters worse. The Soviet government initially denied knowledge of the attack, but within hours it acknowledged that one of its planes shot down the 747. Soviet officials claimed the airliner was on a "pre-planned" spy mission over restricted territory. "As we can see from what has happened, everything was wrong. The liner was crawling, as it were, over our territory. And there is no doubt that it was a deliberate action designed as a crude provocation," said Colonel General Semyon Romanov, the head of Soviet air defense forces.[69]

This official position fueled additional protests and condemnations, further isolating the Soviet Union. Several governments, including the United States and Canada, banned Aeroflot airplanes from landing and refueling at their airports. Mass marches, many drawing large numbers of Koreans, moved through New York, Manila, Paris, London, Berlin, and Seoul. In Washington, D.C., protesters in front of the White House burned an effigy of Yuri Andropov, and one zealous resister began beating the flaming object with a baseball bat.[70]

The KAL 007 incident, more than any other event of the Reagan era, moved U.S.-Soviet relations dangerously close to the breaking point.[71] Other troubling flashpoints followed in rapid succession that tense autumn. On October 25, U.S. Marines invaded the tiny Caribbean island nation of Grenada. Their mission was to restore order after a chaotic coup overthrew the country's popular Marxist leader Maurice Bishop, head of the New Jewel Movement that had come to power in 1979 and established the People's Revolutionary Government (PRG). The coup plotters executed Bishop and several of his allies, paving a way for a takeover by his political rivals. Murdering Bishop, a charismatic writer and speaker with close ties to Fidel Castro in Cuba and the Sandinistas in Nicaragua, sealed the doom of the PRG in Grenada. Millions of people in the Caribbean and Latin America revered Bishop, and his brutal slaying transformed him into a martyr. His bloody ouster led to unrest on the island, and chaos ensued. Reagan justified his decision to send an invading force of army, navy and marine units, along with support servicemen from other Caribbean nations, under the pretext of protecting American medical students—a thousand or so in number—in Grenada. The American forces encountered little resistance, and the invasion brought an end to the PRG, leading to the installment of a government friendlier to American political and economic interests.[72]

Code-named Operation Urgent Fury, American intervention in Grenada was a brief affair. Within days, it was over, and the island secured. Aside from a handful of Caribbean leaders, most heads of state around the world condemned the invasion. Even British prime minister Margaret Thatcher, Reagan's staunchest ally, opposed sending American troops to the former British colony. Protests failed to sway the White House, where the invasion was seen as a decisive victory following a period of foreign policy setbacks. The event demonstrated Reagan's willingness to flex his muscle in international affairs at a time when the Second Cold War was at is coldest. Soviet vice president Vasili Kuznetsov thought Operation Urgent Fury showed that

Washington was "making delirious plans for world domination" and "pushing mankind to the brink of disaster."[73]

Worse things lay in store. A week after the Grenada invasion, Able Archer 83, a massive, ten-day-long NATO exercise, lasting from November 2 to November 11, simulated an escalation to nuclear war, nearly setting off World War III. Although it had been conducting Able Archer preparedness exercises since 1975, NATO activities in November 1983 were unprecedented in size, scope, and authenticity. "Extending from Scandinavia to the Mediterranean, the drill employed more than three thousand military and civilian personnel according to some estimates. Able Archer 83 was also more realistic than its predecessors," observed historian Beth Fischer.[74] Unlike the Cuban Missile Crisis in October 1962, neither the American public nor the rest of the world knew anything about Able Archer 83. Via KGB communiqués, Kremlin officials followed the mock exercises unfolding on a number of fronts. Soviet intelligence officers in far-flung locations warned of impending chemical weapons and nuclear arms strikes. Soviet leaders, according to historian Nate Jones, "feared that Able Archer 83 was not just a war game, but could potentially be a planned nuclear attack. A classified 1990 study conducted in Washington, D.C., by the President's Foreign Intelligence Advisory Board concluded that NATO's Able Archer 83 exercises "may have inadvertently placed our relations with the Soviet Union on a hair trigger." News of the close brush with nuclear war "surprised" Reagan when he learned about it the following year. He found the revelation "really scary."[75]

Making History on Television

In this volatile atmosphere, ABC aired *The Day After*. The film had been the brainchild of Brandon Stoddard, president of ABC, who came up with the idea after seeing the *China Syndrome*, a 1979 topical thriller starring Jane Fonda, Jack Lemmon, and Michael Douglas, about a meltdown at a nuclear power plant outside Los Angeles. Stoddard left the theater envisioning a made-for-television film with "no political discussion or bent or leaning whatsoever," one that "simply says that nuclear war is horrible."[76] He commissioned Edward Hume, the creator of such beloved shows as *Cannon*, *Barnaby Jones*, and the *Streets of San Francisco*, to write the film's teleplay. Once Stoddard had a script, he began searching for directors.

Novelist, screenwriter, and film director Nicholas Meyer was, by his own admission, the "fourth director ABC had approached."[77] Meyer was born in New York City in 1945 to a psychoanalyst father and a concert pianist mother. Raised in Manhattan, he moved west to attend the University of Iowa, obtaining a bachelor of arts degree in theater and filmmaking. Meyer's 1974 Sherlock Holmes pastiche novel, *The Seven-Per-Cent Solution*, had been made into a 1976 movie of the same name, which gave the author the boost he needed to move into directing film. He wrote and directed *Time After Time*, a clever 1979 science fiction film about British author H. G. Wells (Malcolm McDowell) using a time machine to chase the serial killer Jack the Ripper (David Warner) forward into time to modern-day San Francisco. Three years later, Meyer directed *Star Trek II: The Wrath of Khan,* an acclaimed box office triumph that revived the franchise after the first film in the series fared poorly both critically and commercially. When ABC execs approached Meyer's agent in May 1982 requesting that he direct, Meyer needed time to consider the request. "I thought about it for two weeks and finally decided it was the right thing to do. My civic duty."[78]

Meyer made certain demands. He insisted on no musical score for the film except in the opening credits, which he thought would add to its realism. Set in the heartland, Meyer and crew shot location scenes in the Midwest, mainly in the city of Lawrence, Kansas. Producers felt Lawrence was, geographically, the center of the nation, and the missile silos dotting the nearby landscape made it a prime target for the Soviets in the event of a nuclear war. The network tasked Meyer with the job of showing the nation what a "nuclear war will look like from the point of view of the average American. Don't take us places they can't go, like the White House, the Kremlin, the War Room. Our people will never know what happens there and it will not matter."[79]

The original script extended the story across two nights, in keeping with the network's championing of the miniseries format. But Meyer insisted *The Day After* had to be shown in one night, convinced that "no one is going to tune in two nights to see Armageddon."[80] His bosses at ABC agreed, handing Meyer the formidable task of editing a film originally scheduled to be four hours long down to slightly over two hours in length. *The Day After* was originally set to air in May 1983, but delays ended up pushing back the date until November. Keeping to the show's apolitical mandate, the script did not reveal who started the nuclear war, and Meyer was careful to keep his own political beliefs a closely guarded secret.[81]

Months before the airdate, ABC conducted an advance promotional blitz for *The Day After*. Some network executives doubted a film about nuclear war would be a draw, but their hopes were raised by *WarGames*, a techno-thriller that opened in theaters on June 3. The movie starred Matthew Broderick and Ally Sheedy and went on to become one of the highest-grossing films of 1983. Director John Badham, who had also directed box office leviathan *Saturday Night Fever* in 1977, aimed *WarGames* squarely at a young audience. Its main character, David Lightman (Broderick), is a high school computer geek who inadvertently starts World War III after hacking into the War Operation Plan Response (WOPR) network, a North American Aerospace Defense Command computer system. Lightman gets in trouble with government bureaucrats but manages to escape their clutches to hunt down the network's programmer, Dr. Stephen Falken (John Wood), an embittered man still grieving the death of his son, Joshua. Falken is convinced nuclear war is inevitable. But Lightman and his friend Jennifer (Sheedy) convince the brilliant recluse to help prevent the system he programmed from launching a nuclear attack. In a climactic scene inside a huge high-tech war room, Falken, Lightman, and government officials and military brass watch WOPR launch a nuclear war. It turns out to be a simulation, designed to teach human beings that such a conflict is ultimately unwinnable.[82]

Nuclear war, *WarGames* proved, could be the stuff of summer blockbusters. The surprise hit inspired ABC to redouble its promotional efforts for *The Day After*.[83] In the weeks leading up to airtime, the network distributed guides to half a million viewers with information about the movie and the arms race. For the first time, a major network encouraged Americans to see the film in groups, in public settings—at churches, schools, civic meeting spaces, and auditoriums—and untold viewers followed that advice. An army of peace activists encouraged people to see the movie with others and invited speakers to address gatherings in churches and community centers. In St. Louis, for example, the Committee for a Nuclear Weapons Freeze organized "The Night after *The Day After*," a panel with four experts speaking in a packed hall at St. Louis University.[84] Meantime, Robert A. Papazian, the film's producer, announced at a press conference that ABC would limit commercial interruptions, with none shown during the eighty minutes following the graphic depiction of nuclear war. In the fall, ABC held advance viewings for different groups: television critics and journalists, residents of Lawrence, Kansas, and President Reagan, who watched the film for the first of several times on October 10. After viewing it, a deeply shaken Reagan wrote in his diary: "Columbus Day. In the morning at Camp D. I ran the tape of the movie ABC is running on the air Nov. 20. It's called 'The Day After.' It has Lawrence, Kansas, wiped out in a nuclear war with Russia. It is powerfully done—all $7 mil. worth. It's very effective & left me greatly depressed. So far they haven't sold any of the 25 spot ads scheduled & I can see why. Whether it will be of help to the 'anti nukes' or not, I can't say. My own reaction was one of our having to do all we can to have a deterrent & to see there is never a nuclear war."[85] The film would stay with Reagan for a long time and leave an even deeper impression on him upon subsequent viewings.

Sunday night, November 20, at 8:00 p.m. eastern time, *The Day After*—an event as much as a movie—opened with a breathtaking aerial vista of midwestern farms and a fleeting film score heavy on Americana by motion picture composer David Raskin, the only segment with music. Multiple characters are immediately introduced: Kansas City physician Dr. Russell Oakes (Jason Robards) and his wife Helen (Georgann Johnson); science professor Joe Huxley (John Lithgow), attending a packed football game in Lawrence when the war breaks out; a farming family called the Dahlbergs, residents of rural Kansas, living next to missile silos; University of Kansas student Stephen Klein (Steve Guttenberg), who's hitchhiking his way to Joplin, Missouri; and missile silo worker Airman First Class Billy McCoy (William Allen Young). The action escalates rapidly, with radio and television alerts in the background offering occasionally audible details about a crisis overseas and the shrill alert of the Emergency Broadcast System. Documentary-like footage of the military mobilizing for nuclear attack is mixed with scenes of the characters responding to the impending strike. During a University of Kansas football game, Professor Huxley and thousands of sports fans gaze up at intercontinental ballistic missiles launching into the sky. "What's going on?" asks a female spectator. "Those are Minuteman missiles," Huxley explains. "Like a test sort of? Like a warning?" the woman asks. Huxley shakes his head. "They're on their way to Russia," he says. "They take about thirty minutes to reach their targets." "So do theirs. Right?" asks a man next to Huxley.

Moments later, after scenes of a frenzied evacuation of Kansas City, three high-yield nuclear weapons detonate high above the city, emitting electromagnetic pulses (EMPs) that shut down all electrical power. Dr. Oakes is driving toward Kansas City when his car stalls on the freeway, along with thousands of the other vehicles, from the massive EMP wave. Seconds later, three gigantic mushroom clouds surge tens of thousands of feet high. The devices vaporize humanity, flatten buildings, and terrorize eyewitnesses watching from afar in a memorable segment that lasts four minutes. The rest of *The Day After* is filled with agonizing scenes of doctors caring for legions of dying people, martial law violence, survivors sifting through rubble, and radiation sickness killing off characters. Eventually, Dr. Oakes returns to the ruins of what was once his house, his wife presumably dead. The doctor is dying of radiation poisoning, but he works up the energy to yell at haggard survivors huddled around a fire on what was once his property. One of the squatters offers Oakes an onion, and the grief-stricken physician falls to his knees and begins sobbing. The man with the onion approaches the sobbing doctor and they embrace in a moment of compassion. The film fades to black and a message appears: "The catastrophic events you have just witnessed are, in all likelihood, less severe than the destruction that would actually occur in the event of a full nuclear strike against the United States. It is hoped that the images of this film will inspire the nations of this earth, their peoples and leaders, to find the means to avert the fateful day."[86]

With more than 100 million people—or 46 percent of the nation's television households—watching, *The Day After* was the most successful made-for-television movie of all time. Due to its timing, *The Day After* overshadowed two lesser-seen but equally powerful films about nuclear war: *Testament*, a low-budget, made-for-PBS (Public Broadcasting Service) drama starring Jane Seymour as the head of a family living in a small Northern California town that is not hit directly by nuclear arms but where all the inhabitants die slowly of radiation poisoning; and *Threads*, a 1984 British docudrama made for the British Broadcasting Corporation about the impact of nuclear war on Sheffield in northern England. Both films had a brief run in American movie theaters. Paramount released *Testament* three weeks before *The Day After* aired, and PBS showed the film in 1984, but it was largely forgotten in the aftermath of *The Day After*. *Threads*, filled with a cast of unknowns, was more widely seen in Great Britain, but the handful of American critics who reviewed it compared it favorably to *The Day After*.

As soon as *The Day After*'s credits rolled on millions of TV screens, critics got busy attacking the film and downplaying its importance. They pointed to a series of nationwide polls taken before and after the movie that showed little shift in public opinion about the nuclear arms buildup, President Reagan's policies, or the need for arms control. Dr. William Adams, in charge of one poll conducted by George Washington University, interpreted his findings thusly: "Those who predicted the movie would produce at least a short-term bonanza in additional antinuclear sentiment among the general public were completely wrong. . . . *The Day After* failed to change existing views on the horror of nuclear war, the need for mutual arms control, and the strategy of deterrence." Historian and Reagan chronicler Steven Hayward put it even more bluntly: "The freeze movement had made its last throw, and lost."[87]

These dismissive criticisms missed a larger contextual point: no other television movie in the history of the medium had resulted in multiple public opinion polls being administered to gauge the public's reaction to it. Long before the movie aired, Americans sensed this was a film with historical gravitas on its side, and they were correct. No other television movie had ever generated such extensive advance publicity, with hundreds of newspapers devoting multiple pages of coverage to it. Before *The Day After*, public opinion pollsters had never once considered the likelihood that a television movie—based on a fictional story, no less—might actually change the minds of viewers about an issue. Indeed, no other television movie had ever been held to such high expectations. The film's critics thus applied a standard to *The Day After* not used in any other instances.

One had only to look across the country on November 20, 1983, to detect the nationwide sensation caused by the film. In churches and schools and public meeting places in every state in the Union, men, women, and children encircled televisions and watched the movie in rapt attention on a scale never before seen—and one that has not repeated itself since. In a rebuttal to the naysayers, University of Kentucky political scientists Stanley Feldman and Lee Sigelman, who wrote the definitive study on the film's polling data, observed: "*The Day After* focused on the relatively narrow issue of the aftermath of a nuclear strike, not on what led to the attack (a question the moviemakers deliberately avoided), what should be done to avoid such an attack, or the chances that an attack will actually occur. In this light we would argue that assessing the impact of *The Day After* as having little or no effect on attitudes toward issues the movie did not directly address constitutes a very hard test of its effects."[88]

Not all of *The Day After*'s attackers attempted to sweep it aside or shrug it off as insignificant. Many of its attackers feared its influence and faulted it for being, in their view, strongly biased in favor of the antinuclear movement. The Reverend Jerry Falwell fell into this category. He was invited by ABC to an advance screening of the film, which he disliked, so much so that he threatened to boycott advertisers, which never materialized. "The movie says we'd be better off just to disarm and trust the Russians to treat us nicely," Falwell insisted.[89]

Other hawkish right-wing figures registered their disapproval. Young Americans for Freedom, the country's largest conservative youth group, picketed ABC headquarters in New York City during the showing of *The Day After*. Phyllis Schlafly, president of the right-wing Eagle Forum, described the movie as "a two-hour political editorial showing the core of the nuclear-freeze argument: that survivors would wish they were dead, that there is no way to defend yourself against it. What should be shown is that there are ways to defend ourselves." Reed Irvine, head of the right-wing watchdog group Accuracy in Media, called *The Day After* "extremely depressing" and worried it would "have a negative effect on morale and the American determination to have a strong defense."[90]

Persistent right-wing criticism of *The Day After* bothered Brandon Stoddard. To show his fair-mindedness, he announced plans to make a film based on a suggestion from Ben Stein, a former Richard Nixon speechwriter. Displeased with *The Day After*, Stein proposed a different kind of made-for-television movie: "Let's have a movie called *In Red America*," Stein wrote in the *Los Angeles Herald Examiner*, a film that would show "a few days or weeks in the life of several American families after the Soviet Union had taken over America."[91] Stoddard turned Stein's idea into a miniseries called *Amerika* about a Soviet takeover of the United States. *Amerika* enjoyed a lavish budget ($40 million, as opposed to $7 million for *The Day After*) and seven episodes, totaling fourteen and a half hours, from ABC. The show caused controversy before it aired, resulting in protests from the Soviet Union, the United Nations, and American peace groups.

Televised February 15 to February 22, 1987, *Amerika* focused on the United States ten years in the future, in 1997, after the Soviet Union had seized control of the country in a "bloodless" coup, made possible by the widespread complacency of the American masses, unwilling to fight for their freedom in the face of an insidious communist power grab. *Amerika* involves numerous characters, mainly zeroing in on a Soviet KGB official (Sam Neill), a puppet governor (Robert Urich), and a strong-willed, risk-taking dissident (Kris Kristofferson) and the challenges they face living under the authoritarian regime. The first two episodes pulled in respectable ratings, then viewership plummeted. It fell so low so fast, in fact, that in the week *Amerika* was shown, ABC finished third overall of the three networks in the Nielsen ratings.[92]

Timing was a key factor in the show's tanking. By 1987, glasnost and perestroika were under way in the Soviet Union, Mikhail Gorbachev and Ronald Reagan were holding historic summit talks, and the Soviet leader was openly talking about the country's economic woes and the dire need to withdraw troops from Afghanistan. Détente was once again a top priority of superpower leaders. Thus, ABC's overblown response to *The Day After* proved a massive flop. "*Amerika* became an anachronism before it ever saw the light of day," observed social critic and journalist Andrew Kopkind.[93]

As for *The Day After*, while it enraged many people on the right, it influenced the most important conservative in America: Ronald Reagan. The fortieth president watched the film several times. *The Day After* haunted him, and he spoke of it repeatedly. At a Pentagon briefing on nuclear war in late October 1983, Reagan listened intently as military brass discussed different plans for the unthinkable: a superpower clash involving the use of nuclear weapons. The meeting, which Reagan found a "sobering experience," reminded him of *The Day After*. "In several ways, the sequence of events in the briefings paralleled those in the ABC movie. Yet there were still some people in the Pentagon who claimed a nuclear war was 'winnable.' I thought they were crazy."[94]

A reporter at a Rose Garden event the morning after the film aired asked Reagan what he thought of it. "I think it was pretty well handled. It didn't say anything we didn't know, that is, that nuclear war would be horrible and that's why we're doing what we're doing, so there won't be one." Privately, however, Reagan took *The Day After* seriously. According to journalist and former secretary of state Leslie Gelb, Reagan thought "anecdotally, not analytically," and film provided an effective means of influencing the president.[95] Reagan could relate to *The Day After*, a film about ordinary Americans caught in the unimaginable horror of nuclear war. *The Day After*, writes historian Beth Fischer, presented Reagan with "visual images of nuclear annihilation" that changed his thinking and "made a lasting impression on him."[96]

Three years after he first watched *The Day After*, Reagan was in the midst of negotiating a historic arms control agreement with Mikhail Gorbachev to eliminate intermediate-range nuclear weapons based in Europe, which marked a radical shift for Reagan in the direction of détente. The president took time out of his busy schedule to send a telegram to the director of *The Day After*, Nicholas Meyer, to praise him for the role he played in inspiring the superpower negotiations. "Don't think your movie didn't have any part of this, because it did," the telegram read.[97] Years later, Meyer met Edmund Morris, author of Reagan's authorized biography, who confirmed to Meyer that "the only time he ever saw Reagan depressed was after viewing *The Day After*. Reagan who had come to power contemplating a winnable nuclear war . . . had changed his mind."[98]

The broadcast of *The Day After* occurred at the high point of antinuclear activism. The movement began to decline in the months and years following the landmark television movie. But the grassroots struggle to abolish nuclear weapons had been effective in helping create a rich and visible antinuclear culture, and the movement enjoyed ample public backing. A poll conducted by the Warner-Amex Qube cable television network of 5,500 viewers of *The Day After*, one of those cited by the film's detractors as showing no significant change of public opinion after the movie, found 49 percent surveyed "still support" arms control, with an additional 12 percent indicating they "now support" arms control.[99]

By the time of Reagan's reelection in November 1984, the tide of history was shifting inexorably toward détente. Backed by a moderate secretary of state, George Shultz, Reagan began to pursue arms control talks with the Soviets during his second term in the White House. The death of hard-line Soviet Communist Party general secretary Konstantin Chernenko in March 1985 and his replacement with reformer Mikhail Gorbachev raised hopes for improved relations between Washington and Moscow, as well as the possibility of new, far-reaching arms control treaties. Years of hard work and obstacles lay ahead, but a great reversal was under way, and the antinuclear movement—in all of its grassroots and cultural manifestations—helped pave the way for that shift.

In the weeks and months following a nuclear reactor meltdown at the Three Mile Island Nuclear Generating Station in Pennsylvania, countless grassroots antinuclear protests occurred across the United States. Mass marches such as this one in Washington, D.C., on May 6, 1979, helped fuel the growth of America's peace movement. MPVHistory/Alamy Stock Photo.

Architect and designer Maya Lin poses here with a scale model of her winning design for the Vietnam Veterans Memorial, May 6, 1981. While in its planning stages, the memorial touched off a firestorm of controversy and criticism for not sufficiently celebrating the heroism of Vietnam veterans. But once it was dedicated, it became one of the most revered monuments in the United States. Science History Images/Alamy Stock Photo.

Warren Beatty portrays radical activist and journalist John Reed and Diane Keaton plays his lover, Louise Bryant, in the Oscar-winning film *Reds* (1981). Reed (1887–1920), a globe-trotting writer who covered the Mexican and Russian Revolutions, died at age thirty-two after an eventful life spent in left-wing and bohemian circles. *Reds* proved to be a rarity: a mainstream Hollywood film featuring a sympathetic portrayal of a real-life communist. Ronald Grant Archive/Alamy Stock Photo.

In Managua, Nicaragua, women of the Sandinista army celebrate the second anniversary of the Nicaraguan revolution outside of a cathedral on July 17, 1981. Women played a pivotal role in the Nicaraguan revolution, fighting alongside men to oust the country's reviled dictator, Anastasio Somoza Debayle, bringing an end to a longtime Washington-backed ruling dynasty. Mike Goldwater/Alamy Stock Photo.

Bumper stickers were a popular way of expressing dissent during the Cold War of the 1980s. Here is a truck from New York State in 1982 plastered with antinuclear and peace bumper stickers, mixed with classic rock band favorites. Emanuel Tanjala/Alamy Stock Photo.

The nuclear war sequence from *The Day After*, which aired on the American Broadcasting Company on November 20, 1983, left a lasting impression on millions of Americans who watched the made-for-TV movie. One of its viewers, President Ronald Reagan, credited film with helping him to embrace détente with the Soviet Union. Photo 12/Alamy Stock Photo.

Patrick Swayze, C. Thomas Howell, and Charlie Sheen fend off a Soviet invasion in the fantasy film *Red Dawn* (1984). The movie, about a group of Colorado youngsters who form a deadly guerilla army called the "Wolverines" (named after their high school mascot) to resist a takeover of the United States by Soviet, Cuban, and Nicaraguan troops, was the first American film to receive a PG-13 rating, due to excessive violence. AA Film Archive/Alamy Stock Photo.

Sylvester Stallone as John Rambo in *Rambo: First Blood Part II*, the second highest-grossing film of 1985, manages to do what roughly 2.5 million Americans in the 1960s and 1970s could not accomplish: single-handedly defeat the Vietnamese communist foes, and a Soviet heavy thrown in for good measure. Allstar Picture Library Ltd./Alamy Stock Photo.

Oliver Stone directs actors James Woods and Elpidia Carrillo in Mexico during the making of the film *Salvador* (1986). Director Stone's gritty and brutal drama, set in war-torn El Salvador, depicts events from earlier in the decade when repressive paramilitary death squads—backed by Washington—murdered countless civilians and triggered a bloody civil war across the countryside. Ronald Grant Archive/Alamy Stock Photo.

The British 7-inch 45 RPM of the Genesis hit single "Land of Confusion," released in the fall of 1986. Both the British and American versions featured the memorable caricature puppets of the band from the song's music video. Designers Peter Fluck and Roger Law, the duo responsible for the popular U.K. satirical TV puppet series *Spitting Image*, also created likenesses of Ronald Reagan and a number of other celebrities and world leaders to appear in the "Land of Confusion" video. Records/Alamy Stock Photo.

Soviet leader Mikhail Gorbachev and President Ronald Reagan sign the Intermediate-Range Nuclear Forces (INF) Treaty on December 8, 1987. Reagan endured a barrage of criticism from hardened Cold Warrior conservatives, who attacked him for not being sufficiently hard-line in his dealings with the Soviets. World History Archive/Alamy Stock Photo.

CHAPTER 6

The Wars for Central America

I've been called a Communist. I'm not. I'm a humanist and I'm involved in El Salvador because our government is responsible for much of the violence. The U.S. is sounding increasingly like it did in Vietnam 15 years ago, and I'm very aware of what that led to.

—*Dr. Charlie Clements,* Witness to War, *1984*

The Agony of Central America

"Be calm. Act with maturity. The moment is coming when all Nicaraguans, regardless of their beliefs, can go into the streets together and rejoice."[1] So began the broadcast on Nicaragua's national radio station in the early morning of July 19, 1979. Unlike the usual Latin music of the past, the radio station now played songs sung by leftist rebels when they waged war against the government. Within hours of that announcement, truckloads of Sandinista guerrillas in green fatigues entered Managua, Nicaragua's capital, greeted by cheering crowds lining the roads. Black and red, the colors of the Sandinistas, appeared everywhere: on banners and homemade flags, in people's clothing, in graffiti on buildings. Similarly ubiquitous were paintings and silhouettes of Augusto César Sandino (1895–1934), the instantly recognizable Nicaragua liberator, with his iconic sombrero and tall boots. In the 1920s and 1930s, Sandino had boldly led a peasant insurgency against U.S. Marines occupying the country. Captured and executed by the National Guard in 1934, Sandino did not live to see his vision of independence come to pass. Rebels carried on the fight in his name over the decades, and by the 1970s, conditions were turning in their favor. A final offensive, launched in May 1979, resulted in weeks of savage warfare, leading to the collapse of Anastasio Somoza's regime. The dictator fled the country with all the wealth he could transport. His reviled National Guard, which he and his father—also named Anastasio Somoza—had used for decades to murder, torture, and intimidate ordinary Nicaraguans, now scattered into neighboring countries or the United States. The Somoza dynasty, backed by Washington since the Great Depression, was no more.[2] Church bells pealed all day when the Sandinistas swept into Managua. The revolution enjoyed strong support among religious Nicaraguans, and many Sandinista leaders were Catholics. "It is a traditional principle of the church that there can be a just war in the legitimate defense of the people against an oppressive regime," said Father Ernesto Cardenal, a Catholic priest, poet, and Sandinista revolutionary, in July 1979.[3]

In neighboring El Salvador, a country also beset by turmoil, leftist guerrillas in the Farabundo Martí National Liberation Front (FMLN) waged war against a U.S.-backed military dictatorship. State-supported paramilitary units consisting mainly of military personnel, known by the morbid nickname "death squads," targeted students, farmers, religious workers, and other opponents of the government, real and imagined. Between 1980 and 1992, an estimated seventy-five thousand Salvadorans died in the country's civil war. Thousands of others disappeared, never to be seen or heard from again. Among the multitudes of missing were children, as many as three thousand, abducted—often in the night—by the army.[4] Death squads left a bloody calling card wherever they went. Bodies were piling up in ditches, fields, rivers, landfills, backyards, alleys, and the ocean. Lorena Peña, a young Salvadoran woman who later joined the guerrillas, recalled the systematic fashion in which death squads in her hometown of Santa Ana City carried out their grim task: "One week only students' bodies appeared, the next week market vendors, the next tailors, the next nurses and the next workers. . . . I was constantly distressed by the scenes of death along the way, decapitated and dismembered bodies."[5] Father Paul Schindler, a Catholic activist who worked in El Salvador from 1972 to 1982, never got used to the ordeal of finding corpses attracting swarms of flies. Even worse were the regular visits he got from panicked Salvadorans looking for missing loved ones. Desperate searches often ended tragically. "I buried 37 mutilated bodies that were left along the road, or thrown in the ocean," Schindler recalled.[6]

The bloodbath in El Salvador worsened in 1980, when guerrillas launched a new offensive and a death squad crackdown resulted in an orgy of killings. On

March 24, 1980, the world took notice of the tiny Central American country when sixty-two-year-old Archbishop Óscar Romero, outspoken champion of human rights, the poor, and nonviolence, was assassinated after delivering a sermon. In his final homily, spoken the day before he was murdered at San Salvador's Church of the Divine Providence, Romero made a memorable plea for justice: "In the name of God and this suffering population, whose cries reach to the heavens more tumultuous each day, I beg you, I beseech you, I order you, in the name of God, cease the repression."[7] Romero's assassin shot him in the heart, killing him instantly. Multiple investigations later revealed that Romero's killers—many men were involved in carrying out his assassination—were acting under the orders of Major Roberto D'Aubuisson, the far-right head of the death squads.[8]

Archbishop Romero's death shocked the world and revealed the brutality of the country's reign of terror. Eight months later, the spotlight returned once more to El Salvador when four women from the United States, all Catholic missionaries, were raped, tortured, and murdered by the death squads on December 2, 1980. Maryknoll sisters Maura Clarke and Ita Ford, Ursuline sister Dorothy Kazel, and lay missionary Jean Donovan had all been active in a rural humanitarian relief operation. They were aware of the dangers of staying in El Salvador. "People are being killed daily," wrote Jean Donovan in May 1980. "We just found out that three people from our area had been taken, tortured, and hacked to death." Donovan, only twenty-seven at the time, considered returning to the United States, leaving the bloodletting behind. "I almost could," she wrote, "except the children, the poor, bruised victims of this insanity. Who would care for them?" Likewise, Sister Maura Clarke could not conceal her anxiety about the grisly violence surrounding her. "My fear of death is being challenged constantly," Clarke wrote near the end of her life, "as children, lovely young girls, old people, are being shot, and some cut up with machetes, bodies thrown by the road, and people prohibited from burying them."[9]

The four churchwomen fell under the watchful eye of the death squads. Far-right military officers inside of the murderous clandestine unit regarded the four Americans as meddlesome communist sympathizers whose actions were aiding the guerrillas. Under the cloak of night, the death squads followed the women, tailing their minivan on a lonely stretch of road after Jean and Dorothy picked Maura and Ita up from the airport on their return from a trip to Nicaragua. Like the countless Salvadorans murdered by the death squads, the churchwomen must have known unimaginable pain and terror in their final moments. A villager found their bodies on December 3, each shot in the head execution style and partially buried in a shallow grave outside of San Salvador.[10]

When President Jimmy Carter learned of the murdered American workers, he temporarily suspended $25 million in aid to the ruling junta in San Salvador, at the advice of his ambassador to El Salvador, Robert White, a staunch proponent of human rights. Ambassador White had befriended the nuns during his time in El Salvador and knew them well. Deeply shaken by the murders, White drove out to the temporary gravesite where the nuns had been buried to help retrieve the bodies. "The bastards won't get away with it," he said, as he stood over the remains.[11] President Carter condemned the murders but concluded there was no evidence linking the killings directly to high-level Salvadoran officials. Concerned about the growing strength of the leftist FMLN rebels, Carter resumed aid shipments to the Salvadoran government, fearing a repeat of the Nicaraguan revolution if Washington continued to withhold support. Carter's commitment to human rights in Central America was lukewarm and inconsistent and ultimately subordinated to his Cold War focus. He had ignored pleas from Archbishop Romero to suspend military aid to the Salvadoran government. At the same time, Carter halted aid to the new regime in Nicaragua after he became convinced the Sandinistas were backing the FMLN's armed struggle in El Salvador.[12]

The Reagan administration, on entering the White House in January 1981, assumed a harder line than its predecessor against the Salvadoran guerrillas and Nicaragua's Sandinista revolution. The hawkish new commander in chief made it a top priority to wage Cold War against communism around the world, especially in Central America, which Reagan called "our backyard."[13] Alexander Haig, Reagan's newly appointed secretary of state, took the first drastic step of dismissing Robert White as Ambassador to El Salvador, a casualty of excessive devotion to human rights. The Reagan administration displayed striking callousness when it came to the suffering and deaths unleashed by the military on El Salvador's civilian population. Haig even suggested that the four churchwomen played a role in bringing about their deaths. "Perhaps the vehicle the nuns were riding in may have tried to run a roadblock . . . and there may have been an exchange of fire. And perhaps those who inflicted the casualties sought to cover it up," Haig told the House Foreign Relations Committee in March 1981.[14]

President Reagan imposed a Cold War template on Central America that fit poorly over the conflicts there. He viewed the region as a vital East-West ideological battleground between communist and anticommunist proxies, rather than a north-south conflict between a wealthy imperial power and impoverished nations being exploited for their economic resources and labor. Prior to the 1980s, Central America had been regarded—when regarded at all—as an insignificant backwater, subject to recurring military interventions by Washington. The turmoil and revolutions of the late 1970s changed that, pulling Central America—especially El Salvador and Nicaragua—out of the shadows and into the global spotlight. In the case of El Salvador, President Reagan threw his unwavering support behind the Salvadoran military in its counterinsurgency war against FMLN guerrillas. Cold Warriors in Congress and the White House conceded that the Salvadoran government was not ideal, insisting that the rebels were worse. However, as historian Doug Rossinow points out, during the early 1990s, the Truth Commission for El Salvador, a UN-approved body, "compiled accounts of twenty-two thousand atrocities committed in that country between 1980 and 1991, and revealed, in its thorough and impartial report, that testimony by Salvadorans attributed almost 85 percent of this violence to the regime and its death squads, and only about 5 percent to the insurgents."[15]

Further south, in Nicaragua, the Reagan administration was backing the Contras by December 1981, a coalition of armed exiles waging war against the government.[16] Reagan insisted the Sandinistas intended to establish a Soviet and Cuban beachhead in the region, which threatened U.S. security. By contrast, the Contras were "freedom fighters," Reagan proclaimed. "You know the truth about them, you know who they're fighting and why. They are the moral equal of our Founding Fathers and the brave men and women of the French Resistance."[17] But Reagan's lofty descriptions did not match the record of the Contras, who routinely resorted to rape, torture, kidnapping, murder, and other acts of terrorism.[18]

Elsewhere in the region, Guatemala and Honduras, too, experienced varying levels of repression and human rights violations. Abject poverty plagued both countries, particularly Honduras, the poorest of the Central American nations. Military officers dominated political institutions in Guatemala and Honduras, with U.S. advisers maintaining a significant presence in each country.[19] Human rights abuses were rampant in both countries. Civil war in Guatemala, a permanent condition there since the early 1960s, pitted the military against leftist guerrillas and peaceful dissenters alike. "All they do in Guatemala is give orders and kill," Pope John Paul II famously lamented in the 1980s. Meantime, Honduras served as a base for the Contras, who trained and launched attacks against Nicaragua along the border between the two countries.[20] As a result of the government's close ties to Washington and its willingness to allow the Contras to operate inside the country, Honduras was often on the verge of going to war against Nicaragua. In the summer of 1982, when a bloody armed conflict between the two nations appeared imminent, a Honduran military officer remarked, "In a war the United States will send some aid, some body bags, and the journalists to cover it. But we'll provide the bodies."[21]

Anatomy of a Protest Movement

The Reagan administration exacerbated conditions in Central America by furnishing military aid to repressive dictatorships and treating nations as Cold War battlegrounds. In response to the region's deepening turmoil, a grassroots Central America peace and solidarity movement began to spread across the United States. The Second Cold War thus birthed yet another resistance struggle, driven largely by fears of American military intervention in El Salvador and Nicaragua. With the Vietnam War was still fresh in people's minds, organizers aimed events—marches, rallies, vigils, and the like—at resisting the looming threat of their country going to war in Central America. "We have phone trees set up in every town. As soon as anyone hears about an invasion, they'll get in contact with us. We'll contact one person in each town, and then they'll contact a group of people. Each of the people in that group will contact their own group of people," noted Sarah Murray, coordinator of the Michigan Interfaith Committee on Central American Human Rights, explaining the group's plans in the event of Washington intervening in El Salvador or Nicaragua.[22]

Like antinuclear campaigns, the Central America peace movement was a decentralized coalition of organizations, with no single group exercising control over activities. Historian Bradford Martin offered a modest guesstimate of the movement's size in his 2011 account of the decade's activism, *The Other Eighties*, pegging its "core" at "about twenty thousand people."[23] In all likelihood, Martin erred on the side of modesty with his head count. Sociologist Christian Smith, author of *Resisting Reagan*, the first history of the Central America peace movement in the United States, acknowledged the existence of "fifteen hundred to two thousand social-movement organizations spread throughout the U.S."[24] While it is impossible to pinpoint the precise number of men and women involved at different points in Central America–related activism, at its height in the mid-1980s, combined efforts on multiple fronts resulted in one of the Reagan era's most energetic and creative protest movements. At least once a year in the 1980s—in some years, several times—the movement would flex its muscle and mobilize demonstrations of fifty to one hundred thousand in Washington, D.C.[25]

The movement's goals and tactics changed over time in ways that mirrored shifting policies in Washington. In the early 1980s, the war in El Salvador dominated its agenda. Activists placed a high priority on educating Americans about their government's role in the violence that racked the country daily. The most visible and effective organization behind many early protests was the Committee in Solidarity with the People of El Salvador (CISPES), founded in October 1980 to pressure politicians to stop supporting El Salvador's ruling junta and death squads. By the spring of 1981, CISPES boasted over 120 chapters across the country, and its members routinely organized rallies, teach-ins, and lobbying campaigns.[26] The committee maintained an especially active presence on university campuses, where activists arranged to bring critics of the administration's policies to speak and planned showings of the Oscar-nominated documentary *El Salvador: Another Vietnam*, an exposé of Washington's involvement in the country's civil war.[27]

The Committee in Solidarity with the People of El Salvador and other Central America peace groups stoked the American public's fears of another Vietnam War–style conflict happening in El Salvador. Activists in CISPES often relied on documentary films about El Salvador, which abounded in the 1980s, to help educate Americans about the country's agonizing violence. The Academy Award–winning *Witness to War*, for example, released in 1985, told the story of Charlie Clements, an American physician who traveled to El Salvador to attend to poor Salvadorans living in rural war zones. Years earlier, during the Vietnam War, Clements had been an Air Force officer who flew more than fifty missions over Southeast Asia before leaving the armed forces early to protest the war. He returned to the United States, received his discharge, and got involved with peace activism. In 1981, Clements, then a recently trained physician, picked rebel-controlled areas in El Salvador as his destination, aware of the risks posed to his life by working there. He regarded his decision as partly a political act to resist his government's policies and partly a humanitarian act to help people who might not otherwise have access to medical care.

Clements traveled to El Salvador with seventy-five pounds of supplies—all he could carry—on an odyssey that exposed him to the civil war's stark brutality. He worked tirelessly with Salvadorans to establish a network of fifteen clinics, all the while living in an adobe hut with two couples who had six children between them. He trekked through guerrilla-held zones on foot or horseback, and the two constants he faced on a daily basis were mosquito bites (he came down with malaria in El Salvador) and violence. His harrowing story became the subject of his 1984 book, *Witness to War*, and the documentary of the same name, directed by Deborah Shaffer, a veteran film editor. At the 58th Academy Awards in March 1986, Shaffer's film won an Oscar for best documentary short subject. "You didn't have to be a genius to know that this was a compelling story," said the film's producer, David Goodman.[28]

Photography and documentaries made by politically conscious men and women heightened awareness of the conflict, especially among peace activists, who despaired at the news of constant bloodletting. Violence in El Salvador was routine and woven into daily life. However, every now and then, it reached such appalling depths of depravity that it was capable of shocking even the most seasoned human rights advocates. Such was the case in the early months of 1982, when details of a gigantic massacre of civilians—mostly the elderly, women, and children—by the Salvadoran military in the remote village of El Mozote in December 1981, came to light. The Salvadoran government and military engaged in a massive cover-up of the event, yet Raymond Bonner of the *New York Times* learned of it and wrote an exposé that ran on January 27, 1982. "When we reached El Mozote, evidence of the massacre was still abundant. Skeletons were being picked over by vultures, the stench of death carried by the breeze," Bonner later recalled. Coincidentally, Alma Guillermoprieto, a freelance journalist reporting from Central America, wrote about El Mozote for the *Washington Post* on the same day as Bonner.[29]

The Salvadoran government and the Reagan administration denied claims by Bonner and Guillermoprieto of a huge, assembly line type of killing field at El Mozote. Apologists for Washington's El Salvador policies—including the *Wall Street Journal* and *Time* magazine—launched a concerted effort to discredit the two journalists. However, subsequent investigations of El Mozote over the years, including one conducted by the U.N.-sponsored Truth Commission for El Salvador in the early 1990s, revealed that, if anything, Bonner and Guillermoprieto did not realize the enormous scope or severity of the mass killings. Estimates varied, but between eight hundred and twelve hundred Salvadoran civilians—no one will ever know the exact number—were murdered at El Mozote by the Salvadoran military. In an emotional speech to the nation in 2012, more than thirty years after the killings, El Salvador's president, Mauricio Funes, addressed the crimes committed by the military: "In three days and three nights, the biggest massacre of civilians was committed in contemporary Latin American history. For this massacre, for the abhorrent violations of human rights and the abuses perpetrated in the name of the Salvadoran state, I ask forgiveness of the families of the victims."[30]

The horrors in El Salvador and, more broadly, the violence and abject poverty across much of Central America, sent hundreds of thousands of refugees streaming northward in the 1980s to escape. Half a million Salvadorans and Guatemalans made the perilous trek to "el norte" between 1980 and 1984, entering through Texas, New Mexico, Arizona, or California.[31] From this refugee crisis arose another nationwide protest campaign: the sanctuary movement, a coalition of Jewish, Catholic, and Protestant activists. Half a dozen churches formed the core of the movement when it began in 1982. Four years later, the sanctuary movement had multiplied into a vast network of hundreds of churches.[32] Activists transformed places of worship into safe havens for impoverished Central Americans escaping the wars and brutality of their homelands. California, home to 160 (or 36 percent) of the more than 450 refugee sanctuaries in the United States, was a hotbed of sanctuary activism. In addition to the Southwest, the movement grew rapidly in the Northeast, especially New York and Pennsylvania, and in the Midwest, particularly Illinois, Wisconsin, and Ohio.[33]

"All we're doing is providing transportation, medical care, food and shelter to people who would be dead if we didn't take them," explained Jim Fife, a pastor at the Southside Presbyterian Church in Tucson, Arizona.[34] One of the many people saved by the movement was a nineteen-year-old refugee, too fearful to reveal his name, who fled El Salvador in 1983 after the death squads murdered his uncle, aunt, three cousins, and brother. The young man walked to Guatemala, boarded a ramshackle bus to Mexico, and continued north, eventually crossing into the United States with the help of Jim Corbett, a rancher who played a vital role in launching the sanctuary movement. Corbett transported countless Central Americans across the border. Thanks to him, the young man made his way to Chicago, where the sanctuary movement provided him with a place to live, regular meals, and moral support. In exchange, he risked deportation by speaking at schools and public events about the plight of ordinary Salvadorans. "The most frequent question I am asked is, 'Is communism taking over El Salvador?' I haven't seen communism, just repression with the rich getting richer. . . . I would return to my country immediately if the repressive situation were to clear up."[35]

In a case of art imitating life, the acclaimed film *El Norte* (1984) dramatized the ordeal of Central Americans who took part in the mass northward exodus of the 1980s. Latino filmmaker Gregory Nava directed the movie, based on a screenplay he cowrote with his wife, Anna Thomas, a fellow University of California at Los Angeles film school graduate. Nava and Thomas spent years trying to raise funds to make *El Norte*, which was the type of film the big studios eschewed. The duo finally found a backer in Lindsay Law, executive producer of *American Playhouse*, a long-running anthology program on the Public Broadcasting System. Additional funds trickled in from Great Britain's Channel Four Films, and a handful of sympathetic investors. Nava, an American of Mexican descent who grew up in San Diego, had relatives in the United States and Mexico, so he crossed the border often and witnessed Central Americans streaming into his hometown on a daily basis. "These people are like shadows—they wash our clothes, they clean our dishes, they work in our yards, yet we know nothing about them," Nava explained.[36]

In *El Norte*, an Indigenous sister and brother, Rosa (Zaide Silvia Gutiérrez) and Enrique (David Villalpando), escape their impoverished, violence-torn village in Guatemala after government soldiers kill their father. The siblings head north through Mexico, where they fall prey to so-called coyotes—men who specialized in transporting people across the U.S.-Mexican border. They finally reach San Diego, California, after literally crawling through a long, narrow drain pipe to get there. In Los Angeles, Rosa and Enrique look for employment and hold down menial jobs, but they struggle to survive. Shot in documentary style, *El Norte* depicts the quest of two Guatemalans searching for a better life so authentically that critic Roger Ebert likened it to John Steinbeck's Depression-era novel *The Grapes of Wrath*, about the plight of Oklahoma migrants moving to California during the Dust Bowl.[37]

Yet *El Norte* came perilously close to not being made. Studio executives wanted no part of it. Too dreary, not enough romance or car chases, and—worst of all—it's in Spanish, they said. One executive suggested it might get financed if Nava and Thomas cast Brooke Shields and Robby Benson in the main roles.[38] The pair insisted on casting Indigenous actors from Mexico, to heighten *El Norte*'s realism. Shooting the movie in southern Mexico on a tiny budget was fraught with peril. At one point, bandits kidnapped the film's location manager, stole the footage, and demanded a ransom. Nava and Thomas bribed the culprits with 1.3 million pesos—a big share of their budget—to secure the return of the crew member and negatives. Another tense incident involved angry villagers appearing at a location shoot with guns and machetes, menacing cast and crew.[39] When the film was completed, the finished product was widely hailed as a masterpiece for capturing the desperation of its two main characters, who are forced to confront painful challenges in their new home, including raids by immigration authorities and struggles to find work. Near the end of the film, a weary Rosa—hospitalized with an illness that suddenly overtakes her—laments the endless hardships they face and their inability to find a safe haven. "When will we find a home, Enrique? Perhaps we'll find a home when we die," an ailing Rosa tells her brother. Enrique encourages Rosa to stay hopeful: "Don't say that, Rosita. It's hard, but we'll be lucky from now on. We'll have everything we want. We'll make a lot of money. And we'll go back to our village, and when we walk down the street, people will look at us with envy."[40]

But Enrique's optimistic declaration does not come to pass. The film ends on a tragic note, with Rosa dying and Enrique finding temporary employment on a Los Angeles construction crew. *El Norte* was a unique film, infused with a mix of humor, pathos, and magical realism. Its politics were subtle yet apparent, woven seamlessly into a script that prioritized the personal story of a brother and sister. It did not shy away from showing the bloodletting in Guatemala, which Reagan regarded as a bastion of freedom in the Cold War struggle against communism, or the tragic endurance test that the life of a refugee entailed. *El Norte* had a limited run in movie theaters before being shown on PBS, at a time when the sanctuary movement was flourishing. For Gregory Nava and Anna Thomas, *El Norte* was a profoundly personal film, near and dear to their hearts. "What I'd like *El Norte* to accomplish," Nava said at its release, is to "take people's fear of immigrants away."[41]

Targeting Nicaragua

Even as *El Norte* flickered on a handful of theater screens in early 1984, the Central America peace movement's focus had begun to shift toward Nicaragua, where the Contra war was gaining momentum. Tens of millions of dollars of aid from the United States made it to the Contras—totaling between $40 million and $90 million—in 1982 and 1983. Were they the "freedom fighters" Reagan claimed they were, waging a good fight against a Marxist regime and attracting farmers and peasants dissatisfied with the excesses of the Sandinista revolution?[42] Or were they the creation of Central Intelligence Agency, controlled by former Somoza National Guardsmen, as the war's critics asserted? Regardless of whether the Contras were an authentic guerrilla movement or a proxy army imposed by the U.S. government, they wasted no time in committing atrocities in small towns and isolated rural areas. The Reagan White House and its hawkish backers in Congress held the Sandinistas under a microscope, assailing every act that gave off the slightest whiff of totalitarianism, including the temporary closure of the opposition press, the forced removal of Miskito Indigenous peoples from war zones along the east coast, and the harassment of dissidents. Yet far worse human rights violations committed by the Contras failed to stir the same indignation among the rebels' zealous defenders. Indeed, Contra atrocities occurred with such alarming frequency that even the Defense Intelligence Agency, an information-gathering branch of the Department of Defense, described the Contras a "terrorist group."[43]

Former Contra leader Édgar Chamorro, scion of a prominent Nicaraguan family, arrived at a similar conclusion. Chamorro left the rebels in disgust in 1984 in protest against their excessive use of violence and their reliance on a CIA training manual titled *Psychological Operations in Guerrilla Warfare*, which taught the use of terrorist methods. Chamorro became a prominent critic of the rebels, describing them as "mere mercenaries" with "no democratic goals." "They are very ruthless," he said, and "believe they can get away with anything if they are fighting communists. And communists, for them, is a very broad definition. Anybody who is not ultraright, you know, is a communist." Persistent rumors of the Contras selling cocaine to raise funds to wage war against their fellow Nicaraguans further tarnished their reputation.[44]

So shocking and routine were abuses committed by the Contras that Congress passed the Boland Amendment—really, three separate amendments, enacted between 1982 and 1984—placing limits on Washington's support for the Nicaraguan rebels. Named for Representative Edward P. Boland, a Massachusetts Democrat who headed the House Intelligence Committee and opposed Contra aid, the amendments amounted to an effort by Congress to apply the brakes on the Reagan administration's not-so-secret covert war in Nicaragua. To get around the restrictions, Reagan's team worked closely with friendly regimes abroad, including South Korea, Taiwan, and Saudi Arabia, to divert aid to the Contras.[45]

Unknown to the American public, the White House had also begun to sell advanced high-tech weaponry to America's avowed enemy, the Islamic Republic of Iran, in a complex trading arrangement designed to benefit the Contras. Lieutenant Colonel Oliver North ran the scheme out of the Old Executive Office Building near the White House. The plan involved the Israeli government shipping large numbers of deadly MIM-23 Hawk surface-to-air missiles and BGM-71 TOW antitank missiles to Tehran, in exchange for payments diverted to the Contras to circumvent the Boland amendments. During Reagan's second term, revelations of the Iran-Contra scheme erupted into a full-blown scandal. It coincided with a historic World Court ruling in The Hague that the U.S. government had violated international laws by supporting the Contras and covertly mining Nicaragua's harbors.[46]

On the home front, Reagan's Central America policies enjoyed little public support. A 1982 Harris poll found that two-thirds of Americans opposed the administration's El Salvador policies, while 74 percent told a *Time* magazine pollster they feared their government would enter into a Vietnam War–like conflict in El Salvador.[47] The Contra war was equally unpopular. A 1983 Harris survey found that two-thirds of the American people expressed opposition to "arming and supporting the rebels in Nicaragua who are trying to over-throw the Sandinista government."[48] Sixty-three percent of those polled in a July 1985 Harris survey supported Congress in its dispute over Contra aid with President Reagan, and 61 percent shared that view in a 1987 poll by the same firm.[49] Opposition to military aid for the Contras peaked at 76 percent by mid-decade. By contrast, support for military aid to the Contras yo-yoed between 13 percent and 29 percent in the years 1983 to 1986, depending on the poll and the time.[50] A brief upward spike of support during the Iran-Contra hearings to 43 percent was due to Lt. Col. North's dramatic televised testimony. The numbers plummeted again, however, and at no point did military aid to the Contras ever enjoy a plurality of support, much less majority backing, in the United States.[51]

Such weak poll numbers emboldened Central American peace activists, who were more motivated than ever by the mid-1980s to challenge their government's policies. The widespread practice of Americans traveling to Nicaragua to witness the Sandinista revolution firsthand was one effective way to resist the Contra war. By 1986, more than one hundred thousand U.S. citizens had made the journey to tour the country and see conditions for themselves.[52] Nonprofit groups and progressive travel agencies sponsored and planned trips of American delegations to Nicaragua. One such organization, TecNica, sent hundreds of technical experts—including computer scientists, engineers, electricians, machinists, and an array of other specialists—to assist in different areas. Founded in 1984 by economist Michael Urmann, TecNica had amassed over 350 volunteers within four years.[53] These men and women paid their own way to travel to Nicaragua to perform challenging technical duties, such as installing computer networks, repairing medical equipment, advising on infrastructure developments, instructing Nicaraguans to use machines, including seismographs to detect earthquake activity. The country was still reeling from a devastating earthquake in December 1972, which left large sections of downtown Managua flattened and killed as many as eleven thousand people. By the 1980s, Nicaragua was desperately in need of the technical aid that TecNica provided. "I'd say two-thirds of our volunteers have no history of political activism. They just want to do something meaningful to help others," explained Urmann.[54]

Most Americans who journeyed to Nicaragua did so to bear witness, and they returned to the United States to report on what they saw. The nonprofit Witness for Peace, founded in 1983 by Christians seeking to step up nonviolent resistance against the Contra war, organized contingents from all fifty states to travel to Nicaragua. The visitors interviewed government officials and representatives of human rights organizations, labor unions, and nongovernmental organizations. Americans also saw the devastating effects of the war, which never failed to shock them. A typical Witness for Peace delegate to Nicaragua was Mary Schoen, a teacher from Cincinnati, who spent two weeks crisscrossing the country in the spring of 1984 with other American travelers, interviewing Nicaraguans from all walks of life. It horrified Schoen to see the destruction of the Contra war for herself. In addition to "the kidnappings, the rape," the Contras "destroy their food supplies, . . . burn grain storage bins, . . . blow up food fuel supplies and ports. . . . Those people are extremely poor. They live on rice and beans and tortillas—there is nothing in the stores."[55]

Anti-Contra protests thrived mid-decade as a result of an influx of activists like Schoen who'd recently returned from Nicaragua and joined the resistance. Many protesters affiliated with Pledge of Resistance, a nationwide network of religious activists and peace groups dedicated to collecting the signatures of Americans vowing to engage in mass civil disobedience in the event of a U.S. invasion in Central America. The Pledge of Resistance was formed at a religious retreat weeks after the U.S. invasion of Grenada in the fall of 1983. By the spring of 1987, it had the support of more than ninety thousand individuals and organizations.[56] "People from all walks of life have signed the Pledge of Resistance, people who normally wouldn't have come together," said Rose Anne Braniff, Ohio coordinator for the group, in April 1985. Even without a large-scale U.S. invasion of Nicaragua or El Salvador, Pledge of Resistance sponsored hundreds of protests across the country. In one dramatic day of civil disobedience in June 1985, around nine hundred arrests occurred in twelve cities in protests against Contra aid.[57]

Soon to Be a Major Motion Picture

Popular culture reflected the widespread dissatisfaction with Reagan's Central America policies. While an array of movies, books, and songs brimmed with protest themes, it was hard to find any pop culture specimens that contained even a hint of a positive take on the White House's position.[58] A rare exception was *Last Plane Out*, a low-budget action movie released in 1983, set against the backdrop of the Nicaraguan revolution, directed by David Nelson, son of Ozzie and Harriett (and famous for playing himself on TV in the 1950s). *Last Plane Out* told the story of real-life journalist Jack Cox (Jan-Michael Vincent), who befriended dictator Anastasio Somoza (played sympathetically by actor Lloyd Battista) while covering the tumultuous events in Nicaragua in the late 1970s.[59] In the movie version, Cox falls in love with the beautiful, aristocratic Nicaraguan, Maria Cardena (Julie Carmen), who turns out to be an undercover Sandinista agent. When the Sandinistas take over, Cox and two members of an American television crew hide before the totalitarian Marxists in green fatigues can execute them as CIA spies. The Americans befriend a likable young taxi driver and his kid brother, who deliver them to the last plane out of Managua, enabling them to escape the ravages of revolution.[60]

Released by New World Pictures, *Last Plane Out* crashed at the box office. It lacked adequate distribution pull, opening in only a dozen theaters in Miami in September 1983, and twice that many across the state of Florida, where the local press panned it.[61] Aside from scattered drive-in showings outside Florida, mainly in Texas, *Last Plane Out* seemed destined for a straight-to-video release, airing sporadically on cable movie channels before sliding into obscurity. The movie remains significant, however, for being the only meaningful attempt in the Reagan era to present a critical view of the Sandinista revolution and a sympathetic portrayal of Somoza.[62] In addition to *Last Plane Out*, Nicaraguan characters turned up in bit parts and cameos in various right-wing Cold War revenge fantasy movies, such as *Red Dawn* (1984) and *Invasion U.S.A.* (1985), a paranoid Chuck Norris action vehicle about a polyglot invasion of Florida involving nearly every ne'er-do-well (in the minds of the filmmakers) imaginable: Arabs, Cubans, Nicaraguans, and Vietnamese.[63]

Most films about Latin America from the 1980s bluntly critiqued U.S. foreign policy. Setting the tone was the 1982 drama *Missing*, directed by the leftist Greek filmmaker Constantin Costa-Gavras, the man responsible for such influential political thrillers as *Z* (1969) and *State of Siege* (1972). *Missing* takes place in Chile after the 1973 coup that brought General Augusto Pinochet to power and toppled the popularly elected government of socialist Salvador Allende. It tells the true story of Ed Horman (Jack Lemmon), who travels to Santiago to search for his missing son, left-wing political journalist Charlie Horman (played in flashbacks by John Shea). Ed is helped by his daughter-in-law, Beth Horman (Sissy Spacek) in his efforts to locate Charlie. Early in the film, Beth's left-wing politics clash with Ed's deeply held Cold War assumptions and faith in the U.S. government. "I know, I know. God bless our way of life," Beth protests during an argument. "Oh, a very good way of life it is, young lady, no matter how much people like you and Charles try to tear it down with your sloppy idealism," Ed snaps back. During his search, Ed works with U.S. officials, but they repeatedly deceive him about the fate of his son. In one particularly agonizing scene, Ed is allowed to enter a stadium in Santiago where thousands of political prisoners are being held, many of whom will be executed. Ed is escorted out into the middle of the stadium field and allowed to use a public address loudspeaker to call out to Charlie, who is nowhere to be found. A tour of a morgue filled with the dead bodies of political dissidents is equally painful for Ed, who cannot believe his government is supporting this mass violence.

The distraught father eventually learns that his son was murdered by the Chilean military, backed by the CIA. Before leaving Chile, Ed has a tense exchange with the two U.S. officials who failed to help him in his heartbreaking quest to locate his son. "Listen, Mr. Horman, I wish there was something we could say or do," one of the officials tells Ed. "Well, there's something I'm going to do," Ed replies. "I'm going to sue you, Phil. And Tower and the ambassador and everybody who let that boy die. We're going to make it so hot for you you'll wish you were stationed in the Antarctic." The official replies: "Well, I guess that's your privilege." "No," snaps Ed. "That's my right! I just thank God we live in a country where we can still put people like you in jail." Then a voiceover at the end of the film informs viewers of the outcome of the tragedy: "Ed Horman filed suit charging eleven government officials, including Henry A. Kissinger, with complicity and negligence in the death of his son. The body was not returned home until seven months later, making an accurate autopsy impossible. After years of litigation, the information necessary to prove or disprove complicity remained classified as secrets of state. The suit was dismissed."[64]

Missing opened in theaters in February 1982 at a time when real-life Washington officials—like the ones in the movie—were wading deeper into entanglements in faraway countries, this time further north, in Central America. The film's timing was not accidental. Director Costa-Gavras deliberately avoided identifying the film's setting as Chile in the screenplay so as to "give some kind of universality to the story. People are disappearing all over the world. This is why I did the film. People disappearing for political reasons is one of the major problems of our time."[65] *Missing* was a critical success, garnering multiple Academy Award nominations (including for best picture) and winning an Oscar for best adapted screenplay. It performed respectably at the box office, especially for an overtly political film lacking summer blockbuster aspirations. The success of *Missing*, in fact, led to what the *New York Times* called "a highly unusual move": it prompted State Department officials to issue a three-page critique of the film, a rarity in the history of cinema. "The Department of State undertook intensive and comprehensive efforts to locate Charles Horman from the moment it was learned he was missing, to assist his relatives in their efforts to locate him and also to learn the circumstances of his disappearance and death," the statement said.[66]

In addition to upsetting State Department officials, *Missing* helped establish a cinematic trope recycled in other films critiquing the Cold War: that of the naive American who, on becoming aware of destructive policies of his government, resolves to resist the harm caused by Washington: in Ed Horman's case, by suing his government to protest the murder of his son by the Chilean military. By utilizing this narrative structure, Costa-Gavras hoped that an American audience—moved by Horman's tragedy—would come to empathize with him and, by extension, turn against their government's policies. Conspicuously absent in *Missing*, however, were actual Chileans. Nearly all the film's characters are Americans, which a few observers noted in 1982. "Why," wrote critic Andrew Sarris, "should the death of any one American weigh so much more heavily on the human scales than the deaths of so many Chileans?"[67]

Two other notable Reagan-era movies that recycled *Missing*'s trope of the apolitical American naïf who's transformed into a firebrand critic of foreign policy were Roger Spottiswoode's *Under Fire* (1983), starring Nick Nolte, Gene Hackman, and Joanna Cassidy, and Oliver Stone's *Salvador* (1986), with James Woods and Jim Belushi. Both films were shot in southern Mexico but set in Central America—*Under Fire* in Nicaragua during the 1979 Sandinista revolution, *Salvador* in El Salvador against the backdrop of the horrific violence of 1980. *Under Fire* dramatized the chaotic final days of Somoza's regime, whereas *Salvador* focused on the assassination of Archbishop Romero, the rapes and murders of the four American Catholic church workers, death squad terror, and civil war violence. Both films featured main characters who are American press photographers: Nolte stars as fictional Russell Price in *Under Fire*, and James Woods plays real-life pot-smoking, pill-popping gonzo journalist Richard Boyle in *Salvador*. At the start of both films, Price and Boyle are detached and politically neutral. They both have hopes of snapping photos of Central American war zones that will win them fame and a steady paycheck. "If I get some good combat shots for [the Associated Press], I can make some money," Boyle tells his sidekick, unemployed disc jockey Doctor Rock (Belushi), during their long, dope-filled drive from San Francisco to El Salvador in a beat-up Mustang.[68]

In *Under Fire*, Nolte's photojournalist character Price is torn between his commitment to remain a dispassionate chronicler of events and his deepening sympathy for the Sandinista cause. Sandinista rebels persuade him to snap a photo of their recently deceased leader, the mysterious "Rafael," staged to look like he is still alive. By doing this, the Sandinistas reason, ordinary Nicaraguans will be more likely to rally behind the revolution, which is already overtaking towns and villages, and Washington will abandon Somoza. Price takes the photo, compromising his journalistic integrity by throwing his support behind the revolution. Complicating matters, he is also caught in a love triangle with fellow journalist Claire (Joanna Cassidy), romantic partner of his onetime editor Alex Grazier (Gene Hackman). In a scene that re-creates the real-life execution-style murder of ABC News reporter Bill Stewart in June 1979, a Somoza National Guardsman forces Alex to lie facedown on a street outside of Managua and shoots him. Price snaps a picture of the execution as it happens (in the case of Stewart, an ABC cameraman caught the incident on film). Between Price's staged photo of Rafael and his gruesome picture of Alex being executed by the National Guard, the photojournalist helps the Sandinista revolution, which triumphs at the conclusion of the film.[69]

But *Salvador*—after taking its audience through one horror after another, all based on actual events—ends on a darker note. Richard Boyle (Woods) fails in his efforts to rescue his Salvadoran lover, Maria (Elpidia Carrillo), and her children from the war-ravaged nation. After their bus enters California, immigration officials pull Maria and her children off of the vehicle to send them back to their homeland, and a hysterical Boyle is arrested for resisting their efforts to do so. Despite outward similarities, *Under Fire* and *Salvador* look strikingly different from each other. *Under Fire* is more lavish, bankrolled by a major studio (MGM), giving it slick production values. *Salvador* is rougher around the edges, due to its threadbare $4 million budget, which came from English and Mexican investors and the small British production company Hemdale.[70] Neither *Under Fire* nor *Salvador* broke box office records, yet they were not commercial fiascos. The success of Stone's follow-up hit, *Platoon*, in fact, led to a short-lived theatrical revival for *Salvador* in early 1987, a year after its initial release. *Salvador* earned two Oscar nominations, one for James Woods's manic performance, the other for the screenplay by Boyle and Stone. "I am thrilled . . . that *Salvador* has been rescued from obscurity," Stone said, on learning about the nominations in February 1987.[71]

A spate of lesser-known films about Central America drew modest-sized audiences to art house theaters and activist fundraisers. In 1985, Oscar-winning cinematographer Haskell Wexler sat in the director's chair to make *Latino*, a film about a Hispanic Vietnam veteran, Eddie Guerrero (Robert Beltran), who is sent to Central America as part of a covert U.S. government operation to advise and assist the Contras.[72] He falls in love with Nicaraguan Marlena (Annette Cardona), whose father is murdered by the Contras. The killing deepens Guerrero's disillusionment with the "freedom fighters," which was under way when he set foot on Honduran soil and saw their violent tactics. Unlike other films about Central America, *Latino* was filmed in Honduras and Nicaragua, enhancing its authenticity. Much of its minuscule budget came from Wexler's friend, George Lucas, whose production company, Lucasfilm, released the movie. Wexler put $1 million of his own money into the film and borrowed funds from his widowed mother, whose husband—Wexler's father—had been a wealthy manufacturer of radio parts in Chicago.[73] Unfortunately for Wexler, *Latino* had only a fleeting run in major U.S. cities in the fall of 1985 and failed to recoup its meager costs.[74]

An even bigger bomb than *Latino* was Alex Cox's notorious historical epic *Walker* (1987), about nineteenth-century American mercenary William Walker (Ed Harris), who briefly seized control of Nicaragua to become its ruler in the 1850s, before his abrupt downfall and execution. Cox, an iconoclastic whose credits included the cult sci-fi sleeper *Repo Man* (1984) and the Sid Vicious biopic *Sid and Nancy* (1986), opted to inject heavy doses of black humor into *Walker*, turning it into a middle finger at imperialism. The title character goes to Nicaragua—where the movie, like *Latino*, was actually filmed—with an army of sixty mercenaries, backed by financier Cornelius Vanderbilt (Peter Boyle), to help establish a profitable pre–Panama Canal overland shipping route across the impoverished land. But Cox, a British director with punk sensibilities, packed the movie full of deliberate historical anachronisms, such as characters reading recent issues of *Time* and *Newsweek*, using Zippo lighters, owning personal computers, and a being rescued by a modern American helicopter. The decision to insert such heavy-handed anachronisms was agreed on by Cox, screenwriter Rudy Wurlitzer, and producer Lorenzo O'Brien. "We thought they were important," explained Cox years later, "because we were making a film about a contemporary political and moral problem, not a museum piece."[75] The result was a chaotic mess, so relentlessly offbeat that not even Ed Harris's earnest performance could help it. Critics savaged *Walker*, and the public steered clear of it. A movie that cost $6 million to make earned a quarter of a million dollars at the box office—a disaster by anyone's calculations. *Walker* effectively killed Cox's career in Hollywood, which led to his bitter assertion thirty years later that the major studios had "blacklisted" him for directing it.[76]

The cautionary tale that was *Walker* did not deter Australian director John Duigan from helming *Romero*, a sympathetic biopic of Archbishop Óscar Romero released in 1989. The film's coproducer, Rev. Ellwood Kieser, a pacifist with a passion for the project, raised a third of the film's $3.5 million budget from the Catholic Church and released it through Paulist Pictures, a Catholic production company.[77] Visiting El Salvador in 1983 with screenwriter John Sacret Young, Kieser witnessed death squad violence and the exhumation of a mass grave, which inspired him to tell Romero's story on film. He hired Duigan, a rising star in the Australian film industry, director of an acclaimed 1987 coming-of-age-drama, *The Year My Voice Broke*, to direct *Romero*. Puerto Rican actor Raul Julia—who took a major pay cut to be in the film—played Romero. His dignified and understated performance earned wide praise.[78]

Romero's grim subject matter did not appeal to the movie-going masses, and while higher grossing than *Latino* and *Walker*, it had a limited run in theaters and failed to generate a profit. However, *Romero*'s significance, like that of other political movies about Latin America made in the 1980s, transcends box office performance. Whether these films were profitable (such as *Missing*), broke even or lost a little money (e.g., *Under Fire* or *Salvador*), or flopped, their relative popularity or lack thereof is not the only yardstick by which their importance may be measured. Making even a low-budget movie was a major undertaking that involved many people, ample financing, and a great deal of labor. The mere existence of so many leftist Latin America–themed movies in the 1980s, most set in Central America, as well as an absence of contrasting pro-government films to counter them, speaks volumes about the state of Cold War culture in the Reagan years. With the exception of *Last*

Plane Out, filmmakers on the right showed no interest in contesting films from the left about Central America's Cold War battlegrounds. Moreover, the men and women involved in making these politically charged movies regarded their efforts as acts of resistance. "*Romero* was really a labor of love," Raul Julia explained in 1989.[79] Julia could have been describing most of the politically left-leaning movies about Latin America made in the Reagan era, even the caustic *Walker*.

Arguably, Hollywood's most scathing critique of Reagan's Central America policies appeared not in movie theaters but on television. Michael Mann's trendsetting *Miami Vice*—thriving in a Friday prime-time night slot—had become a network juggernaut during its first two seasons on NBC. The phenomenal show, a pop culture offspring of Music Television (MTV) and Brian De Palma's 1983 gangster epic *Scarface*, wielded massive influence in the mid-1980s, shaping the nation's fashion and music tastes, not to mention spawning rip-offs on movie and TV screens alike. Its two main characters, Miami police detectives James "Sonny" Crockett (Don Johnson) and Ricardo "Rico" Tubbs (Philip Michael Thomas), were household names by 1985, and the show's pastel color scheme and edgy rock music soundtrack left an indelible imprint on the period's styles.[80]

Utilizing an exotic Florida setting, *Miami Vice* often featured story lines with Latino characters, and a few episodes were set—partially or fully—in Latin American countries. For example, in the sixteenth episode of the first season, "Smuggler's Blues" (airdate February 1, 1985), a pilot played by Glenn Frey (of the Eagles) flies Sonny and Rico to Cartagena, Colombia, where they participate in an undercover drug deal.[81] Midway through the following season, Don Johnson directed an episode titled "Back in the World" (airdate December 6, 1985), about gonzo journalist and Vietnam vet Ira Stone (Bob Balaban), who discovers that renegade U.S. Army colonel William Maynard (played by famed Watergate "plumber," ex-FBI agent, and Nixon associate G. Gordon Liddy) is shipping heroin into the United States from Southeast Asia.[82]

The characters Stone and Maynard were so memorable that the show's writers brought them back in the second episode of the third season, "Stone's War" (airdate October 3, 1986). In the hands of writer/director David Jackson, "Stone's War" emerged as the most daring, politically charged episode in *Miami Vice*'s five-season run, as well as television's most pointed criticism of U.S. foreign policy in the 1980s. The episode opens in a remote Nicaraguan village, seamlessly lifting scenes of Contra warfare from Haskell Wexler's *Latino*. Journalist Ira Stone and a cameraman traveling with him are in a village that comes under attack by the Contras. The cameraman films U.S. military personnel fighting alongside the rebels, blowing up buildings and killing civilians, including an American priest volunteering in a relief mission. After the cameraman is shot, Stone manages to smuggle the videotaped footage out of the country. He heads to Miami, where he connects with his old friend and fellow Vietnam veteran, Sonny Crockett.

The flashy vice cop is initially skeptical of Stone's conspiratorial tales. But when the shadowy figures chase down Sonny and Stone in Sonny's new Ferrari Testarossa, the hard-bitten vice detective starts to believe his fast-talking journalist friend.[83] Covert agents, headed by Col. Maynard (Liddy), doggedly pursue Stone, even murdering a television journalist to get back the video footage shot by his cameraman. Maynard and his henchmen abduct Stone, which leads to a violent shootout between the kidnappers and Crockett and Tubbs at an airfield near the Everglades. Stone and two of Maynard's goons are killed in the confrontation, but Maynard—having successfully destroyed Stone's video footage—escapes in an airplane with a fresh battalion of Americans bound for Nicaragua. Later, Crockett sits on the deck of his boat docked in a marina, mourning the loss of his friend Ira. A radio news bulletin announces that State Department sources confirmed the Sandinistas executed an American priest in Nicaragua, despite attempts by the Contras to save his life. A visibly disgusted Crockett bows his head in shame.[84]

The End of the Tunnel?

In addition to its bold criticism of the Contra war, the timing of "Stone's War" made it particularly prescient. On Sunday, October 5, 1986, two days after the episode aired, the Sandinistas shot down a Fairchild C-123K military transport aircraft flying supplies to the Contras. Eugene Hasenfus, a Vietnam veteran, former Marine, and contractor for the CIA, parachuted to safety but was captured by the Sandinistas. A Nicaraguan court sentenced Hasenfus to thirty years in prison, but the country's president, Daniel Ortega, ordered his release days before Christmas to the custody of Senator Christopher Dodd, a Democrat from Connecticut. "Since [the Sandinistas] captured me, every day these people could be doing whatever they want to me, I believe with justification. And they have treated me well," Hasenfus told the CBS news program 60 Minutes.[85] Then, in early November, less than a month after the shooting down of the C-123K, Al Shiraa, an obscure Lebanese newspaper, broke the story about the United States selling weapons to Iran. Four weeks later, on November 25, Attorney General Edwin Meese confirmed that the U.S. government had sold weapons to Iran and resupplied the Contras with the profits from those sales, to get around the Boland Amendment.[86]

Fueled by Iran-Contra revelations, the nationwide debate over Contra aid reached a fever pitch in the spring of 1987, when the counterrevolutionaries murdered Benjamin Linder, a twenty-seven-year-old American engineer volunteering on a hydroelectric project in rural Nicaragua. The combination of a grenade attack and being shot in the head at close range killed Linder instantly. He died on April 28 in a remote forest, along with two Nicaraguan volunteers, Sergio Hernández and Pablo Rosales, in the Contra ambush.[87] Predictably, Linder was instantly turned into a martyr by the Left and a naive dupe of communism (or, worse, a villain in a few cases) by the Right. "He did not arrive in a flight full of weapons, or with millions of dollars. He arrived in a flight full of dreams, which were born in his belief that the ethical values of the American people were much greater than the illegal policy of the United States government," eulogized Nicaraguan president Daniel Ortega at Linder's funeral.[88] Not so, balked former New Left radicals–turned–far right pundits David Horowitz and Peter Collier. "Linder was not a dewy-eyed noncombatant. . . . His cause was not that of the Nicaraguan people but of Ortega and the other commandantes," they wrote.[89]

The Central American peace movement experienced a second shock four months after the Linder killing, when, on September 1, a train carrying weapons to the Contras left the Concord Naval Weapons Station in Concord, California, and struck Vietnam veteran and activist Brian Willson, who was blocking the railroad tracks with other activists in an act of civil disobedience. The diesel engine hit and dragged Willson for thirty feet while his fellow protesters watched in horror, resulting in multiple injuries and severing his legs below the knees. A subsequent Navy investigation found the train crew had been advised there would be activists blocking the tracks, but they refused to stop.[90] A few days after the grisly incident, around ten thousand people showed up to protest Contra aid and show support for Willson. After being fitted with artificial limbs, Willson—who had no memory of being hit by the train—returned to protesting Contra aid. "The life of a Nicaraguan or an El Salavadoran or an Angolan is worth no less than my life and we kill them every day with our policies," he reasoned.[91]

But by the time of the Linder killing and the Willson incident, the Contras' days were numbered. Mired down in the Iran-Contra scandal, Reagan was effectively disempowered during his final eighteen months in the White

House. Even pro-Contra Republicans, like Iowa congressman Fred Grandy—former star of TV's *The Love Boat* and a staunch backer of the rebels—conceded that public support had bottomed out by February 1988, when he voted in favor of Reagan's request to send $36.2 million in aid to the Contras. "If you read the polls you vote the other way. I think even a majority of Republicans are opposed to Contra aid," Grandy said prior to the vote.[92]

Sure enough, Contra aid was defeated in the House of Representatives on February 4, 1988. With the Nicaraguan government participating in regional peace talks, allowing antigovernment demonstrations, and lifting restrictions on the opposition press, along with the American public's support for financing the "freedom fighters" in a state of free fall in the polls, Washington's war against Nicaragua was grinding to a halt.[93] The combination of a well-organized and unceasing grassroots protest movement, coinciding with a groundswell of cultural resistance that was especially potent in cinema, formed an effective counterweight to the narrative preferred by President Reagan and his backers in Congress that the United States government stood steadfastly behind the forces of democracy and freedom in Central America.

CHAPTER 7

The End of the Line

The Cold War now belongs to the age of political dinosaurs, when the Earth was dominated by two overgrown empires each claiming to stand for rival principles of economics and politics, as easily distinguished from each other as black from white. The choice between them—even the abstract choice between socialism and capitalism—no longer interests the rest of the world.

—*Christopher Lasch*, St. Louis Post-Dispatch, *July 16, 1990*

Tearing Down the Walls

When President Reagan delivered his memorable "Mr. Gorbachev, tear down this wall" speech at the Brandenburg Gate in Berlin on June 12, 1987, neither he nor anyone who heard his speech that day among the forty thousand invited guests cheering him on in person, or the millions listening from afar, knew the Cold War was hobbling through its final lap. The speech, one of the defining moments in Reagan's presidency, came during the twilight of the long ideological contest between the superpowers. Ever since the historic Geneva Summit in November 1985, at which Reagan sat down for the first time with Soviet general secretary Mikhail Gorbachev to discuss relations between the United States and the Soviet Union, the Cold War had been waning in intensity. Two days of meetings at Geneva produced nothing of substance in the way of arms control agreements, but Reagan and Gorbachev established a rapport that would carry them through subsequent summits.[1] "The personal chemistry was apparent. The easy and relaxed attitude toward each other, the smiles, the sense of purpose, all showed through," observed Secretary of State George Shultz.[2]

Gorbachev and Reagan raised the stakes further at the Reykjavík Summit in October 1986. Still mired down in the aftermath of Chernobyl, the worst nuclear disaster in human history, Gorbachev brought dramatic arms reduction proposals to the table. He stunned the world on the summit's third day by calling for the elimination of all nuclear weapons within a decade. Reagan and Shultz liked what they heard. "Let's do it," Shultz replied. A giddy Reagan told Gorbachev, "I can imagine both of us in ten years getting together again in Iceland to destroy the last Soviet and American missiles under triumphant circumstances. By then, I'll be so old that you won't even recognize me. And you will ask in surprise, 'Hey, Ron, is that really you? What are you doing here?' And we'll have a big celebration over it."[3] Although Reagan and Gorbachev both voiced a desire to abolish all nuclear weapons during their talks, the two men left Iceland without reaching any concrete arms control agreements, leading to the perception at the time that the meetings ended in failure. Sticking points impeded progress, especially Reagan's insistence on maintaining his Strategic Defense Initiative (SDI), despite Gorbachev's objections. Nonetheless, the vision of a world without nuclear weapons articulated by both leaders was nothing less than revolutionary. "Despite the perception by some that the Reykjavik summit was a failure, I think history will show it was a major turning point in the quest for a safe and secure world," Reagan wrote in his autobiography.[4]

The summit further highlighted conflicts in Reagan's mind between his longtime militant anticommunism and his deepening concerns about the threat of nuclear war. Reagan's shift during the summits from Cold Warrior to champion of détente had actually been years in the making. Nobody doubted his anticommunist credentials, but few knew the extent to which he had been grappling—especially recently—with his deeply held concerns about the looming prospect of World War III. Reagan's transformation was on display for the world to see at the yearly U.S.-Soviet summits.

Reagan's newfound cooperation with Gorbachev infuriated hard-liners on the American right. Future house speaker Newt Gingrich warned during the Geneva Summit that the talks might very well be "the most dangerous summit for the West since Adolf Hitler met with in 1938 at Munich."[5] The following year, conservative pundit George Will, alarmed by developments at Reykjavik, warned *Newsweek* readers: "The Reagan administration is losing credibility by taking actions radically inconsistent with its past rhetoric."[6] Will's fears of creeping détente proved well founded. Talks in Reykjavík paved the way for the most dramatic nuclear arms reduction treaty in modern history, the INF (Intermediate-Range Nuclear Forces) Treaty of 1987. The INF Treaty banned the United States and the Soviet Union from developing or deploying any ground-launched missiles with an intermediate range of between 500 and 5,500 kilometers, or 300 to 3,400 miles. Although the treaty did not address missiles launched from air and sea, it amounted to a dramatic breakthrough in nuclear disarmament negotiations.

Even before Reagan and Gorbachev met in Washington, D.C., on December 8, 1987, to sign the landmark treaty, conservative Cold Warriors went on the warpath. Former president Richard Nixon and ex-secretary of state Henry Kissinger cowrote an article in *National Review* detailing the agreement's weaknesses. Howard Phillips, founder of the Conservative Caucus, a far-right public policy advocacy organization, called Reagan a "useful idiot for Soviet propaganda."[7] Echoing Phillips, right-wing activist Richard Viguerie insisted Reagan was an "apologist for Gorbachev" and had "changed sides and he is now allied with his former adversaries, the liberals, the Democrats and the Soviets."[8] To resist the president's revised outlook, Phillips and Viguerie founded the Anti-Appeasement Alliance, which sought to block the treaty's ratification. The Munich analogy frequently came up to describe Reagan's actions. Congressman Jack Kemp called the INF Treaty a "nuclear Munich," and evangelist Pat Robertson, preparing to enter the 1988 presidential race, insisted that Reagan "sounded like Neville Chamberlain." "Reagan's Suicide Pact," cried a cover of William F. Buckley's conservative *National Review* magazine in May 1987. "The search for a conservative successor to Ronald Reagan has now begun in earnest," lamented *National Review*.[9]

These comments irked Reagan, whose worldview was undergoing striking transformations during the summits. He justifiably felt like he was moving forward and adapting to changing times, while his erstwhile comrades on the right were calcified in a permanent state of bellicosity. However, it encouraged Reagan that opinion polls taken in late 1987 and early 1988 revealed overwhelming public approval for his support of the INF Treaty.[10] In early December 1987, he responded to his right-wing critics by lashing out in a television interview: "Now, I think that some of the people who are objecting the most and just refusing to even accede to the idea of ever getting an understanding, whether they realize it or not, those people, basically, down in their deepest thoughts, have accepted that war is inevitable and that there must come to be a war between the two superpowers."[11]

Reagan further fanned the flames on the right during his visit Moscow in 1988, when he gave the Soviet Union a clean bill of health, telling an interviewer the country was no longer the "Evil Empire." "No, I was talking about another time, another era," Reagan confirmed.[12] Reagan spelled out his newfound perspective in the weeks following the signing of the INF Treaty. "Possibly the fundamental change is that in the past, Soviet leaders have openly expressed their acceptance of the Marxist theory of the one-world communist state; that their obligation was to expand in the whole world. They no longer feel that way," he said.[13]

Thus, when Reagan stood at the Brandenburg Gate in June 1987, imploring Gorbachev to "tear down this wall," his retreat from Cold War ideologue was already under way. On the home front, his reversal helped defuse Cold War cultural friction, which had reached high tide by mid-decade. Opposition to Cold War policies on multiple fronts—grassroots and cultural alike— remained formidable throughout the 1980s. But something had undeniably changed during Reagan's second term as president, perhaps owing as much or more to Gorbachev than to Reagan. Two Russian words entered the American vocabulary in 1987, thanks to Gorbachev: *glasnost* ("openness") and *perestroika* ("restructuring"), the former used to describe a shift in political culture toward greater accountability, the latter applied to market-oriented economic reforms intended to offset stagnation. "Today our main job is to lift the individual spiritually, respecting his inner world and giving him moral strength," Gorbachev wrote in his best-selling 1987 book *Perestroika*. The optimal means to achieve such uplift, Gorbachev argued, was through "broad democratization of all aspects of society."[14]

"Washington was seized by Gorbachev-mania," wrote veteran journalist Wilbur Landrey in December 1987, during Gorbachev's visit to the nation's capital.[15] "Gorby fever" swept through the rest of the country as well. The Soviet leader appeared on the cover of news magazines, and his face—mostly smiling, less dour than past communist apparatchiks—graced newspaper front pages throughout the land. Fans could buy Gorbachev coffee mugs, Gorbachev T-shirts and sweatshirts, and Gorbachev Halloween masks.[16] Meantime, Gorbachev's wife, Raisa, fell under the watchful eye of American fashionistas, who critiqued her style of dress. "For a Russian lady, . . . she looked smashing!" said Claire Dratch, wedding dress designer for the wealthy and famous. Famed fashion designer Oscar de la Renta exercised greater restraint when asked his opinion of Raisa's wardrobe by *Women's Wear Daily* magazine: "She's not chic at all, but she's better than anything else that has come out of Russia recently."[17] Meantime, public opinion polls found Gorbachev elevated by a wave of support, with 71 percent of American respondents in an October 1987 survey agreeing he "is different from other Soviet leaders." Gorbachev's popularity in the United States, in turn, helped boost Reagan's sagging poll numbers. During the Washington Summit in December 1987, Reagan's approval ratings rose above 60 percent for the first time since the Iran-Contra scandal. By May 1988, nearly as many Americans had a favorable view of Gorbachev as they did Reagan, according to a Media General-Associated Press poll.[18]

The Decline of Dissent

The resurrection of détente and Gorbachev's runaway popularity influenced the course of domestic dissent. Of all the protest campaigns associated with the Cold War, the antinuclear movement, not surprisingly, was the most heavily impacted by these developments. The movement had been in a state of decline even before the Reagan-Gorbachev summits. Most startling of all was the unraveling of the nuclear freeze campaign, after a remarkable period of growth in the early 1980s. Once upon a time, the mighty grassroots movement seemed unstoppable. "The rise of the nuclear freeze movement displays a fundamental strength of representative democracy at its best—the power of individual citizens to influence their government, and even to change the course of history," noted Senator Ted Kennedy.[19]

But the movement's heyday was cut short in March 1983, with Reagan's announcement of the Strategic Defense Initiative—or "Star Wars," as it came to be known. Even with its colossal $1 trillion price tag and large segments of the scientific community questioning its feasibility, Star Wars left nuclear freeze activists scrambling to search for new ways to keep opposition to the arms race relevant. Reagan's rhetoric about a protective "shield in space," which he insisted would make nuclear weapons "obsolete," undermined the momentum of a protest movement focused on reversing the steady buildup of the arms race. Reagan used SDI to allay the public's nuclear anxieties and undercut resistance in the process.[20]

The freeze campaign's setbacks continued with the landslide defeat of Democratic presidential candidate Walter Mondale in November 1984. During the campaign for the White House, Mondale had backed the goals of the nuclear freeze movement and—in doing so—lured some activists away from the streets to work for him.[21] "The freeze is the most important citizen initiative of modern time," Mondale declared at a primary debate in May. But Mondale's defeat, a year and a half after SDI's debut, demoralized even seasoned stalwarts. "After the 1984 election," wrote journalist Cody Shearer three years later, "the movement virtually disappeared; it couldn't straighten out its own decision-making apparatus and subsequent turf battles."[22]

The freeze campaign did not disappear, at least not immediately, but it lost direction and exerted little influence after 1984.[23] Fatigue also claimed one of its most visible champions. In April 1986, Dr. Helen Caldicott—the most famous spokeswoman of the worldwide struggle to abolish nuclear weapons—triggered an avalanche of headlines when she announced she was leaving the peace movement. "I can't go on if I've got nothing more to give," she declared. For years, Caldicott had maintained a Herculean schedule, jetting all over the world in her capacity as a celebrated opponent of the nuclear arms race. Her books and speeches, her radio and television appearances, and her eloquent critiques of the arms race helped elevate her to the stature of Gandhi or Martin Luther King Jr. But she was burned out by April 1986, fed up with the nonstop infighting in the movement, and eager to turn inward to her family and personal life after sixteen years of working tirelessly for disarmament. "I've always had this tremendous sense of responsibility that I've got to save the world," she said. "It's just too much now. I just can't keep going. I'm exhausted both mentally and physically."[24]

Pushing herself beyond the limits of endurance only partially accounted for Caldicott's weariness. Her impassioned one-woman crusade required that she gaze into the abyss on a daily basis and grapple with the stark possibility that all life on the planet might be eliminated and that nuclear winter would engulf earth for thousands of years. Because of these staggering stakes, antinuclear activism inflicted a worse psychological toll than had some other protest movements. The movement often attracted people who were sensitive to begin with, and dedicating oneself passionately to the cause could leave the psyche badly scarred. "No one," wrote psychiatrist Robert Jay Lifton and international law scholar Richard Falk, "psychologically speaking, can live in a world of nuclear weapons all time."[25] Caldicott was no exception. When asked what she planned to do after leaving the movement, her reply contained a mix of resignation and relief: "I'm just going to be in the garden and grow my flowers and swim every day and stop reading the newspapers."[26]

Caldicott was not alone. Antinuclear campaigners left the movement in droves in the mid-1980s. Longtime Los Angeles antinuclear activist Chris Brown partially explained the losses in 1987: "There seems to be an expectation that if you work in the peace movement, somehow you shouldn't get paid for it. That and the long hours lead to a lot of burnout."[27] But there was more to it than no pay and grueling schedules. Sectarian infighting often made for a toxic working environment in local freeze chapters. Anecdotal evidence suggests many people who dropped out of antinuclear work gravitated to other protest campaigns, such as resisting Contra aid, or the newly emerging antiapartheid movement on university campuses.[28]

Meantime, a smaller, more fragmented version of the peace movement endured. Those who maintained their commitment revised agendas and adopted new approaches. Some acts of resistance were more effective than others. The decade's most ambitious antinuclear protest, the Great Peace March, took place over a period of eight and a half months, beginning in March and ending in November of 1986. Organized by antiwar and civil rights veteran David Mixner and his Los Angeles–based group PRO-Peace (PRO stood for People Reaching Out for), the Great Peace March started out strong with around thirteen hundred "hardy idealists," ranging in age from ten months old to seventy-eight, who planned to walk from Los Angeles to Washington, D.C., to protest the nuclear arms race.[29]

Mixner envisioned many more thousands joining the march while it was in progress. He used celebrity endorsements from the likes of Paul Newman, Madonna, Barbra Streisand, Carole King, Demi Moore, Rob Lowe, Richard Dreyfuss, Emilio Estevez, and Ted Danson to publicize the pilgrimage. Yet the march immediately encountered problems. Less than two weeks into it, PRO-Peace, the organization sponsoring the event, declared bankruptcy. David Mixner later referred to the Great Peace March as "my biggest political failure and my biggest regret."[30] The march stalled in the California desert for twelve days. About half the marchers went home; the other half erected an encampment while planners scrambled to maintain the protest's momentum. "We had windstorms, sandstorms, dust in your face and your teeth. We had some snow last night and very cold rains," reported marcher Karen Jeffers.[31]

Organizers managed to salvage the Great Peace March with a last-minute infusion of cash from wealthy sympathizers, and the transcontinental walk resumed at the end of March, its numbers cut in half. For months, hundreds of marchers walked alongside highways, crossing entire states, joined by sympathizers who would journey either part or the rest of the way. "I've got calluses on top of calluses," said former Marine J. J. Corber.[32] A five-day stop in New York City in October offered a much-needed pause filled with teach-ins, rallies, and a benefit concert. On November 15, the marchers—now totaling eighteen hundred, swollen by new additions—arrived at their destination: Washington, D.C.

Despite being canceled by its organizer days after it began, the Great Peace March was one of the most heavily publicized antinuke protests in the second half of the decade. "The March was the biggest event to happen to some of the smaller towns in years," noted one enthusiastic account at the time.[33] Other pockets of antinuclear protest thrived but drew less attention. For years, large-scale civil disobedience occurred on a near-daily basis at the Nevada Test Site, north of Las Vegas, the scene of underground nuclear tests conducted by the Department of Energy. Some of the confrontations between test site security and activists at the front gates of the desert facility could be quite dramatic. On March 12, 1988, for example, a clash led to the arrests of 1,113 men and women, most for trespassing. The group American Peace Test organized most of these protests, calling for an underground nuclear test ban similar to the treaty signed by President John F. Kennedy in 1963 ending atmospheric tests. But the test site protests occurred out of sight of the American public, and although covered by the press, the campaign failed to generate the same nationwide buzz as the nuclear freeze movement.[34]

Diminishing Cold War tensions had a similar impact on the Central America peace movement. On February 25, 1990, the Nicaraguan general election ushered in a new government, led by Violeta Chamorro, head of the National Opposition Union, an anti-Sandinista party. By this time, the Contra war was essentially over, but the destruction it had caused had been extensive and the loss of life staggering. "After tens of thousands of deaths, perhaps $10 billion worth of damage, and a 90 percent decline in the standard of living—with no end in sight—60 percent of Nicaragua gave up and cried uncle," wrote Pulitzer Prize–winning reporter Randolph Ryan, who spent years covering Central America for the *Boston Globe*.[35] Chamorro's victory in Nicaragua, along with the end of the Contra war, eased the pressure on Central American peace groups. More than that, it left thousands of Sandinista sympathizers in the United States feeling discouraged.

A revolution that toppled decades of dynastic dictatorship and brought literacy, medical and dental care, and improved diets to ordinary Nicaraguans, without the totalitarian excesses of Castro's Cuba, had been defeated, at least in the short term, by the very government that kept the Somozas in power for so long. That was a bitter pill to swallow for Central American solidarity activists. Those heady days earlier in the decade, when thousands of Americans visited Nicaragua and returned home with stories about a revolution that appeared to be working, had passed into history. The revolutionary mystique was gone. After the election, the number of American delegations visiting Nicaragua plummeted, and legions of American volunteers working in the country returned to the United States, citing a loss of purpose and feeling less welcome by the new government. "The only thing I can compare it to is the day Kennedy was shot," explained Lynda Sharp, an activist affiliated with the Nicaragua Solidarity Network of Greater New York, months after the election.[36]

In the United States, government repression dealt another blow to the Central America peace movement. In 1988, a Freedom of Information Act request filed by New York's Center for Constitutional Rights resulted in the release of seventeen hundred pages of declassified documents revealing that the Federal Bureau of Investigation had engaged in a long and expensive program of surveillance and harassment of the Committee in Solidarity with the People of El Salvador (CISPES).[37] Between 1981 and 1985, the FBI investigated all 180 CISPES chapters in the United States and expanded its investigation to include probes of nearly two hundred peace groups with ties to the organization. But the FBI did more than merely investigate. The bureau wiretapped phone lines, photographed protesters, recorded license plate numbers, monitored activists' movements, maintained dossiers on around seven hundred people (including a former ambassador, a member of the House of Representatives, and two United States senators), and broke into CISPES offices to steal files.[38] Acting on intelligence provided by a Salvadoran-born informant, Frank Varelli, the FBI instructed its agents to look for evidence showing that CISPES was engaged in domestic "terrorism" by supporting the leftist guerrillas in El Salvador. Varelli worked as an informant, infiltrating the Dallas chapter of CISPES and furnishing regular reports on its activities. The investigation was so rife with abuses that it led to congressional hearings and an internal FBI inquiry in which multiple agents were disciplined. "The mistakes in judgment that took place during the investigation of CISPES were serious ones," FBI director William Sessions told the Senate Intelligence Committee in September 1988.[39]

The FBI's "investigation"—which amounted to a full-scale attempt to neutralize CISPES—was not an aberration.[40] In fact, the federal government's assault on the Left in the 1980s was expansive and far-reaching, carried out by multiple agencies against a long list of groups. Private, nongovernment entities were also involved. The FBI in the 1980s relied extensively on information from private individuals with links to such extremist far-right groups as Young

Americans for Freedom, the John Birch Society, the World Anticommunist League, and the Reverend Sun Myung Moon's CAUSA.[41] "Numerous Central America peace movement groups were penetrated by undercover operatives— typically FBI or INS [Immigration and Naturalization Service] agents and informers—who posed as concerned activists in order to infiltrate Central America organizations and spy from the inside on movement activities," writes sociologist Christian Smith.[42] Internal Revenue Service tax audits, phone tampering, break-ins, confiscations by U.S. Customs Service officers of routine items being brought back from Nicaragua, and visits by inquisitive FBI agents to Americans who traveled to Nicaragua became all-too-regular occurrences in the Reagan era.[43]

The Last Hurrah

Persistent government harassment had a chilling effect, but there is little evidence that it curtailed protest. On the contrary, dissent was made of stronger stuff than that. Of all the grassroots protests in the Cold War's twilight years, resistance against South Africa's apartheid system stirred the passions of youthful campus radicals more than any other issue since the Vietnam War.[44] By 1984, universities—especially those with investments in South Africa—offered fertile ground to antiapartheid groups. Flickering televised images and daily headlines about government crackdowns on Black protesters in South Africa helped inflame youthful passions. Students gravitated to activism and pressured their universities to divest. Rallies, marches, boycotts, teach-ins, film screenings, and benefit concerts were among the nonviolent weapons in the arsenals of activists. The Free South Africa Movement (FSAM), founded in 1984, soon emerged as the largest and most influential antiapartheid coalition in the United States. Political scientist Donald R. Culverson described its burst of activity in the mid-1980s: "The FSAM was not one organization but a broad coalition of anti-apartheid organizations, elected officials, labor unions, and student, civil rights, and church groups that successfully orchestrated a series of publicized arrests outside the South African embassy and at other sites around the country. Over a five-month period, more than 3,000 Americans, including members of Congress, were arrested at these demonstrations."[45]

While the movement's primary focus was apartheid, which provided South Africa's five million whites with a much higher standard of living than its twenty-four million Black people, it also contained opposition to Cold

War policies within its ranks. Southern Africa had become an ideological battleground in the 1980s. President Reagan and his fellow Cold Warriors in Washington regarded the African National Congress (ANC), South Africa's armed insurgency, as a communist threat determined to transform the country into a pro-Soviet stronghold. But apartheid was so unpopular in the United States that its stealthy allies in government trod carefully around the issue. The Reagan administration opposed sanctions and divestment, instead supporting a policy called "constructive engagement," which involved exerting diplomatic pressure on the apartheid regime to adopt reforms. Further complicating matters, since the mid-1970s, the White House and its allies in Congress had been backing the anticommunist National Union for the Total Independence of Angola (UNITA) and its charismatic leader, Jonas Savimbi, in a bloody proxy war against a Marxist regime in Angola. In fact, support for UNITA was one of the cornerstones of the so-called Reagan Doctrine, a White House policy of backing rebel groups in Nicaragua, Angola, Mozambique, and Cambodia. Hence, Reagan was already predisposed to view the conflicts in southern Africa through a Cold War lens.[46]

But efforts to turn the region into a Cold War theater sparked protest, mainly among politicized university students. On a number of campuses, students erected makeshift shanties, crudely built out of lumber, cardboard, and other materials and often painted over with political graffiti. "We believe we have the right to be here, and we won't leave until the university divests. We're prepared to be here for a long, long time," said Yale student Margo Pave. In April 1986, an entire shantytown went up on the lawn adjacent to the state capitol building in Madison, Wisconsin, built by students from the nearby University of Wisconsin. Faculty even joined in on the action at Cornell University in November 1986, when a group of antiapartheid professors built shanties in defiance of a court order banning them on campus.[47]

The shanty controversy revealed the intensity of the Cold War culture wars on America's university campuses when the eyesores led to heated debates about the limits of free speech. Many shanties became targets of destruction, usually at night. At Dartmouth College in Hanover, New Hampshire, a dozen vandals—most of them associated with the right-wing student newspaper, the *Dartmouth Review*—used sledgehammers to demolish the recently built shanties on campus. Elsewhere, shanties suffered at the hands of attackers at the University of Pittsburgh, the University of Missouri at St. Louis, the University of Texas, the University of Washington, the University of California at Berkeley, California State College at Long Beach, and the University of

Utah.[48] At Johns Hopkins, student activist Kevin Archer suffered severe burns as a result of three other students dumping gasoline over a campus shanty and set fire to it, burning it to the ground.[49]

Amid the shanty battles, popular culture yet again nurtured opposition. And once more, cultural expression was lopsided to the left, in favor of apartheid's foes, with its apologists virtually silent in the realm of artistic endeavors. Bookstore shelves filled up with new titles on apartheid, fueled by a heightened awareness of atrocities in South Africa. Furthermore, a golden age of antiapartheid literature blossomed in the 1980s, with such world-renowned South African writers as Nadine Gordimer, J. M. Coetzee, André Brink, Bessie Head, Lewis Nkosi, Alan Paton, and Zakes Mda active during the decade, turning their attention to conditions in their rigidly segregated country.

In 1982, the South Africa–born playwright Athol Fugard wrote what many regarded as his finest play, his semiautobiographical antiapartheid drama *"Master Harold"* . . . *and the Boys*. "Master Harold" opened at Broadway's Lyceum Theatre in May 1982 and ran for 344 performances. The coming-of-age play focused on a teenager boy named Hally (also known as "Master Harold") and his close—yet complex—relationship with two Black waiters, Sam and Willie, who worked in a tea shop owned by Hally's mother. The relationship is thrown into a tailspin with the news that Hally's father, a violent and abusive alcoholic who was absent for a lengthy period after losing his leg in World War II, is returning home. Hally, upset by the news, turns his rage and anguish against Sam and Willie, who had shown him love and kindness all his life. The play got rave reviews and cemented Fugard's fame as a dramatist. Fugard, who lived outside Port Elizabeth, South Africa, and turned fifty in 1982, had been writing plays critical of apartheid for decades, and he paid a price for his dissent. Government security forces monitored Fugard and his wife, Sheila, who was also an antiapartheid writer. They opened and read his mail before giving it to him, tapped his phones, and withdrew his passport privileges at various points. These human rights violations emboldened Fugard to continue writing antiapartheid drama. "I have a responsibility in a time of oppression to bear witness, to tell the truth, the whole truth, so help me God. And I do draw strength from that," Fugard told an interviewer in 1982.[50]

Hollywood purchased the rights to *"Master Harold"* . . . *and the Boys* and turned it into a made-for-TV movie starring Matthew Broderick. It aired first on the cable movie channel Showtime, then on Public Broadcasting

Service stations nationwide, thus exposing Fugard's antiapartheid drama to a wider audience. It was one of the first of many films about apartheid made in the 1980s. Subsequent movies picking up the theme included Richard Attenborough's *Cry Freedom* (1987), an epic about the murder of antiapartheid activist Stephen Biko (played by Denzel Washington); *A World Apart* (1988), a coming-of-age drama centered on the daughter (Jodhi May) of antiapartheid activists Diana Roth (Barbara Hershey) and Gus Roth (Jeroen Krabbé); and *A Dry White Season* (1989), starring Donald Sutherland, Susan Sarandon, and Marlon Brando, directed by Martinique-born director Euzhan Palcy, based on a novel of the same name by André Brink, about a Johannesburg school-teacher Ben Du Toit (Sutherland) who endangers his life as he digs deeper into the murder of his gardener, Gordon Ngubene (Winston Ntshona), and Gordon's son, by government security forces. Brando is only in the film for 12 minutes, but he makes a memorable appearance as weary human rights attorney Ian McKenzie, who helps Du Toit. "Justice and the law are distant cousins," McKenzie tells Du Toit. "But here in South Africa, they're not on speaking terms at all."[51]

But the box office behemoth of antiapartheid movies was *Lethal Weapon 2*, the sequel to the blockbuster 1987 cop-buddy action movie starring Mel Gibson as Los Angeles Police Department detective Martin Riggs and Danny Glover as Detective Roger Murtaugh. The second installment in the franchise pits Riggs and Murtaugh against racist white South African consul diplomats in Los Angeles who hide behind their diplomatic immunity to make massive drug deals. The bludgeoning of apartheid in *Lethal Weapon 2* was impossible to miss.[52] In fact, South African officials lashed out at the action-packed movie as biased. Peter Bryant, vice consul for the Republic of South Africa in New York, complained about what he termed Hollywood's "villainization of South Africa in films." "In the film industry, all of a sudden, Cuba and the Soviet Union are good boys. Now they cast around for another country as the villain, and they've picked us," Bryant lamented.[53] Such criticisms failed to dampen the film's box office draw. *Lethal Weapon 2* was the third-highest-grossing film of 1989.

Like filmmakers, musicians played a pivotal role in the antiapartheid cultural explosion. Protest songs could be heard on the airwaves and filled record store shelves: "Biko" (1980), British singer-songwriter Peter Gabriel's tribute to the martyred South African protester; "Free Nelson Mandela" (1984), by British ska band The Specials; "It's Wrong (Apartheid)" (1985), by Stevie Wonder; and "Sing Our Own Song" (1986), by British pop reggae band

UB40, were but a few of the more pointed antiapartheid songs from the era. The star-studded 1985 album *Sun City*, produced by Steven Van Zandt of the E Street Band, brought over fifty famous talents together to collaborate on an antiapartheid protest album. The impressive collaboration, which included Bruce Springsteen, Bono of U2, Pat Benatar, Pete Townshend, Jimmy Cliff, Keith Richards, Darlene Love, Miles Davis, Kurtis Blow, Nona Hendryx, Lou Reed, Bonnie Raitt, Joey Ramone, David Ruffin, Daryl Hall, John Oates, Bob Dylan, Jackson Browne, and a host of others, sold modestly in the United States, climbing to thirty-one on the Billboard 200 album chart. More significant, its title track, "Sun City," a mix of many vocalists imploring musicians not to play at an infamous segregated South African luxury resort, became an anthem for the antiapartheid movement. Ultimately, "Sun City" was an edgier, more politicized version of such recent supergroup hits as "Do They Know It's Christmas?" (1984) and "We Are the World" (1985). The album and the song also helped reinforce a boycott of Sun City, resulting in fewer bands and singers performing there in the late 1980s.[54]

Not all performers adhered to the cultural boycott of South Africa. Singer-songwriter Paul Simon touched off a furor in antiapartheid circles when he traveled to South Africa in February 1985 to record portions of his album *Graceland*. Simon journeyed to Johannesburg to record at Ovation Studios with a group of Black South African musicians. Despite his best efforts to keep the trip a secret, Simon's two-week stay in South Africa ignited a heated backlash. The African National Congress banned Simon from the country, a symbolic act given that the ANC did not actually have the power to keep him out of South Africa. The United Nations added him to a "blacklist" reserved for musicians who refused to adhere to the cultural boycott of the apartheid state, although what exactly Simon was blacklisted from remained a mystery. Musicians affiliated with Artists United Against Apartheid, as well as British antiapartheid musicians Paul Weller and Billy Bragg, scolded Simon for his decision to travel to South Africa, even though he declined an invitation to play at Sun City.[55] Solly Simelane, an ANC representative to the United Nations, explained the organization's rebuke of Simon: "The UN calls for comprehensive sanctions. . . . Just spending money on a hotel and food is incorrect, because they need foreign currency to survive."[56]

The release of *Graceland*, Simon's seventh solo studio album, on August 25, 1986, abruptly muted much of the outcry. The album won instant acclaim and soared to the top spot on album sales charts. Critics hailed it as a milestone in world music and an innovative composite of styles, blending African genres (particularly those rooted in Zulu traditions), zydeco, rock, a cappella and Tex-Mex. *Graceland* went on to win a Grammy for album of the year in 1987, and for decades after its release, it enjoyed a vaunted status as a game changer and one of the greatest albums in rock history. It did far more to promote awareness of Black South African music than did any other album. Yet criticisms of Simon's decision to record in Johannesburg persisted beyond *Graceland*'s astonishing success. Simon endured accusations of exploiting South African musicians, and antiapartheid purists railed against him for singing a duet on the album with Linda Ronstadt, who performed in Sun City in 1983.[57] Allegations of cultural appropriation dogged Simon for years, with some on the far left regarding him as a colonialist oppressor extracting labor from South African musicians rather than collaborating with them.[58] Simon bristled at these attacks. "This was just musician to musician," he told an interviewer when the album was released. "I'm sharing my royalties, and I paid the people I worked with. . . . My feeling is that these guys are really talented musicians—why should they be penalized twice? They have to live there, and you're not allowed to make music with them. Why?"[59]

The Paul Simon imbroglio aside, the antiapartheid movement stood as a textbook example of an effective protest movement that accomplished most of its goals. Economic statistics confirmed its potency: by late 1986, more than a hundred educational institutions had divested close to $500 million dollars from companies doing business in South Africa or reaping profits from apartheid. Divestment policies by this time had been adopted by twenty-one states and sixty-eight cities. Likewise, corporations began to retreat from the apartheid state. United States investments in South Africa plummeted from nearly $2.8 billion in 1983 to $1.3 billion in 1985. Of the 350 American corporations operating in South Africa in 1984, eighty had left the country by 1987, among them such giants as Exxon, GM, Coca-Cola, IBM, Xerox, and Honeywell.[60]

The antiapartheid movement represented the last hurrah of anti–Cold War culture wars. And with the exception of the shanty controversy, it was not much of a culture war. Nor was it as burdened by the Cold War baggage of the antinuclear and Central America peace movements. With the Reagan administration weakened by the Iran-Contra scandal, zealous defenders of "constructive engagement"—often the same people who regarded the region as a Cold War battleground—were a near-extinct species by the late 1980s. A handful of conservatives wrote op-ed pieces criticizing perceived excesses of the antiapartheid movement and pop culture portrayals of apartheid, while ignoring human rights abuses under the Pretoria regime. But the impact of such punditry on public opinion was negligible at best.[61] Lacking a compelling counternarrative to the antiapartheid movement's forceful moral critique, the apologists found themselves at a distinct disadvantage in the court of public opinion.[62]

More than any other protest campaign of the 1980s, opposition to apartheid fell victim to its own success. With so many universities divested from South Africa or in the process of divesting, resistance had dissipated, and most campuses were placid by 1988. Historian and antiapartheid activist Matthew Countryman blamed the decline of activism on "serious organizational and strategic weaknesses in the student movement." To maintain the movement's momentum, Countryman encouraged students to join in "a broad movement against university complicity with racism."[63] However, the ebbing of the divestment tidal wave left no other movements of comparable size, scope, and influence in its wake.

Triumphalism and the End of History

The Cold War culture wars, like the Cold War that drove them, had run their course. Commentary about the "end" of the Cold War filled airwaves and the press in the late 1980s, with experts and syndicated columnists weighing in regularly on the matter. "It's hard to distinguish a change like this when you're right in the middle of it, but I personally think we are seeing the end of the Cold War as a dominant foreign policy concept," said John Steinbruner, a scholar with the Brookings Institution, during the Reagan-Gorbachev Moscow Summit in May 1988.[64] On the campaign trail in the fall of 1988, Vice President George Bush—running for his boss's job—spoke about the Cold War at Westminster College in Fulton, Missouri, where Winston Churchill had delivered his famous "Iron Curtain" speech nearly forty years earlier. "The Iron Curtain," Bush reminded his audience, "still stretches from Stettin to Trieste. But it's a rusting curtain. Shafts of light from the western side are piercing the gloom and failure and despair on the other side. . . . There is new hope of change."[65] British prime minister Margaret Thatcher was more decisive in her verdict of November 1988. "We're not in a Cold War now," Thatcher said, but rather in a "new relationship much wider than the Cold War ever was." "Margaret Thatcher had it right," wrote Secretary of State George Shultz in his memoirs. He concluded that the "Cold War was over" by the time he left the White House in January 1989. Around the time Thatcher declared the Cold War dead, a national poll found that Mikhail Gorbachev's popularity rivaled that of President Bush.[66]

By decade's end, joyful bouts of self-congratulatory triumphalism seized American Cold Warriors. "What we may be witnessing is not just the end of the Cold War, or the passing of a particular period of postwar history, but the end of history as such: that is, the end point of mankind's ideological evolution and the universalization of Western liberal democracy as the final form of human government." So wrote political economist Francis Fukuyama in the neoconservative journal the *National Interest* in the summer of 1989.[67] The impact of Fukuyama's "End of History" essay when it first appeared in print cannot be overstated, and it provoked years of debate. It was among the first—and perhaps most influential—of a long line of articles and books full of triumphalist themes. Fukuyama's piece was so successful, in fact, that he revised it into a best-selling book published in 1992.[68]

Fukuyama was not the first person, nor would he be the last, to revel in victory. The late 1980s was full of such pronouncements. "Bulletin: We won!" chimed a May 24, 1989, headline in the *Wall Street Journal*, with an accompanying article proclaiming "containment plus the Reagan doctrine worked. If the Cold War is over, the West has won." "We've won it, and the Soviets are suing for peace," said Admiral Ronald J. Hayes as he stepped down from his position as commander in chief of the United States Pacific Command in September 1988. Days after Christmas 1989, right-wing columnist Patrick Buchanan credited his former boss, Ronald Reagan, for the "the triumph of freedom" and "the global retreat of communism." Buchanan rejoiced: "Of him, more than any other man in 50 years, it may fairly be said: He won the Cold War!" Or as humorist Dave Barry, less weighed down by ideological baggage than Buchanan, put it: "I'm happy to announce that, while you were outside trying to get the barbecue started, we won the Cold War."[69]

With each new unraveling of the Cold War—the fall of the Berlin Wall, the collapse of communist regimes in Eastern Europe, the dissolution of the Soviet Union in the late summer of 1991—America's televised talking heads, newspaper pundits, and assorted experts expanded the list of victors responsible for "winning" the Cold War: Reagan won the Cold War.[70] "We"— meaning the United States—won the Cold War.[71] Franklin D. Roosevelt won the Cold War.[72] Democrats and Republicans working together, in a bipartisan effort, won the Cold War.[73] The "Western democracies" won the Cold War.[74] The "strong economies" of Japan and West Germany won the Cold War.[75] George H. W. Bush won the Cold War.[76] Capitalism won the Cold War.[77]

Rarely did anyone in this celebratory atmosphere give credit to the people of Eastern Europe or the Soviet Union for helping to bring an end to the Cold War. Fewer still worked up the nerve to question whether a perilous resurgence of Cold War hostilities a decade earlier—which put the entire world at risk—should have happened in the first place. Boasting and immodesty came effortlessly during that whirlwind of rapid change, and triumphalists, basking in the glow of victory, did not stop to consider whether the thing they were rejoicing should have ever transpired. Quiet reflection would have to wait. A longer passage of time was needed before Americans could begin to come to terms with the real costs—in money, resources, and human lives—of the Cold War's revival in the late 1970s and throughout the 1980s.

CONCLUSION

It all ended so quickly. Revolutionary transformations occurred at a rapid-fire pace at the end of the 1980s and beginning of the 1990s. The USSR's Eastern European satellites had been liberated. The Warsaw Pact was no more. Yugoslavia was breaking apart and would eventually become seven countries. The Union of Soviet Socialist Republics no longer existed, seventy-four years after the Bolshevik revolution overthrew Czar Nicholas II. The Russian Federation took its place. East and West Germany had merged into one country, united once more. Communism continued in name only in China and Vietnam. North Korea's twenty million–plus inhabitants still lived under a stark dictatorship that has remained in place for decades, run by a cult of rigid ideologues in Pyongyang. Fidel Castro prided Cuba on being the keeper of the flame, the one true surviving bastion of communism, delivering universal health care and housing for its people. But the island nation struggled economically through a devastating U.S. embargo, which outlasted the Cold War's demise for years.

By start of 1992, the Cold War—which had defined the global order since 1945—had passed into history. Predictably, self-congratulatory commentary abounded in the United States. Words such as "win," "victory," and "triumph" appeared often in print and could be heard frequently on television in those heady days of the early 1990s. Even knowledgeable experts with nuanced perspectives on world affairs opted for absolutist language, referring to communism as "dead" and market economies as "victorious."

In time, rejoicing gave way to uncertainty. More than just world maps required updating. Worldviews also had to be reoriented to adapt to changing realities and an unpredictable world. Diplomats, politicians, pundits, and scholars immediately began to speak of a "post–Cold War" world. Around the time the Gulf War ended in late February 1991, President George H. W. Bush popularized the term "new world order" to signify the international system that had replaced the Cold War.[1] Surveying the transformed landscape in the fall of 1992, liberal historian H. Stuart Hughes—a scholar not inclined to subscribe to neoconservative doctrines—conceded that Francis Fukuyama might have a point, that history may well be over and done with. "It is conceivable that if nations continue to turn democratic," he wrote, "the old history in the sense of diplomacy and war may virtually cease."[2]

But shortsighted victory culture, like the Cold War itself, would eventually slip into oblivion with the passage of time. A decade after the collapse of the Soviet Union, militant jihadists launched the horrific September 11, 2001, terrorist attacks, which took the lives of nearly three thousand innocent civilians and offered a stark refutation, on a giant scale, of the End of History. The so-called post-9/11 wars in Iraq and Afghanistan extended the devastation beyond America's borders and continued to raise the death toll and destabilize the already volatile Middle East and parts of South Asia. The financial crisis of 2007–8 showed that capitalism also rested on precarious foundations and required massive infusions of government capital to survive, forcing Washington, D.C., to run up staggering deficits to keep its economy functioning.

Against this backdrop of increased volatility, a small coterie of conservative scholars and Ronald Reagan hagiographers spent years fashioning a myth that the fortieth president had followed a grand plan to "win" the Cold War in the 1980s. "The legend goes like this," wrote journalist and scholar Peter Beinart. "Reagan came into office, dramatically hiked defense spending, unveiled the Strategic Defense Initiative (his 'Star Wars' missile shield), and aided anti-communist rebels in the Third World. Unable to keep pace, the Kremlin chose Gorbachev, who threw in the towel."[3] A plethora of books appeared that gave Reagan much of the credit for ending the Cold War.[4] These accounts contained valuable information and insights, capturing certain important truths about the Cold War in its twilight years. But they also tended to be hyperpartisan celebrations of Reagan that singled him out as the main—if not sole—architect of Cold War victory.

In the triumphalist narratives of the first two decades of the twenty-first century, one could hear the distant echoes of President Reagan calling the Vietnam War a "noble cause." These accounts amounted to celebrations of Reagan's unwavering support for the military–industrial complex, his escalation of the arms race to perilously high levels, and his insistence on financing bloody proxy wars in less developed countries.

But it is worth taking a moment to remember that the Cold War was not merely the doing of one man. The Second Cold War of the Reagan era depended on broad, bipartisan support from Democrats and Republicans in Congress. In the wars of the Reagan era, hot and cold, and in the astonishing defense spending, adding up to $3 trillion, and in the existential threats to human existence posed by the accompanying nuclear buildup, Reagan's supporters have desperately sought to find redeeming qualities and reasons to celebrate his legacy.

Theirs, however, is far from the sole interpretation of the past.[5] History has always been contested terrain. Turn the historical prism slightly, and one finds another aspect of America that went largely overlooked for decades after the Cold War ended but nevertheless illustrates where redemption might be found in America's Cold War revival of the 1980s. Victory celebrations in the late 1980s and early 1990s invariably overlooked the men and women—and sometimes children—who lent their voices to a national resistance movement and challenged Cold War policies and assumptions at every turn.

Like peace activists elsewhere in the world, these Americans, driven by a deep love of their country and concerns for the future of the planet, recognized the deadly stakes involved in escalating superpower tensions and acted accordingly. Ominous developments in the 1980s stirred the energies of those who opposed the Cold War far more than they inspired comparable displays of public support for the policies backed by Reagan and other Cold Warriors in high positions of influence and authority.

Ordinary Americans from all walks of life rose to challenge the dangers posed by the Cold War, to speak up and resist, to make art and to march in the streets, and, in some cases, to put their bodies on the line to push back, collectively, against the Second Cold War in all of its manifestations. In so doing, they forged an adversarial culture strikingly different from the culture of the First Cold War of the late 1940s to the early 1960s, showing the rest of the world that dissent in the United States was alive and well in the age of Reagan.

Notes

Introduction

1. Hedrick Smith, "Reagan's Gaffe: Jest on Bombing Soviet Casts Shadow on Elections and Diplomatic Efforts," *New York Times*, August 16, 1984, A4.
2. Anthony Bennett, *The Race for the White House from Reagan to Clinton: Reforming Old Systems, Building New Coalitions* (New York: Palgrave Macmillan, 2013), 68.
3. *Washington Post*, August 13, 1984, A6.
4. Lou Cannon, "Bombing Joke Shook GOP Strategists More Than They Let On," *Washington Post*, August 20, 1984, A2.
5. R. W. Apple Jr., "Europe Reacts Mildly to Bomb Quip," *New York Times*, August 17, 1984, A3.
6. Antero Pietila, "Soviet Is Using Reagan Joke to Its Advantage," *Baltimore Sun*, August 15, 1984, 1.
7. Mark W. LaVoie, "Telling the Soviet Redemption Story: Ronald Reagan's Changing Soviet Rhetoric" (PhD diss., University of Illinois at Urbana-Champaign, 2016), 121–22, ProQuest (10609674).
8. Steven R. Weisman, "President Jokes about War Quip," *New York Times*, August 17, 1984, A3; *Arizona Daily Star*, August 20, 1984, 4.
9. Stephen J. Whitfield's *Culture of the Cold War*, 2nd ed. (Baltimore, MD: Johns Hopkins University Press, 1996).
10. In addition to Whitfield, other key works on Cold War culture in the United States from roughly 1947 to 1964 include Greg Barnhisel, *Cold War Modernists: Art, Literature, and American Cultural Diplomacy* (New York: Columbia University Press, 2015); Paul Boyer, *By the Bomb's Early Light: American Thought and Culture at the Dawn of the Atomic Age* (Chapel Hill: University of North Carolina Press, 1994); Lisa Davenport, *Jazz Diplomacy: Promoting America in the Cold War Era* (Jackson: University Press of Mississippi, 2009); Thomas Doherty, *Cold War, Cool Medium: Television, McCarthyism, and American Culture* (New York: Columbia University Press, 2003); Thomas Doherty, *Show Trial: Hollywood, HUAC, and the Birth of the Blacklist* (New York: Columbia University Press, 2018); Andrew J. Falk, *Upstaging the Cold War: American Dissent and Cultural Diplomacy, 1940–1960* (Amherst: University of Massachusetts Press, 2010); Victoria M. Grieve, *Little Cold Warriors: American Childhood in the 1950s* (New York: Oxford University Press, 2018); Cyndy Hendershot, *Anti-Communism and Popular Culture in Mid-Century America* (Jefferson, NC: McFarland, 2002); Margot A. Henriksen, *Dr. Strangelove's America: Society and Culture in the Atomic Age* (Berkeley: University of California Press, 1997); Michael Kackman, *Citizen Spy: Television, Espionage, and Cold War Culture*, 2nd ed. (Minneapolis: University of Minnesota Press, 2005); Robert A. Jacobs, *The Dragon's Tail: Americans Face the Atomic Age* (Amherst: University of Massachusetts Press, 2010); Arthur Redding, *Turncoats, Traitors, and Fellow Travelers: Culture and Politics of the Early Cold War* (Jackson: University Press of Mississippi, 2008); John Sbardellati, *J. Edgar Hoover Goes to the Movies: The FBI and the Origins of Hollywood's*

Cold War (Ithaca, NY: Cornell University Press, 2012); Tony Shaw, *Hollywood's Cold War* (Amherst, MA: University of Massachusetts Press, 2007); Penny Von Eschen, *Satchmo Blows Up the World: Jazz Ambassadors Play the Cold War* (Cambridge, MA: Harvard University Press, 2006).

Chapter 1: Setting the Stage

1. William Safire, "Cold War II," *New York Times*, December 29, 1975, 25.
2. *Daily Courier* (Connellsville, PA), March 6, 1976, 1.
3. Phillips's syndicated column on the Cold War's resurgence appeared in numerous newspapers, including the *El Paso Times*, March 31, 1978, 6.
4. Kevin Phillips, *The Emerging Republican Majority*, rev. ed., with a new preface by the author (Princeton, NJ: Princeton University Press, 2015), xv, 247.
5. *El Paso Times*, March 31, 1978, 6.
6. Patrick Buchanan, "U.N.: 'Mankind's Last Hope' Now Seen as a Great Wasteland," *Waterloo (IA) Courier*, April 6, 1979, 4.
7. *Times Colonist* (Victoria, BC), October 17, 1980, 28.
8. *Hartford Courant*, February 16, 1976, 15.
9. *Edmonton Journal*, February 14, 1980, 6; *Guardian Third World Review* (London), February 4, 1980, 15.
10. Fred Halliday, *The Making of the Second Cold War* (London: Verso, 1983). The book sold so well that Verso published a second edition in 1986.
11. Raymond L. Garthoff, "The U.S. Role in Winding Down the Cold War," in *The Last Decade of the Cold War: From Conflict Escalation to Conflict Transformation*, ed. Olav Njølstad (London: Routledge, 2005), 149–50.
12. Betty Glad, *An Outsider in the White House: Jimmy Carter, His Advisors, and the Making of American Foreign Policy* (Ithaca, NY: Cornell University Press, 2009), 95–96, 142–53; Randall Balmer, *Redeemer: The Life of Jimmy Carter* (New York: Basic Books, 2014), 82–85; Craig Shirley, *Reagan Rising: The Decisive Years, 1976–1980* (New York: HarperCollins, 2017), 83–98.
13. Balmer, *Redeemer*, 89.
14. For the definitive Zbigniew Brzezinski biography, see Justin Vaïsse, *Zbigniew Brzezinski: America's Grand Strategist* (Cambridge, MA: Harvard University Press, 2018).
15. Mark Kramer, "Anticipating a Grand Failure," in *Zbig: The Strategy and Statecraft of Zbigniew Brzezinski*, ed. Charles Gati (Baltimore, MD: Johns Hopkins University Press, 2013), 42–61.
16. Fred Halliday, *The Making of the Second Cold War*, 2nd ed. (New York: Verso, 1986), 214–27.
17. Brian J. Auten, *Carter's Conversion: The Hardening of American Defense Policy* (Columbia: University of Missouri Press, 2009), 258–63.
18. Mark Rosenwasser, "Soviet Press Steps Up Criticism of Reagan," Associated Press, February 1, 1981.
19. Richard Falk, "Interventionist Mood Returns, Transforms Doves into Hawks," *Ukiah (CA) Daily Journal*, December 9, 1979, 72.
20. Richard A. Harris and Daniel J. Tichenor, eds., *A History of the U.S. Political System: Ideas, Interests, and Institutions* (Santa Barbara, CA: ABC-CLIO, 2009), 348.
21. *Arizona Republic*, January 23, 1980, 11.

22. Elizabeth Drew, "On the Campaign Trail: Reagan," Reporter at Large, *New Yorker*, March 24, 1980, 57.

23. Gil Troy, *Morning in America: How Ronald Reagan Invented the 1980s* (Princeton, NJ: Princeton University Press, 2005), 36.

24. To date, the finest book on the 1980 election is Andrew E. Busch's outstanding *Reagan's Victory: The Presidential Election of 1980 and the Rise of the Right* (Lawrence: University Press of Kansas, 2017). Other key titles include Elizabeth Drew, *Portrait of an Election: The 1980 Presidential Campaign* (New York: Simon & Schuster, 1981); Jack W. Germond and Jules Witcover, *Blue Smoke and Mirrors: How Reagan Won and Why Carter Lost the Election of 1980* (New York: Viking, 1981); Jeffrey D. Howison, *The 1980 Presidential Election: Ronald Reagan and the Shaping of the American Conservative Movement* (New York: Routledge, 2013); Craig Shirley, *Reagan's Revolution: The Untold Story of the Campaign That Started It All* (Nashville, TN: Thomas Nelson, 2013); John Stacks, *Watershed: The Campaign for the Presidency, 1980* (New York: Times Books, 1981); and Timothy Stanley, *Kennedy vs. Carter: The 1980 Battle for the Democratic Party's Soul* (Lawrence: University Press of Kansas, 2010).

25. James Reston, "Reagan's Startling Victory," *New York Times*, November 5, 1980, A31.

26. Examples include *Dayton Journal Herald*, November 8, 1980, 4; *New York Daily News*, November 8, 1980, 52; *Morning Call* (Allentown, PA), November 6, 1980, 1; *Palm Beach Post*, November 9, 1980, 307; *Santa Maria (CA) Times*, November 20, 1980, 4; *Baltimore Sun*, November 24, 1980, 15; *San Francisco Examiner*, November 15, 1980, 40; and *Atlanta Constitution*, November 17, 1980, 4, to name a few.

27. Sean Wilentz, *The Age of Reagan: A History, 1974–2008* (New York: HarperCollins, 2008), 125–26.

28. Essential volumes on Sixties protest movements include Terry Anderson, *The Movement and the Sixties* (New York: Oxford University Press, 1994); Clayborne Carson, *In Struggle: SNCC and the Black Awakening of the 1960s* (Cambridge, MA: Harvard University Press, 1981); Charles Debenedetti, with Charles Chatfield, *An American Ordeal: The Antiwar Movement of the Vietnam Era* (Syracuse: Syracuse University Press. 1990); Jim Downs, *Stand by Me: The Forgotten History of Gay Liberation* (New York: Basic Books, 2016); Alice Echols, *Daring to Be Bad: Radical Feminism in America, 1967–1975* (Minneapolis: University of Minnesota Press, 1989); James J. Farrell, *The Spirit of the Sixties: Making Postwar Radicalism* (New York: Routledge, 1997); Michael Stewart Foley, *Confronting the War Machine: Draft Resistance during the Vietnam War* (Chapel Hill: University of North Carolina Press, 2003); Todd Gitlin, *The Sixties: Years of Hope, Days of Rage* (New York: Bantam Books, 1987); Andrew Hunt, *The Turning: A History of Vietnam Veterans against the War* (New York: New York University Press, 1999); Maurice Isserman, *If I Had a Hammer: The Death of the Old Left and the Birth of the New Left* (New York: Basic Books, 1987); Arthur Marwick, *The Sixties: Cultural Revolution in Britain, France, Italy, and the United States* (New York: Oxford University Press, 1998); John McMillian, *Smoking Typewriters: The Sixties Underground Press and the Rise of Alternative Media in America* (New York: Oxford University Press, 2011); James Miller, *Democracy Is in the Streets: From Port Huron to the Siege in Chicago* (New York: Simon & Schuster, 1987); Ruth Rosen, *The World Split Open: How the Modern Women's Movement Changed America*, rev. ed. (New York: Penguin Books, 2006); Douglass C. Rossinow, *The Politics of Authenticity : Liberalism, Christianity, and the New Left in America* (New York: Columbia University Press, 1998); and Tom Wells, *The War Within: America's Battle over Vietnam* (Berkeley: University of California Press, 1994).

29. Ronald R. Krebs, *Narrative and the Making of US National Security* (Cambridge: Cambridge University Press, 2015), 191–18.

30. Most notably by Stephen J. Whitfield, *Culture of the Cold War*, 2nd ed. (Baltimore, MD: Johns Hopkins University Press, 1996). See also Paul Boyer, *By the Bomb's Early Light: American Thought and Culture at the Dawn of the Atomic Age* (Chapel Hill: University of North Carolina Press, 1994); Thomas Doherty, *Cold War, Cool Medium: Television, McCarthyism, and American Culture* (New York: Columbia University Press, 2003); Thomas Doherty, *Show Trial: Hollywood, HUAC, and the Birth of the Blacklist* (New York: Columbia University Press, 2018); Margot A. Henriksen, *Dr. Strangelove's America: Society and Culture in the Atomic Age* (Berkeley: University of California Press, 1997); Robert A. Jacobs, *The Dragon's Tail: Americans Face the Atomic Age* (Amherst: University of Massachusetts Press, 2010); Arthur Redding, *Turncoats, Traitors, and Fellow Travelers: Culture and Politics of the Early Cold War* (Jackson: University Press of Mississippi, 2008); John Sbardellati, *J. Edgar Hoover Goes to the Movies: The FBI and the Origins of Hollywood's Cold War* (Ithaca, NY: Cornell University Press, 2012); and Tony Shaw, *Hollywood's Cold War* (Amherst: University of Massachusetts Press, 2007).

31. Bernard F. Dick's *The Screen Is Red: Hollywood, Communism, and the Cold War* (Jackson: University Press of Mississippi, 2016) is a thorough and engaging history of anticommunist movies.

32. *High Noon*, directed by Fred Zinnemann (Chicago: Olive Films, 2016), Blu-ray. For a gripping history of the making of *High Noon*, see Max Frankel, *"High Noon": The Hollywood Blacklist and the Making of an American Classic* (New York: Bloomsbury USA, 2018).

33. Gabriel Miller, ed., *Fred Zinnemann: Interviews* (Jackson: University Press of Mississippi, 2004), 44.

34. John H. Lenihan, *Showdown: Confronting Modern America in the Western Film* (Champaign: University of Illinois Press, 1990), 119–20.

35. Cynthia Hendershot, *Paranoia, the Bomb, and 1950s Science Fiction Films* (Bowling Green, OH: Bowling Green State University Popular Press, 1999), 23.

36. For a compelling analysis of these films, see Anna Creadick, "Incredible/Shrinking Men: Masculinity and Atomic Anxiety in American Postwar Science-Fiction Film," in *Fear Itself: Enemies Real and Imagined in American Culture*, ed. Nancy Lusignan Schultz (West Lafayette, IN: Purdue University Press, 1998), 286.

37. Mike Bogue, *Apocalypse Then: American and Japanese Atomic Cinema, 1951–1967* (Jefferson, NC: McFarland, 2017), 166–203.

38. Ed Gorman and Kevin McCarthy, *Invasion of the Body Snatchers: A Tribute* (Eureka, CA: Stark House Press, 2006), 59–69.

39. *Pickup on South Street*, directed by Samuel Fuller (New York: Criterion Collection, 2004), DVD.

40. *The Manchurian Candidate*, directed by John Frankenheimer (New York: MGM Home Entertainment, 2006), DVD.

41. Edmund S. Morgan, "Arthur Miller's *The Crucible* and the Salem Witch Trials: A Historian's View," in *Arthur Miller: Bloom's Modern Critical Views*, ed. Harold Bloom, rev. ed. (New York: Chelsea House, 2007), 13.

42. Christopher Bigsby, *Arthur Miller: A Critical Study* (Cambridge: Cambridge University Press, 2005), 154–55.

43. William Boddy, *Fifties Television: The Industry and Its Critics* (Champaign: University of Illinois Press, 1992), 113–86.

44. For many years, the go-to book on Rod Serling and *The Twilight Zone* was Marc Scott Zicree's *The Twilight Zone Companion* (New York: Bantam, 1982). See also Nicholas Parisi, *Rod Serling: His Life, Work, and Imagination* (Jackson: University Press of Mississippi, 2018), and Anne Serling, *As I Knew Him: My Dad, Rod Serling* (New York: Citadel, 2013). It's also worth noting that the poignant Serling-scripted episode "In Praise of Pip" (season 5, episode 1, September 27, 1963) was one of the first television shows to mention the conflict in South Vietnam, before President Lyndon Johnson initiated the American ground war there.

45. In syndication after going off the air in 1964, the reruns became variously known as *The Rocky and Bullwinkle Show* and *The Adventures of Rocky and Bullwinkle and Friends*.

46. The show's colorful history and memorable episodes are detailed in Keith Scott's delightful *The Moose That Roared: The Story of Jay Ward, Bill Scott, a Flying Squirrel, and a Talking Moose* (New York: Thomas Dunne Books, 2000). See also David Bianculli, *The Platinum Age of Television: From "I Love Lucy" to "The Walking Dead," How TV Became Terrific* (New York: Doubleday, 2016), 43–45; June Foray, *Did You Grow Up with Me, Too? The Autobiography of June Foray* (Albany, GA: BearManor Media, 2009); and Ben Ohmart, with June Foray, *Welcome, Foolish Mortals: The Life and Voices of Paul Frees*, rev. ed. (Albany, GA: BearManor Media, 2017).

47. "Pottsylvania," Rocky and Bullwinkle Wiki, http://rockyandbullwinkle.wikia.com/wiki/Pottsylvania (accessed January 26, 2019).

48. Stephen E. Kercher, *Revel with a Cause: Liberal Satire in Postwar America* (Chicago: University of Chicago Press, 2006), 112–18, 229.

49. Accounts of postwar newspaper cartoonists include Paul Conrad, *Drawing the Line: The Collected Works of America's Premier Political Cartoonist* (Los Angeles: Los Angeles Times Books, 1999); Herbert Block, Harry L. Katz, and Haynes Johnson, *Herblock: The Life and Works of the Great Political Cartoonist* (New York: W. W. Norton, 2009); and Todd DePastino, *Bill Mauldin: A Life Up Front* (New York: W. W. Norton, 2008).

50. Kerry D. Soper, *We Go Pogo: Walt Kelly, Politics, and American Satire* (Jackson: University Press of Mississippi, 2012), 11–12, 37–40.

51. *On the Beach*, directed by Stanley Kramer (New York: Kino Lorber Films, 2014), DVD; *Appleton (WI) Post-Crescent*, June 5, 1959, 9.

52. Peter Lev, *The Fifties: Transforming the Screen, 1950–1959* (Berkeley: University of California Press, 2006), 194.

53. Shaw, *Hollywood's Cold War*, 157. See also *Naugatuck (CT) Daily News*, December 22, 1959, 8.

54. Jacobs, *Dragon's Tail*, 73–74.

55. Boyer, *By the Bomb's Early Light*, 353.

56. *Fail Safe*, directed by Sidney Lumet (New York: Sony Pictures Home Entertainment, 2000), DVD.

57. Charles Maland, "*Dr. Strangelove* (1964): Nightmare Comedy and the Ideology of Liberal Consensus," *American Quarterly* 31, no. 5 (Winter 1979): 703–4; David Tully, *Terry Southern and the American Grotesque* (Jefferson, NC: McFarland, 2013), 128–35; Vincent Lobrutto, "The Written Word and the Very Visual Stanley Kubrick," in

Depth of Field: Stanley Kubrick, Film, and the Uses of History, ed. Geoffrey Cocks, James Diedrick, and Glenn Perusek (Madison: University of Wisconsin Press, 2006), 40-41.

58. *Dr. Strangelove, Or: How I Learned to Stop Worrying and Love the Bomb*, directed by Stanley Kubrick (New York: Criterion Collection, 2016), DVD. See also *Gorge Case, Calling Dr. Strangelove: The Anatomy and Influence of the Kubrick Masterpiece* (Jefferson, NC: McFarland, 2014), 32-33.

59. Stephen J. Whitfield, "Review of Tony Shaw's *British Cinema and the Cold War: The State, Propaganda and Consensus*," *Journal of Cold War Studies* 4, no. 4 (Fall 2002): 120-22; Christian G. Appy, *American Reckoning: The Vietnam War and Our National Identity* (New York: Penguin, 2015), 152.

60. Maurice Isserman, *If I Had a Hammer: The Death of the Old Left and the Birth of the New Left* (New York: Basic Books, 1987), 30; Andrew Hunt, "How New Was the New Left? Re-Thinking New Left Exceptionalism," in *The New Left Revisited*, ed. John McMillian and Paul Buhle (Philadelphia, PA: Temple University Press, 2003), 139-55.

61. David M. Oshinsky, *A Conspiracy So Immense: The World of Joe McCarthy* (New York: Oxford University Press, 2005), 495-508. Oshinsky's biography is the gold standard when it comes to McCarthy. A more sympathetic—and far more partisan—account of Senator McCarthy's life can be found in M. Stanton Evans, *Blacklisted by History: The Untold Story of Senator Joe McCarthy and His Fight against America's Enemies* (New York: Crown Forum, 2007). For a view of McCarthy and his impact from the left, see Ellen Schrecker, *Many Are the Crimes: McCarthyism in America* (New York: Little, Brown, 1998).

62. Daniel J. Leab, *I Was a Communist for the FBI: The Unhappy Life and Times of Matt Cvetic* (University Park: Pennsylvania State University Press, 2000).

63. Lewis H. Carlson, "J. Parnell Thomas and the House Committee on Un-American Activities, 1938-1948" (PhD diss., Michigan State University, 1967), 226-28.

64. John A. Farrell, *Richard Nixon: The Life* (New York: Vintage, 2018), 534-58.

65. *Get Smart: The Complete Series* (New York: HBO Home Video, 2015), DVD; *M*A*S*H: The Complete Collection* (New York: 20th Century Fox Home Video, 2018), DVD; *Wait Till Your Father Gets Home*, season 1 (New York: WarnerBrothers Home Video, 2007), DVD. Regrettably, as of May 2020, season 2 of this brilliant animated series has yet to be released on DVD or Blu-ray.

66. *Executive Action*, directed by David Miller (New York: WarnerBrothers Home Video, 2007), DVD; *The Parallax View*, directed by Alan J. Pakula (New York: Paramount Home Video, 1999), DVD; *All the President's Men*, directed by Alan J. Pakula (New York: Warner Home Video, 2010), DVD; *Three Days of the Condor*, directed by Sydney Pollack (New York: Paramount Home Video, 2017), DVD; *The Marathon Man*, directed by John Schlesinger (New York: Paramount Home Video, 2017), Blu-ray; *Apocalypse Now*, directed by Francis Ford Coppola (New York: Paramount Home Video, 1999), DVD.

67. *The Bedford Incident*, directed by James B. Harris (New York: Sony Pictures Home Entertainment, 2003), DVD; *The Russians Are Coming, the Russians Are Coming*, directed by Norman Jewison (New York: Kl Studio Classics, 2015), DVD.

68. *In the Year of the Pig*, directed by Emile de Antonio (New York: Sony Pictures Home Entertainment, 2005), DVD; *Hearts and Minds*, directed by Peter Davis (New York: Criterion Collection, 2014), DVD.

69. Vincent Canby, "*Hearts and Minds*, a Film Study of Power," *New York Times*, March 24, 1975, L-38; David Grosser, "'We Aren't on the Wrong Side, We Are the Wrong Side': Peter Davis Targets (American) Hearts and Minds," in *From Hanoi to Hollywood: The Vietnam War in American Film*, ed. Linda Dittmar and Gene Michaud (New Brunswick, NJ: Rutgers University Press), 269–82.

70. John Henry Faulk, *Fear on Trial* (New York: Simon and Schuster, 1964); Lloyd Larrabee, "Faulk Tells His Story," *San Antonio Express and News*, November 15, 1964, 8-H.

71. Lillian Hellman, *Scoundrel Time (Boston: Little, Brown,* 1976), 39.

72. Quoted in Alice Griffin and Geraldine Thorsten, *Understanding Lillian Hellman* (Columbia: University of South Carolina Press, 2010), 122.

73. Lillian Hellman, *Three: "An Unfinished Woman," "Pentimento" and "Scoundrel Time"* (Boston: Little, Brown, 1979), 726.

74. Paul Gray, "An Unfinished Woman," *Time*, May 10, 1976, 83.

75. Mandy Merck, *Hollywood's American Tragedies: Dreiser, Eisenstein, Sternberg, Stevens* (Oxford: Berg Publishers, 2007), 144–45.

76. The efforts to shut down and blacklist *Salt of the Earth* are documented in James Lorence's *The Suppression of "Salt of the Earth": How Hollywood, Big Labor, and Politicians Blacklisted a Movie in the American Cold War* (Albuquerque: University of New Mexico Press, 1999). See also Herbert Biberman, *"Salt of the Earth": The Story of a Film*, rev. ed. (New York: Harbor Electronic Publishing, 2003); Larry Ceplair, *The Marxist and the Movies: A Biography of Paul Jarrico* (Lexington: University Press of Kentucky, 2007), 137–57; and Danny Peary, *Cult Movies 2* (New York: Dell, 1983), 135.

77. *The Front*, directed by Martin Ritt (New York: Sony Pictures Home Entertainment, 2004), DVD.

78. Hilton Kramer, "The Blacklist and the Cold War," *New York Times*, October 3, 1976, 63.

79. *Julia*, directed by Fred Zinnemann (New York: 20th Century Fox Home Entertainment, 2016), DVD.

80. Quoted in Richard Gid Powers, *Not without Honor: The History of American Anticommunism* (New Haven, CT: Yale University Press, 1998), 345.

Chapter 2: Nostalgia Wars

1. *The Big Chill*, directed by Lawrence Kasdan (New York: Sony Pictures Home Entertainment, 1999), DVD.

2. Pauline Kael, *5001 Nights at the Movies* (New York: Henry Holt, 1991), 69. Kael's reviews in the book originally appeared in the *New Yorker*.

3. Geoffrey Himes, "'Big Chill,' 'Secaucus Seven' Differ on '60s Idealism," *Baltimore Sun*, October 14, 1983, 27.

4. *Return of the Secaucus 7*, directed by John Sayles (New York: MGM Home Video, 2003), DVD; Lou Cedrone, "Kasdan Details Birth of 'Big Chill,'" *Central New Jersey Home News*, September 28, 1983, 32.

5. Jack Ryan, *John Sayles, Filmmaker: A Critical Study and Filmography*, 2nd ed. (Jefferson, NC: McFarland, 2010), 53–54.

6. Janet Maslin, "Tracing the Long Shadow Cast by the *Big Chill*," *New York Times*, July 14, 1985, H15.

7. Sociologist Rebecca Klatch refutes the film and its myth in *A Generation Divided: The New Left, the New Right, and the 1960s* (Berkeley: University of California Press, 1999), 328.

8. Kasdan, *The Big Chill*.

9. Bob Kasper, "Jerry Rubin Goes Wall Street, but Still Can't Tie a Tie," *Baltimore Sun*, August 19, 1980, B1; *Los Angeles Times*, January 26, 1981, V-1; Bob Greene, "Jerry Rubin's Business is Business," *Chicago Tribune*, March 23, 1983, 69; *San Francisco Examiner*, October 11, 1987, 6.

10. Joan Morrison and Robert K. Morrison, *From Camelot to Kent State: The Sixties Experience in the Words of Those Who Lived It*, 2nd ed. (New York: Oxford University Press, 2001), 291; *Austin-American Statesman*, August 7, 1980, C6.

11. Jack Hoffman and Daniel Simon, *Run, Run, Run: The Lives of Abbie Hoffman* (New York: Putnam, 1994), 307–8.

12. Larry Sloman, *Steal This Dream: Abbie Hoffman and the Countercultural Revolution in America* (New York: Doubleday, 1998), 376.

13. Todd Gitlin, *The Sixties: Years of Hope, Days of Rage* (New York: Bantam Books, 1987), 420. In fairness to Gitlin, in his previous book, *The Whole World Is Watching: Mass Media in the Making and Unmaking of the New Left* (Berkeley: University of California Press, 1980), he made more of an effort to emphasize continuities between the 1960s and the 1980s by briefly tracing the antinuclear movement's rise to prominence in the 1970s and 1980s. He has also emphasized the importance of activism and its continuing legacies in a lot of his other writings as well.

14. Many of the books written after Gitlin's *The Sixties* take a more fluid approach to protest movements of the 1960s, one that emphasizes legacies and historical continuities between that era and subsequent periods.

15. Alex Callinicos, *Against Postmodernism: A Marxist Critique* (Cambridge: Polity Press, 1989), 168.

16. *Tampa Bay Times*, March 14, 1982, 19.

17. *Casper Star-Tribune*, October 18, 1981, 1; Morrison and Morrison, *Camelot to Kent State*, 322–25.

18. Peter Collier and David Horowitz, "We Aren't Marching Anymore," This World, *San Francisco Examiner*, May 19, 1985, 6. Horowitz tells the story of his ideological shift in his autobiography *Radical Son: A Generational Odyssey* (New York: Free Press, 1997).

19. Pete Szilagyi, "First Liddy-Leary Confrontation Was a Bust," *Austin American-Statesman*, October 28, 1981, B3.

20. Despite Callinicos's bleak assessment in *Against Postmodernism*, other books written around the same time emphasized the lifelong commitment of sixties radicals to progressive causes, including Doug McAdam, *Freedom Summer* (New York: Oxford University Press, 1988), and Jack Whalen and Richard Flacks, *Beyond the Barricades: The Sixties Generation Grows Up* (Philadelphia: Temple University Press, 1989).

21. *New York Times*, July 13, 1982, 1.

22. *Boston Globe Magazine*, March 15, 1981, 15; *Boston Globe*, October 16, 1983, 378; *Baltimore Sun*, April 27, 1980, 15.

23. David Sirota, *Back to Our Future: How the 1980s Explain the World We Live in Now—Our Culture, Our Politics, Our Everything* (New York: Ballantine Books, 2011), 4.

24. For the single finest treatment of these themes, see Christian Appy's brilliant *American Reckoning: The Vietnam War and Our National Identity* (New York: Penguin, 2015).

25. Sean Wilentz, *The Age of Reagan: A History, 1974–2008* (New York: Harper Perennial, 2009), 151–57.
26. Ryan Lizardi, *Mediated Nostalgia: Individual Memory and Contemporary Mass Media* (Lanham, MD: Lexington Books, 2016), 2–3.
27. Garfield quoted in the *Cincinnati Inquirer*, December 17, 1989, 155.
28. *New York Times*, November 29, 1989, D19.
29. *American Graffiti*, directed by George Lucas (New York: Universal Pictures Home Entertainment, 1998), DVD. The Broadway musical *Grease* actually predated *American Graffiti* by about two years, although it did not have the same profound cultural impact as Lucas's phenomenally successful film.
30. Examples include *Arizona Republic*, January 15, 1974, 12; *Atlanta Constitution*, March 24, 1974, 21F; *Fort Lauderdale News*, February 15, 1974, 14E; TV Section, *Fresno Bee*, January 6, 1974, 6; *Waterloo Courier*, February 15, 1974, 29; *Windsor Star*, September 10, 1974, 21.
31. Michael D. Dwyer, *Back to the Fifties: Nostalgia, Hollywood Film, and Popular Music of the Seventies and Eighties* (New York: Oxford University Press, 2015), 6.
32. *Asbury Park Press*, April 8, 1982, B7; *Boston Globe*, August 3, 1980, D5; *Los Angeles Times*, November 18, 1980, 1, 34; *New York Daily News*, October 7, 1984, B1, B3; *Philadelphia Inquirer*, January 20, 1980, I-1, I-6; *Pottsville Republican*, May 16, 1980, 14.
33. *Cincinnati Enquirer*, August 27, 1982, D10.
34. *Morristown (NJ) Daily Record*, November 17, 1982, 42.
35. *Pittsburgh Press*, March 13, 1983, TV3; *Arizona Daily Star*, February 7, 1982, 124.
36. *Morristown (NJ) Daily Record*, November 17, 1982, 42.
37. Shales quoted in Dwyer, *Back to the Fifties*, 1.
38. *Back to the Future 30th Anniversary Trilogy*, directed by Robert Zemeckis (New York: Universal Pictures Home Entertainment, 2015), DVD.
39. Sirota, *Back to Our Future*, 4–5.
40. *Peggy Sue Got Married*, directed by Francis Ford Coppola (New York: Sony Pictures Home Entertainment, 1998), DVD; Gene D. Phillips, *Godfather: The Intimate Francis Ford Coppola* (Lexington: University Press of Kentucky, 2004), 256.
41. Daniel Marcus, *Happy Days and Wonder Years: The Fifties and the Sixties in Contemporary Cultural Politics* (New Brunswick, NJ: Rutgers University Press, 2004), 109.
42. Calendar, *Los Angeles Times*, August 31, 1986, 52.
43. *St. Louis Post-Dispatch*, July 13, 1981, 3D; *St. Louis Post-Dispatch*, September 24, 1986, 4F; Peter Richardson, *No Simple Highway: A Cultural History of the Grateful Dead* (New York: St. Martin's Press, 2015), 4–5.
44. Scott W. Allen, *Aces Back to Back: The History of the Grateful Dead, 1965–2013* (Denver, CO: Outskirts Press, 2014), 75–80.
45. Dennis McNally, "The Grateful Dead in the Academy," in *Reading the Grateful Dead: A Critical Survey*, ed. Nicholas G. Meriwether (Lanham, MD: Scarecrow Press, 2012), 13.
46. *Eyes on the Prize*, directed by Judith Vecchione et al. (New York: PBS Distribution, 2010), DVD. For years after its original airing, the landmark civil rights documentary was unavailable due to copyright issues involving the original film footage used in the episodes. In 2010, PBS finally released it on DVD, nearly 25 years after it was made.
47. Tom Hayden, *Reunion: A Memoir* (New York: Random House, 1988); *Atlanta Constitution*, June 20, 1988, 3D. See also *Akron Beacon Journal*, February 21, 1988, 125, and Tempo, *Chicago Tribune*, July 19, 1988, C1–C2.

48. For key works on the Iran-Contra scandal, see David Bogen and Michael E. Lynch, eds., *The Spectacle of History: Speech, Text, and Memory at the Iran-Contra Hearings* (Durham, NC: Duke University Press, 1996); Robert Busby, *Reagan and the Iran-Contra Affair: The Politics of Presidential Recovery* (New York: Palgrave Macmillan, 1999); Malcolm Byrne, *Iran-Contra: Reagan's Scandal and the Unchecked Abuse of Presidential Power* (Lawrence: University Press of Kansas, 2017); and Theodore Draper, *A Very Thin Line: The Iran-Contra Affairs* (New York: Hill and Wang, 1992).

49. Lou Cannon, *President Reagan: The Role of a Lifetime* (New York: PublicAffairs, 2000), 580; Doug Rossinow, *The Reagan Era: A History of the 1980s* (New York: Columbia University Press, 2015), 181–200.

50. John Sbardellati, "Reagan's Early Years—From Dixon to Hollywood," in *A Companion to Ronald Reagan*, ed. Andrew Johns (Hoboken, NJ: Wiley Blackwell, 2015), 16–17.

51. Thomas W. Evans, *The Education of Ronald Reagan: The General Electric Years and the Untold Story of His Conversion to Conservatism* (New York: Columbia University Press, 2008), 21; Thomas Doherty, *Show Trial: Hollywood, HUAC, and the Birth of the Blacklist* (New York: Columbia University Press, 2018), 323. The finest book on Reagan's conversion to conservatism remains Evans's *Education of Ronald Reagan*.

52. David S. Barrett, "Communist Threat Same as in 1950s, Reagan Says," *Hartford Courant*, March 19, 1980, 1D.

53. Marc Elliot, *Reagan: The Hollywood Years* (New York: Random House, 2008), 216.

54. Kiron K. Skinner and Annelise Anderson, eds., *Reagan in His Own Hand: The Writings of Ronald Reagan That Reveal His Revolutionary Vision for America* (New York: Free Press, 2001), 121–25.

55. Nina Totenberg, "Did America Vote for This Too?," *Christian Science Monitor*, November 24, 1980, 23; Julia Malone, "Civil Liberties Advocates Brace for Assault from America's Right Flank," *Christian Science Monitor*, November 10, 1981, 1; Don Edwards, "HUAC? In '81? Today?," *New York Times*, February 19, 1981, A31.

56. Ira Aranow, "Once Scorned, Jailed, Marxist Dorothy Healey Given Acclaim," *Los Angeles Times*, November 15, 1979, WS13.

57. *Boston Globe*, January 11, 1981, C7.

58. *New York Times*, May 3, 1981, E20.

59. Douglass K. Daniel, *"Lou Grant": The Making of TV's Top Newspaper Drama* (Syracuse: Syracuse University Press, 1996), 148.

60. *Boston Globe*, April 7, 1986, 18.

61. Kenneth H. Ashworth, "McCarthyism in the Classroom: Anti-Intellectualism at Its Worst," *Change: The Magazine of Higher Learning*, November–December 1985, 10.

62. *St. Louis Post-Dispatch*, November 16, 1980, 8A.

63. *New York Times*, June 5, 1974, 46.

64. *New York Times*, October 27, 1980, 19.

65. *New York Times*, March 15, 1984, B18.

66. David Caute, *The Great Fear: The Anti-Communist Purge under Truman and Eisenhower* (New York: Touchstone Books, 1979).

Chapter 3: In the Shadow of Vietnam

1. Quoted in Christian Appy, *American Reckoning: The Vietnam War and Our National Identity* (New York: Penguin Books, 2016), 286. See also *San Francisco Examiner*, August 18, 1980, 2.

2. Geoff Simons, *Vietnam Syndrome: Impact on U.S. Foreign Policy* (London: Macmillan, 1998), 11–20.

3. National Archives and Records Administration, Office of the Federal Register, *Public Papers of the President: Ronald Reagan, 1981–1989* (Washington, D.C.: Government Printing Office, 1984), 1319.

4. Marvin Kalb and Deborah Kalb, *Haunting Legacy: Vietnam and the American Presidency from Ford to Obama* (Washington, D.C.: Brookings Institution Press, 2011), 85.

5. George P. Shultz, *Turmoil and Triumph: Diplomacy, Power, and the Victory of the American Deal* (New York: Charles Scribner's Sons, 1993), 294; Bernard von Bothmer, *Framing the Sixties: The Use and Abuse of a Decade from Ronald Reagan to George W. Bush* (Amherst: University of Massachusetts Press, 2009), 86.

6. Patrick Hagopian, "The Social Memory of the Vietnam War (Volumes I and II)" (PhD diss., Johns Hopkins University, 1994), 86, ProQuest (9419979).

7. Appy, *American Reckoning*, 229.

8. Bob Brown, "Pain, Frustration Only Begins to Fade for Vietnam Veterans," *Eau Claire Leader Telegram*, May 28, 1983, 2; Charlotte Cahill, "Fighting the Vietnam Syndrome: The Construction of a Conservative Veterans Politics, 1966–1984" (PhD diss., Northwestern University, 2008), 165, ProQuest (3336524).

9. Jim Kerr, "Vietnam Legacy: Boy Moves beyond Hometown Values," *Perkasie News Herald*, November 2, 1983, 34.

10. Scruggs tells his story in Jan Scruggs and Joel Swerdlow, *To Heal a Nation: The Vietnam Veterans Memorial* (New York: Harper and Row, 1985).

11. For example, United Press International wire stories ran in the *Minneapolis Star*, July 5, 1979, 7B, the *Chicago Tribune*, July 5, 1979, 16, and numerous other papers mentioning that Scruggs had raised only $144; "Viet Vets Memorial Fund as Unpopular as War," *Chicago Tribune*, July 5, 1979, 16.

12. Robert W. Doubek, *Creating the Vietnam Veterans Memorial: The Inside Story* (Jefferson, NC: McFarland, 2015), 15.

13. Kristin Ann Hass, *Sacrificing Soldiers on the National Mall* (Berkeley: University of California Press, 2013), 15–16; Wilbur J. Scott, *Vietnam Veterans since the War: The Politics of PTSD, Agent Orange, and the National Memorial* (Norman: University of Oklahoma Press, 2003), 138.

14. Don Shannon, "Student Wins Vietnam Memorial Contest," *Los Angeles Times*, May 7, 1981, Part II, 1; Thomas Hine, "Yale Student Wins Contest for War Memorial Design," *Hartford Courant*, May 7, 1981, 18.

15. *Arizona Republic*, May 7, 1981, C8; Richard Cohen, "Roll Call," *Washington Post*, November 14, 1982, B1.

16. Scott, *Vietnam Veterans since the War*, 139–40.

17. Sydney Liam Elsebeth van Beek, "'We Leave You Our Deaths, Give Them Meaning': Memory, Identity, and the Vietnam Veterans Memorial," (PhD diss., University of Western Ontario, 2010), 135, ProQuest (NR73394); James Reston Jr., *A Rift in the Earth: Art, Memory, and the Fight for a Vietnam War Memorial* (New York: Arcade Publishing, 2017), chap. 5, Kindle.

18. Julia Bleakney, *Revisiting Vietnam: Memoirs, Memorials, Museums* (New York: Routledge, 2006), 78–79.

19. Karal Ann Marling and Robert Silberman, "The Statue Near the Wall: The Vietnam Veterans Memorial and the Art of Remembering," *Smithsonian Studies in American Art* 1, no.1 (Spring 1987): 13; Elisabeth Bumiller, "The Memorial, Mirror of Vietnam," *Washington Post*, November 9, 1984, F10; Scott, *Vietnam Veterans since the War*, 143.

178 · NOTES TO PAGES 52-56

20. Scott, *Vietnam Veterans since the War*, 140.

21. Franklin Ng, "Maya Lin and the Vietnam Veterans Memorial," in *Asian American Women and Gender*, vol. 3, ed. Franklin Ng (New York: Garland Publishing, 1998), 65–66.

22. *Clarion-Ledger* (Jackson, MS), February 15, 1982, 3D; Marsha Meskimmon, *Women Making Art: History, Subjectivity, Aesthetics* (New York: Routledge, 2003), 60.

23. Patrick Buchanan, "An Insulting Memorial," *Chicago Tribune*, December 26, 1981, N1; Tom Wolfe, "Art Disputes War: The Battle of the Vietnam Memorial," *Washington Post*, October 13, 1982, B3.

24. *Chicago Tribune*, June 28, 1981, G12; Bill Boldenweck, "One Man's Dream to Honor U.S.'s Viet Dead Nearing Reality," *San Francisco Chronicle*, May 6, 1981, B14; Charles Krauthammer, "Washington Diarist: Memorials," *New Republic*, May 23, 1981, 43; Edward J. Gallagher, "The Vietnam Wall Controversy, Round 3, October 1981–January 1982," History on Trial, Lehigh University Digital Library, http://digital.lib.lehigh .edu/trial/vietnam/r4/1982/.

25. Kali Tal, *Worlds of Hurt: Reading the Literatures of Trauma* (Cambridge: Cambridge University Press, 1996), 62.

26. Ng, "Maya Lin," 214.

27. John Mintz, "Perot's War: Viet Vets' 'Tombstone,'" *Washington Post*, July 7, 1992, A6.

28. "Vietnam Memorial Falls into Place," *U.S. News & World Report*, April 5, 1982, 5.

29. Scott, *Vietnam Veterans since the War*, 163–64.

30. William Broyles Jr., "Remembering a War We Want to Forget," *Newsweek*, November 22, 1982, 83.

31. An extraordinary account of this practice is Thomas B. Allen's *Offerings at the Wall: Artifacts from the Vietnam Veterans Memorial Collection* (Nashville, TN: Turner Publishing, 1995).

32. Watson's letter is quoted in the *Orlando Sentinel*, November 15, 1982, A-9.

33. *Chicago Tribune*, March 6, 2015, 16.

34. Library of Congress, Public Affairs Office, "War and Remembrance: VHP and PBS History Project with Film," *Library of Congress Information Bulletin* 66, no. 6 (June 2007), https://www.loc.gov/loc/lcib/0706/pbs.html.

35. Michael D. Gambone, *Greatest Generation Comes Home: The Veteran in American Society* (College Station: Texas A&M University Press, 2005), 190.

36. Arthur Egendorf, *Healing from the War: Trauma and Transformation after Vietnam* (Boston: Houghton Mifflin, 1985), 115.

37. For more on the Pentagon Papers, see Daniel Ellsberg, *Secrets: A Memoir of Vietnam and the Pentagon Papers* (New York: Penguin, 2003); George C. Herring, ed., *The Pentagon Papers* (New York: McGraw-Hill, 1993); and Neil Sheehan, Hedrick Smith, James L. Greenfield, E. W. Kenworthy, and Fox Butterfield, *The Pentagon Papers: The Secret History of the Vietnam War* (New York: Racehorse Publishing, 2017).

38. Ben A. Franklin, "President Accepts Vietnam Memorial," *New York Times*, November 12, 1984, A1.

39. Scott, *Vietnam Veterans since the War*, 75–76.

40. *Los Angeles Times*, November 11, 1988, Part V, 1; Eric T. Dean Jr., "The Myth of the Troubled and Scorned Vietnam Veteran," *Journal of American Studies* 26, no. 1 (April 1992): 59–74.

41. There are several outstanding books on the tragedy of America's extensive use of Agent Orange in Vietnam, including Edwin A. Martini, *Agent Orange: History, Science, and the Politics of Uncertainty* (Amherst: University of Massachusetts Press,

2012); Fred A. Wilcox, *Waiting for an Army to Die: The Tragedy of Agent Orange* (New York: Seven Stories Press, 2011); and David Zierler, *The Invention of Ecocide: Agent Orange, Vietnam, and the Scientists Who Changed the Way We Think about the Environment* (Athens: University of Georgia Press, 2011).

42. Michael J. Allen, *Until the Last Man Comes Home: POWs, MIAs, and the Unending Vietnam War* (Chapel Hill: University of North Carolina Press, 2012), 215–49.

43. The darker side of the movement is chronicled brilliantly in H. Bruce Franklin's *M.I.A., or, Mythmaking in America*, rev. ed. (New Brunswick, NJ: Rutgers University Press, 1993).

44. Allen, *Last Man Comes Home*, 270–76.

45. *Uncommon Valor*, directed by Ted Kotcheff (New York: Paramount Home Entertainment, 2017), DVD; *Missing in Action*, directed by Joseph Zito (New York: MGM Home Entertainment, 2012), DVD. The three *Missing in Action* films are available in one set, distributed by TGG Direct.

46. *First Blood*, directed by Ted Kotcheff (New York: Live/Artisan, 2002), DVD.

47. *Rambo: First Blood Part II*, directed by George P. Cosmatos (New York: Lionsgate Home Entertainment, 2004), DVD.

48. Cosmatos, *Rambo*.

49. Gil Troy, *Morning in America: How Ronald Reagan Invented the 1980s* (Princeton, NJ: Princeton University Press, 2005), 192.

50. Gibson quoted in Jerry Lembcke, *The Spitting Image: Myth, Memory, and the Legacy of Vietnam* (New York: New York University Press, 1998), 90.

51. Deborah Kaplan, "Nam Vets Doubt Movie Tells It Like It Was," *Detroit Free Press*, December 19, 1986, 2C; Jay Sharbutt, "Reunion: Men of a Real Platoon," *Los Angeles Times*, February 7, 1987, 106; *Shreveport Times*, July 29, 1987, 40; Mark Curnutte, "Veteran's Story Becomes a Documentary," *Wilmington News-Journal*, September 15, 1987, 50.

52. Scott, *Vietnam Veterans since the War*, 143–46; quotation is on 146.

53. Bernard Weinraub, "American Veterans Treated Warmly in a Threadbare Hanoi," *New York Times*, December 22, 1981," A3.

54. *Battle Creek Enquirer*, November 14, 1982, A-9; Bernard Weinraub, "4 Veterans End Hanoi Trip Nervous about Return to U.S.," *New York Times*, December 25, 1981, 2.

55. Walter H. Capps, *The Unfinished War: Vietnam and the American Conscience* (Boston: Beacon Press, 1990), 7. Al Santoli's book, *Everything We Had: An Oral History of the Vietnam War as Told by 33 American Men Who Fought It*, was published by Random House in 1981. He followed it with *To Bear Any Burden: The Vietnam War and Its Aftermath in the Words of Americans and Southeast Asians* (New York: Dutton, 1985). Both books did an exemplary job of capturing a diverse array of experiences and viewpoints of Vietnam veterans.

56. Scott, *Vietnam Veterans since the War*, 146.

57. Michael Harbert's claims of being involved in bombing missions over North Vietnam first fell under scrutiny in an investigative piece in the *New York Daily News* by journalist Richard Sisk headlined, "The War among the Vets," May 30, 1982, 102. Harbert's version of his past was later called into question in B. G. Burkett and Glenna Whitley in *Stolen Valor* (Irving, TX: Verity Press, 1998), 134–37. After the *New York Daily News* article appeared, Harbert dropped out of sight and made no effort to defend his previous claims, which lends credence to the claims that he embellished or falsified his Vietnam War record.

58. *Battle Creek Enquirer*, November 14, 1982, A-9.

59. Steve Pond, "Springsteen and Others Rally to Help Vets," *Rolling Stone*, October 1, 1981, https://www.rollingstone.com/music/music-news/springsteen-others-rally-to-help-vets-194744/ ; James Coates, "Beleaguered Vietnam Vets Group Fighting for Its Life," *Chicago Tribune*, May 23, 1982, 10; *New York Daily News*, May 30, 1982, 102.

60. Jan Barry, Basil T. Paquet, and Larry Rottmann, eds., *Winning Hearts and Minds: War Poems by Vietnam Veterans* (Brooklyn, NY: First Casualty Press/McGraw-Hill, 1972).

61. Wayne Karlin, Basil T. Paquet, and Larry Rottmann, eds., *Free Fire Zone: Short Stories by Vietnam Veterans* (New York: McGraw-Hill, 1973).

62. Tim O'Brien, *If I Die in a Combat Zone, Box Me Up and Ship Me Home* (New York: Delacorte Press, 1973).

63. Ron Kovic, *Born on the Fourth of July* (New York: McGraw-Hill, 1976).

64. Philip Caputo, *A Rumor of War* (New York: Holt Rinehart Winston, 1977); Michael Herr, *Dispatches* (New York: Knopf, 1977).

65. *Los Angeles Times Magazine*, April 15, 1990, 26; Bruce Weber, "Michael Herr, Author of a Vietnam Classic, Dies at 76," *New York Times*, June 24, 2016, A18.

66. John Leonard, "Books of the Times: *Dispatches*," *New York Times*, October 28, 1977, C27.

67. Michael Herr, *Dispatches* (New York: Anchor Books Edition, 1998), 209.

68. James Webb, *Fields of Fire* (Englewood Cliffs, NJ: Prentice-Hall, 1978), 233–34.

69. Tim O'Brien, *The Things They Carried* (New York: Broadway Books, 1998), 69. This book, O'Brien's most influential and acclaimed, was first published in 1990.

70. Robert D. Schulzinger, *A Time for Peace: The Legacy of the Vietnam War* (New York: Oxford University Press, 2006), 151.

71. Santoli, *Everything We Had*; Santoli, *To Bear Any Burden*; Mark Baker, *Nam: The Vietnam War in the Words of the Men and Women Who Fought There* (New York: Berkley, 1983); Wallace Terry, *Bloods: An Oral History of the Vietnam War by Black Veterans* (New York: Random House, 1984); Keith Walker, *A Piece of My Heart: The Stories of 26 American Women Who Served in Vietnam* (Novato, CA: Presidio Press, 1986); Charley Trujillo, *Soldados: Chicanos in Viet Nam* (San Jose, CA: Chusma House, 1990).

72. Studs Terkel, *Hard Times: An Oral History of the Great Depression* (New York: Pantheon, 1970); Studs Terkel, *Working: People Talk about What They Do All Day and How They Feel about What They Do* (New York: Pantheon, 1974); Studs Terkel, *"The Good War": An Oral History of World War II* (New York: Pantheon, 1984).

73. *New York Magazine*, December 8, 1986, 66.

74. Key works on Oliver Stone include Norman Kagan, *The Cinema of Oliver Stone* (New York: Continuum International Publishing Group, 2000); Susan Mackey Kallis, *Oliver Stone's America: Dreaming the Myth Outward* (Boulder, CO: Westview Press, 1996); James Riordan, *Stone: The Controversies, Excesses, and Exploits of a Radical Filmmaker* (New York: Hyperion, 1995); Ian Scott and Henry Thompson, *The Cinema of Oliver Stone: Art, Authorship and Activism* (Manchester: Manchester University Press, 2016); and Robert Brent Toplin, *Oliver Stone's USA: Film, History, and Controversy* (Lawrence: University Press of Kansas, 2000).

75. Charles L. P. Silet, *Oliver Stone: Interviews* (Jackson: University Press of Mississippi, 2001), 41.

76. *Baltimore Evening Sun*, January 14, 1987, 24.

77. *Platoon*, directed by Oliver Stone (New York: MGM Home Entertainment, 2011), DVD.

78. *New York Magazine*, December 8, 1986, 64.

79. Stone, *Platoon*.
80. Pat H. Broeske, "Drawing Flak from Norris," Calendar, *Los Angeles Times*, January 25, 1987, 3.
81. *Hartford Courant*, May 28, 1988, E2.
82. *Akron Beacon Journal*, November 11, 1992, A2.
83. *Boston Globe*, December 28, 1989, 48.
84. *Hartford Courant*, February 9, 1989, A17.
85. Lynda Van Devanter, *Home before Morning* (New York: Beaufort Books, 1983).
86. William Broyles Jr., *Brothers in Arms: A Journey from War to Peace* (New York: Knopf, 1986), 275.

Chapter 4: Seeing Reds

1. Peter Biskind, *Easy Riders, Raging Bulls: How the Sex-Drugs-and-Rock 'n' Roll Generation Saved Hollywood* (New York: Simon & Schuster, 2011), 364. Interestingly, in his biography of Warren Beatty, *Star: How Warren Beatty Seduced America* (New York: Simon & Schuster, 2010), Biskind portrays Diller as more supportive of Beatty's efforts to make *Reds* than he does in *Easy Riders, Raging Bulls*. The Diller quote from *Easy Riders, Raging Bulls* is nowhere to be found in *Star*, which portrays Diller as backing Beatty and the actor going to Charles Bluhdorn to get his blessing. For a detailed chapter on the making of *Reds*, see Biskind, *Star*, 269–303.
2. Robert Sam Anson, "Hurricane Charlie," *Vanity Fair*, April 2001, 308.
3. Peter Biskind, "Thunder on the Left: The Making of Reds," *Vanity Fair*, March 2006, 344–59.
4. *Reds*, directed by Warren Beatty (New York: Paramount Home Entertainment, 2006), DVD.
5. John Reed, *Ten Days that Shook the World* (New York: Boni & Liveright, 1919). The book that Beatty used as a basis for *Reds* was historian Robert Rosenstone's *Romantic Revolutionary: A Biography of John Reed* (New York: Random House, 1975).
6. Steven J. Ross, *Hollywood Left and Right: How Movie Stars Shaped American Politics* (New York: Oxford University Press, 2011), 340.
7. Jonathan Rosenbaum, *Movies as Politics* (Berkeley: University of California Press, 1997), 112.
8. Ross, *Hollywood Left and Right*, 340.
9. Mark Weinberg, *Movie Nights with the Reagans: A Memoir* (New York: Simon & Schuster, 2018), 165. See also Biskind, "Thunder on the Left," 359.
10. For membership figures in the 1980s, see Michael T. Kaufman, "For Gus Hall, the Fight Is Good, if Not the Fortune," *New York Times*, January 24, 1989, A11. For the 1939 figure of one hundred thousand, see Harvey Klehr, John Earl Haynes, and Fridrikh Igorevich Firsov, *The Secret World of American Communism* (New Haven, CT: Yale University Press, 1995), xxxii.
11. *New York Times*, January 24, 1989, A11.
12. Vivian Gornick, "To Be Young, Gifted and Red," *Mother Jones*, September–October 1983, 20.
13. Terry Lawson, "Seeing Red: Dayton Filmmakers 'Made the Outside World Come to Us,'" *Dayton Journal Herald*, October 8, 1983, 25.
14. *Seeing Red*, directed by Jim Klein and Julia Reichert (Newburgh, NY: New Day Films, 2000), DVD. Bill Bailey (1911–95) also appeared in *The Good Fight*, an acclaimed documentary about the American volunteers who fought in the Abraham Lincoln

Brigade against the fascists in Spain in the 1930s. Released in 1984, a year after *Seeing Red*, *The Good Fight* was codirected by Noel Buckner, Mary Dore, and Sam Sills. Bailey's lively autobiography, *The Kid From Hoboken*, was originally published in San Francisco by Circus Lithographic Prepress in 1993. It is available online at http://www.larkspring.com/Kid/Contents.html.

15. Dorothy Healey discussed her lifelong dedication to radical politics in her memoir, which she cowrote with historian Maurice Isserman, titled *Dorothy Healey Remembers: A Life in the American Communist Party* (New York: Oxford University Press, 1990), republished as a paperback under the title *California Red: A Life in the American Communist Party* (Urbana: University of Illinois Press, 1993). The Healey quotation here is from the film *Seeing Red* (1983).

16. Ironically, one of the few negative reviews of *Seeing Red*, written by historian Joshua B. Freeman, appeared in the leftist *Nation* magazine (October 29, 1983, 411-13).

17. A typical example was an afternoon and evening screening of *Seeing Red* at the Sheldon Memorial Art Gallery in Lincoln, Nebraska, on April 26, 1984. "Ms. Reichert will be present at the 7:30 p.m. screening to discuss her work with the audience," said an ad in the *Lincoln Journal Star*, April 26, 1984, 25.

18. Jack Garner, "A 'Red'-Hot Documentary Director," *Rochester Democrat and Chronicle*, October 12, 1984, 1C, 4C.

19. For a history of WACL, see Scott Anderson and Jon Lee Anderson, *Inside the League: The Shocking Expose of How Terrorists, Nazis, and Latin American Death Squads Have Infiltrated the World Anti-Communist League* (New York: Dodd, Mead, 1986).

20. There are surprisingly few works on the John Birch Society. To date, the only scholarly history of the organization is D. J. Mulloy's *The World of the John Birch Society: Conspiracy, Conservatism, and the Cold War* (Nashville, TN: Vanderbilt University Press, 2014). However, Claire Conner's *Wrapped in the Flag: A Personal History of America's Radical Right* (Boston: Beacon Press, 2013) combines scholarly and personal history in a compelling fashion to tell the JBS's story. A helpful brief overview of the organization can be found in Robert A. Goldberg, *Grassroots Resistance: Social Movements in Twentieth Century America*, 2nd ed. (Long Grove, IL: Waveland Press, 1996). For useful scholarly articles, see Eckard V. Toy Jr., "The Right Side of the 1960s: The Origins of the John Birch Society in the Pacific Northwest," *Oregon Historical Quarterly* 105, no. 2 (Summer 2004): 260-83, and Clyde Wilcox, "Sources of Support for the Old Right: A Comparison of the John Birch Society and the Christian Anti-Communism Crusade," *Social Science History* 12, no. 4 (Winter 1988): 429-49. These publications all focus on the JBS in its heyday of the late 1950s and 1960s, so the history of the JBS in the Reagan era has yet to be explored.

21. Suzanne Spring, "John Birch Society Clings to Its Beliefs," *Morning News* (Wilmington, DE), January 22, 1985, 7; Bob Dart, "John Birchers Stick to Old Ways," *Atlanta Constitution*, March 15, 1983, 14.

22. William D. Zaferos, "John Birch Society in 'Metamorphosis,'" *Appleton (WI) Post-Crescent*, April 7, 1985, 6.

23. James Brian McPherson, *The Conservative Resurgence and the Press: The Media's Role in the Rise of the Right* (Evanston, IL: Northwestern University Press, 2008), 131.

24. Emma A. Jane and Chris Fleming, *Modern Conspiracy: The Importance of Being Paranoid* (New York: Bloomsbury Academic, 2014), 46; *Jackson (TN) Sun*, January 21, 1985, 7.

25. Mathis Chazanov, "Defeated Scribner to Try Levine Again," *Los Angeles Times*, November 8, 1984, B3.

26. Mathis Chazanov, "Scribner Denies Any Ties to the John Birch Society," *Los Angeles Times*, November 1, 1984, B10.

27. Mike Barnicle, "A Traitor? Not So Fast," *Boston Globe*, October 22, 1984, 17.

28. Mike Barnicle, "A Traitor? Not So Fast," *Boston Globe*, October 22, 1984, 17.

29. Eileen McNamara, "Shamie Asked Birch Official to Meeting at His Plant in '75," *Boston Globe*, October 11, 1984, 1, 48.

30. *Boston Globe*, November 4, 1984, A26, and November 8, 1984, 43; Mathis Chazanov, "Defeated Scribner to Try Levine Again," *Los Angeles Times*, November 8, 1984, B1.

31. Informative scholarly histories of the Religious Right include Seth Dowland, *Family Values and the Rise of the Christian Right* (Philadelphia: University of Pennsylvania Press, 2015); Frances FitzGerald, *The Evangelicals: The Struggle to Shape America* (New York: Simon & Schuster, 2017); Emily S. Johnson, *This Is Our Message: Women's Leadership in the New Christian Right* (New York: Oxford University Press, 2019); Michael Lienesch, *Redeeming America: Piety and Politics in the New Christian Right* (Chapel Hill: University of North Carolina Press, 1993); William Martin, *With God on Our Side: The Rise of the Religious Right in America* (New York: Broadway Books, 1996); Clyde Wilcox and Carin Robinson, *Onward Christian Soldiers? The Religious Right in American Politics*, 4th ed. (Boulder, CO: Westview Press, 2011); and Daniel K. Williams, *God's Own Party: The Making of the Christian Right* (Oxford: Oxford University Press, 2010). Steven P. Miller, *The Age of Evangelicalism: America's Born-Again Years* (New York: Oxford University Press, 2014), covers a range of evangelical movements across the political spectrum from the 1970s to the presidency of Barack Obama.

32. Lienesch, *Redeeming America*, 48.

33. Jerry Falwell, *Armageddon and the Coming War with Russia* (self-pub., undated booklet, circa 1980); William M. Knoblauch, *Nuclear Freeze in a Cold War: The Reagan Administration, Cultural Activism, and the End of the Arms Race* (Amherst: University of Massachusetts Press, 2017), 4.

34. Robert Scheer, "Q&A: Falwell Doubts There'll Be Any More Witch Hunts," *Los Angeles Times*, March 4, 1981, 15.

35. Beth A. Fischer, *The Reagan Reversal: Foreign Policy and the End of the Cold War* (Columbia: University of Missouri Press, 2013), 107.

36. Lienesch, *Redeeming America*, 48.

37. Jeremy R. Hatfield, "For God and Country: The Religious Right, the Reagan Administration, and the Cold War" (PhD diss., Ohio University, 2013), 56, ProQuest (3708273); Christopher K. Seely, "Fighting the Good Fight: The Religious Right and American Foreign Policy since World War II" (PhD diss., Boston University, 2013), 16–17, ProQuest (3564315); Roger Bruns, *Billy Graham: A Biography* (Westport, CT: Greenwood Press, 2004), 55.

38. John F. Burns, "Billy Graham, Defying Critics, Journeys to Soviet," *New York Times*, May 8, 1982, 2.

39. Serge Schmemann, "Graham Preaches at Church in Moscow," *New York Times*, May 10, 1982, A3.

40. *St. Louis Post-Dispatch*, May 13, 1982, 17.

41. Vladimir Markov, "Soviet Reporter Writes about Graham's Visit," *Shreveport Times*, May 18, 1982, 12.

42. Charles Austin, "Reaction Is Mixed on Graham," *New York Times*, May 13, 1982, A7.

43. Abraham H. Foxman, "The Kremlin's Debt to Billy Graham, *New York Times*, May 19, 1982, A26.

44. *St Louis Post-Dispatch*, May 14, 1982, 8D.

45. William Buckley, "Rebuke for the Rev. Graham," *San Francisco Chronicle*, May 18, 1982, 16.

46. George W. Cornell, "Religious Leaders Defend Evangelist," *San Francisco Chronicle*, July 3, 1982, 6.

47. Wesley G. Pippert, "New Crusade for Billy Graham: World Peace," *San Francisco Chronicle*, July 3, 1982, 6.

48. Seely, "Fighting the Good Fight," 80.

49. Charles Krauthammer, "Dangerous Religion," *Philadelphia Daily News*, October 17, 1986, 114.

50. *Windsor (ON) Star*, June 17, 1985, D7.

51. John Lofton, "'Secular Humanism,' Textbooks at Issue," *St. Louis Post-Dispatch*, October 18, 1987, 4B.

52. *Ithaca (NY) Journal*, January 15, 1985, 14.

53. Seely, "Fighting the Good Fight," 81; *Boston Globe*, May 26, 1985, A18.

54. Richard P. McBrien, *Caesar's Coin: Religion and Politics in America* (New York: Macmillan, 1987), 109.

55. Jeanne Pugh, "The Humanist Counterattack," *St. Petersburg (FL) Times*, November 30, 1985, 80.

56. Jeffrey K. Hadden, "The Rise and Fall of American Televangelism," *Annals of the American Academy of Political and Social Science* 527 (May 1993): 113–30.

57. *Los Angeles Times*, May 21, 1988, Part II, 6; Hadden, "American Televangelism," 126; David Niose, *Nonbeliever Nation: The Rise of Secular Americans* (New York: Palgrave Macmillan, 2012), 20.

58. Alex Klein, "Outmoded or Invaluable?," *Tampa Tribune*, March 10, 1983, 6-B.

59. Bob Morris, "Comrade Bob Recalls Communism Lesson," *Orlando Sentinel*, September 11, 1991, 11.

60. David Lee McMullen, "An Idea as Old as the Cold War," *Tampa Bay Times*, December 17, 2014, 11A.

61. *Miami News*, April 26, 1983, 30.

62. *Tampa Tribune*, March 10, 1983, 6-B, and June 5, 1983, 3-B.

63. *Fort Myers News-Press*, June 1, 1983, 5B.

64. Campbell F. Scribner, "'Make Your Voice Heard': Communism in the High School Curriculum, 1958–1968," *History of Education Quarterly* 52, no. 3 (August 2012): 368.

65. Aryeh Neier, "Comments," *Nation*, February 27, 1982, 232.

66. Norman Cousins, "East/West View," Book Review, *Los Angeles Times*, February 15, 1981, 3; *Ithaca Journal*, November 29, 1986, 12.

67. To add to the confusion, Vladimir Pozner also had a cousin with his same name who was a noted Soviet novelist and translator.

68. For Vladimir Pozner's fascinating story, see his autobiography, *Parting with Illusions* (New York: Atlantic Monthly Press, 1990).

69. *Wilkes-Barre Citizens' Voice*, September 30, 1981, 42.

70. Michael Harrington and Irving Howe, "Voices from the Left," *New York Times Magazine*, June 17, 1984, 24–26.

71. Susan Sontag, "Communism and the Left," *Nation*, February 27, 1982, 231.

72. Mitford quoted in James Lardner, "Susan Sontag Makes a Little Trouble," *Washington Post*, March 16, 1982, C9.

73. Christopher Hitchens, "Comments," *Nation*, February 27, 1982, 232; Christopher Hitchens, "Poland and the U.S. Left," *Spectator*, March 6, 1982, 248.

74. *Washington Post*, March 16, 1982, C9; Lisa Paddock and Carl Rollyson, *Susan Sontag: The Making of an Icon*, rev. and updated (Jackson: University Press of Mississippi), 224.

75. William F. Buckley Jr., "Sontag Sees Red—Clearly," *Washington Post*, March 5, 1982, A7; Jeffrey Hart, "A Prodigal's Return," *Indianapolis Star*, March 16, 1982, 8; John Chamberlain, "Why Do Liberals Ignore the Repentant Sinners?," *Human Events*, April 10, 1982, 42.

76. *Rocky IV*, directed by Sylvester Stallone (New York: MGM Home Video, 1997), DVD.

77. Patrick Taggart, "Dark Side of 'Red Dawn,'" *Austin American-Statesman*, September 7, 1984, C1, C8.

78. *Green Bay Press-Gazette*, August 28, 1984, 8.

79. *Los Angeles Times*, September 19, 1985, 75; *Red Dawn*, directed by John Milius (New York: MGM Home Video, 2005).

80. *Arizona Republic*, September 5, 1984, E2.

81. According to figures from Box Office Mojo, *Red Dawn* grossed $38,376,497 in 1984 to $40,382,659 for *Reds* in 1981. For 1981 figures, see https://www.boxofficemojo.com/yearly/chart/?yr=1981&p=.htm. For 1984 figures, see https://www.boxofficemojo.com/yearly/chart/?yr=1984&p=.htm. Admittedly, 1984 was a robust year for block-busters, with a number of smash hits flooding the theaters in the summer, including *Ghostbusters, Indiana Jones and the Temple of Doom, Gremlins*, and *The Karate Kid*. The year ended off with another massive commercial success, *Beverly Hills Cop*.

82. Several newspaper stories about *Red Dawn* from August 1984 discuss young filmgoers cheering in theaters. For example, as one theater patron described a screening in the *Statesman Journal* (Salem, OR), August 19, 1984, 2: "There were high moments where people were shouting 'Wolverines!'"

Chapter 5: No Nukes

1. Brian Kates, "See N-Rally as Largest Ever in U.S.," *New York Daily News*, June 12, 1982, 5.

2. Given that it was the largest single protest in U.S. history, surprisingly little has been written about the rally and march for nuclear disarmament. The challenges involved in organizing such a large event are covered in Kyle Harvey, *American Antinuclear Activism, 1975–1990: The Challenge of Peace* (New York: Palgrave Macmillan, 2014), 32–40. Bradford Martin, *The Other Eighties: A Secret History of America in the Age of Reagan* (New York: Hill and Wang, 2011), 3–5, examines the event briefly in the opening pages to his first chapter, treating the protest as the movement's high point preceding its decline. William M. Knoblauch also briefly mentions the march in *Nuclear Freeze in a Cold War: The Reagan Administration, Cultural Activism, and the End of the Arms Race* (Amherst: University of Massachusetts Press, 2017), 23–24. Most other accounts of the Reagan years, even those written from a leftist perspective, ignore that this protest gathering occurred under Reagan's presidency. As of this writing, Vincent Intondi, associate professor of history at Montgomery College, is writing a book about the event.

3. Robert D. McFadden, "A Spectrum of Humanity Represented at the Rally," *New York Times*, June 13, 1982, 42.

4. Michael Oreskes, "From a Business View, March Had a Big Impact," *New York Times*, June 13, 1982, 42.

5. *The Record* (Hackensack, NJ), June 13, 1982, A-22.

6. Welles is quoted in Jane O'Hara, "Weapons Protest on Parade, *Maclean's*, June 21, 1982, 23. See also the *Boston Globe*, June 13, 1982, 1.

7. Welles is quoted in John J. Goldman and Doyle McManus, "Largest Ever U.S. Rally Protests Nuclear Arms, *Los Angeles Times*, June 13, 1982, 1.

8. Linda Case, "Colorful Celebration with a Serious Message," *Hartford Courant*, June 15, 1982, 15.

9. *Newark Advocate*, June 21, 1982, 4.

10. *Rochester Democrat and Chronicle*, June 13, 1983, 2.

11. Paul Harvey, "None Want Nuclear War," *Newark Advocate*, November 21, 1982, 4; William F. Buckley, "Better a Cold War Than a Hot One," *Detroit Free Press*, June 22, 1982, 9.

12. Toward the end of 1979, Asylum Records released an LP of the No Nukes concert titled *No Nukes: The Muse Concerts for a Non-Nuclear Future*, produced by event organizers Jackson Browne, John Hall, Graham Nash, and Bonnie Raitt.

13. Dr. Randall Forsberg, *Call to Halt the Arms Race* (1979), Institute for Defense and Disarmament Studies Records, 1974–2007, box 20, folder 90, Rare and Manuscript Collections, Cornell University Library, Cornell University, Ithaca, NY.

14. Martin, *The Other Eighties*, 7.

15. Jonathan Schell, "The Spirit of June 12," *Nation*, July 2, 2007, 4–5; Lawrence S. Wittner, "The Nuclear Freeze and Its Impact," published on the Arms Control Association website, December 5, 2010, https://www.armscontrol.org/act/2010_12/LookingBack.

16. K. Harvey, *American Antinuclear Activism*, 30.

17. Harvey, 31.

18. Bulletin of the Atomic Scientists maintains a historical timeline of the Doomsday Clock on its website at https://thebulletin.org/doomsday-clock/past-announcements/.

19. "Three Minutes to Midnight," editorial, *Bulletin of the Atomic Scientists* 40, no. 1 (January 1984): 2.

20. "Three Minutes to Midnight," 2.

21. Knoblauch, *Nuclear Freeze*, 11.

22. Jonathan Schell, *The Fate of the Earth* (New York: Knopf, 1982), 21.

23. Knoblauch, *Nuclear Freeze*, 17. Surprisingly, Schell refused to go on a nationwide tour and would not appear on television or radio shows to promote *The Fate of the Earth*. See Herbert Mitgang, "How Theodore White Makes a Best-Seller," *New York Times*, July 24, 1982, 9.

24. Helen Caldicott, *Nuclear Madness: What You Can Do!*, rev. ed. (New York: Bantam Books, 1980), 3; Helen Caldicott, *Missile Envy: The Arms Race and Nuclear War* (New York: William Morrow, 1984), 3.

25. Quoted in Mary Kathryn Neal, "Balancing Passion and Reason: A Symbolic Analysis of the Communication Strategies of the Physicians' Movement against Nuclear Weapons" (PhD diss., University of California, San Francisco, 1988), 294, ProQuest (8824679).

26. Scheer's book took its title from Scheer's interview with T. K. Jones, Reagan's deputy undersecretary of defense, who expressed the controversial view that Americans could win a nuclear war by constructing shelters. "If there are enough shovels to go around," Jones told Scheer, "everybody's going to make it." Jones's instructions to survive a nuclear strike were simple: "Dig a hole, cover it with a couple of doors

and then throw three feet of dirt on top. It's the dirt that does it." Quoted in Robert Scheer, *With Enough Shovels: Reagan, Bush, and Nuclear War* (New York: Random House, 1983), 18. See also Sam Roberts, "T. K. Jones, 82, Dies; Arms Official Saw Nuclear War as Survivable," *New York Times*, May 23, 2015, A18.

27. Scheer, *With Enough Shovels*, 3, 24.

28. Scheer, 262, 140, 111.

29. *Akron Beacon-Journal*, April 2, 1982, 6.

30. Richard E. Meyer, "Bush Charges That He Was Misquoted, Denies Saying Nuclear War Can Be Won," *Los Angeles Times*, September 11, 1980, 16. Three years before the publication of *With Enough Shovels*, Scheer's interview with Bush appeared in the *Los Angeles Times*, the same interview the author later used in *With Enough Shovels*. When *New York Times* columnist Anthony Lewis quoted Scheer's interview in the summer of 1980, reporters brought it to Bush's attention, and he denied making the comments that Scheer attributed to him. This was the topic of Meyer's *Los Angeles Times* story cited above. Scheer, however, had kept tapes of his interviews. Interestingly, on publication of *With Enough Shovels* in 1983, Bush made no attempt to refute Scheer's quotes in the book. Opting for silence instead, Bush perhaps sensed that Scheer had evidence on his side.

31. Robert D. Clayton, *Life after Doomsday: A Survivalist Guide to Nuclear War and Other Major Disasters* (New York: Dial Press, 1980); Robert L. Cruit and Ronald L. Cruit, *Survive the Coming Nuclear War: How to Do It* (New York: Stein and Day, 1982); Cresson H. Kearny, *Nuclear War Survival Skills* (Aurora, IL: Caroline House Publishers, 1979); Barry Popkess, *The Nuclear Survival Handbook: Living through and after a Nuclear Attack* (New York: Collier Press, 1980).

32. Gaddis Smith, "Book Reviews," *Bulletin of the Atomic Scientists* 39, no. 6 (June/July 1983): 30.

33. William M. Knoblauch, "Selling the Second Cold War: Antinuclear Cultural Activism and Reagan Era Foreign Policy" (PhD diss., Ohio University, 2012), 53–54, ProQuest (3503950).

34. Wittner, "Nuclear Freeze and Its Impact."

35. *Detroit Free Press*, October 15, 1981, 6C.

36. Don Steinberg, "The Quarter Century," *Philadelphia Inquirer Magazine*, June 22, 1997, 24.

37. Ozzy Osbourne, "Crazy Train," recorded March 22, 1980, track 2 on *Blizzard of Ozz*, Jet Records, compact disc.

38. Iron Maiden, "Two Minutes to Midnight," recorded February–June 1984, track 2 on *Powerslave*, EMI/Capitol Records, 33 1/3 rpm.

39. Pete Bishop, "Queen Still King," *Pittsburgh Press*, May 13, 1984, L5; Queen, "Hammer to Fall," recorded January 8, 1984, track 8 on *The Works*, EMI/Capitol records, 33 1/3 rpm.

40. The Clash, "London Calling," recorded August–September 1979, track 1 on *London Calling*, CBS Records, vinyl LP.

41. Jonathan Kyle Williams, "'Rock against Reagan': The Punk Movement, Cultural Hegemony, and Reaganism in the Eighties" (master's thesis, University of Northern Iowa, 2016), 65.

42. Williams, "'Rock against Reagan,'" 51.

43. Ward Harkavy, "Musicians, Activists Are Gearing Up for 'Rock against Reagan' Festival," *Arizona Republic*, August 9, 1984, B4.

44. Time Zone, "World Destruction," recorded November 1984, track 1 on *World Destruction*, Celluloid Records, 12-inch vinyl LP.

45. For an outstanding history of British New Wave antinuclear pop, see William M. Knoblauch, "'Will You Sing about the Missiles?': British Antinuclear Protest Music of the 1980s," in *Nuclear Threats, Nuclear Fear and the Cold War of the 1980s*, ed. Eckart Conze, Martin Klimke, and Jeremy Varon (Cambridge: Cambridge University Press, 2017), 101–15; David Bowie, "Bombers," recorded July 9, 1971, released as 45 rpm promotional single in 1971, included on the reissue of *Hunky Dory* in 1990, RCA, compact disc.

46. Peter Gabriel, "Games without Frontiers," recorded 1979, track 7 on *Peter Gabriel*, Charisma Records (UK), Mercury Records (U.S.), compact disc.

47. Kate Bush, "Breathing," recorded 1980, track 3 on *Never for Ever*, EMI, compact disc.

48. Among the more successful examples were "Red Skies" and "Stand or Fall" by the Fixx (1982); "I Melt with You" (1982) by Modern English; "Seconds" (1983) by U2; "It's a Mistake" (1983) by Men at Work; "Forever Young" (1984) by Alphaville; "Two Tribes" (1984) by Frankie Goes to Hollywood; "Just Another Day" (1985) by Oingo Boingo; "Everybody Wants to Rule the World" and "Mothers Talk" (1985) by Tears for Fears; "The Future's So Bright, I Gotta Wear Shades" (1986) by Timbuk 3; and "Everyday Is Like Sunday" (1988) by former Smiths lead singer Morrissey, to name a few.

49. James Muretich, "Cute Tune about the Big Boom Propels Group," *Calgary Herald*, June 9, 1984, D1.

50. Nena, "99 Luftballons," recorded 1982, track 6 on *Nena*, CBS Records, vinyl LP.

51. For example, Neal Hall, "Nena Leads the German Rock Invasion, *Vancouver Sun*, March 14, 1984, D20.

52. Examples include Donald Fagen's *New Frontier* (1982); Jackson Browne's *Lawyers in Love* (1983); Depeche Mode's *"People Are People"* (1984); and Ultravox's *"Dancing with Tears in My Eyes* (1984), to name a few. Though not considered New Wave at the time, the music video for Elton John's 1985 song "Nikita," off of his nineteenth studio album, *Ice on Fire*, depicted the singer falling in love with a female communist border guard. The synthesizer solo in the song gave "Nikita" a New Wave feel, and the music video, directed by flamboyant British director Ken Russell, shows a happy yet ultimately doomed relationship between John and the title character, played by British model and athlete Anya Major.

53. Genesis, *Land of Confusion*, YouTube video, 5:28, September 18, 2014, https://www.youtube.com/watch?v=Yq7FKO5DlV0&list=PL9601729BF2F61761.

54. *Baltimore Sun*, January 25, 1987, 7E.

55. Melvin E. Matthews Jr., *Duck and Cover: Civil Defense Images in Film and Television from the Cold War to 9/11* (Jefferson, NC: McFarland, 2011), 166.

56. The three key works on the tensions of 1983 are Marc Ambinder, *The Brink: President Reagan and the Nuclear War Scare of 1983* (New York: Simon & Schuster, 2018); Taylor Downing, *1983: Reagan, Andropov, and a World on the Brink* (Cambridge, MA: Da Capo Press, 2018); and Nate Jones, ed., *Able Archer 83: The Secret History of the NATO Exercise That Almost Triggered Nuclear War* (New York: New Press, 2016).

57. Ronald Reagan, "Remarks at the Annual Convention of the National Association of Evangelicals in Orlando, Florida," in *The Columbia Documentary History of Religion in America since 1945*, ed. Paul Harvey and Philip Goff (New York: Columbia University Press, 2005), 71.

58. Albert J. Mauroni, *Countering Weapons of Mass Destruction: Assessing the U.S. Government's Policy* (Lanham, MD: Rowman & Littlefield, 2016), 80.

59. *Chicago Tribune*, March 24, 1983, 16.

60. Examples of this specific story can be found in the *Detroit Free Press*, June 1, 1984; *Pittsburgh Press*, January 29, 1984, 32; St. Louis Post-Dispatch, December 17, 1985, 17; *San Francisco Examiner*, September 24, 1985, 3; and *Casper (WY) Star Tribune*, August 22, 1984, D7.

61. This one-liner was said repeatedly about both President Reagan and Secretary of Defense Weinberger. For example, see Lee Byrd, "Weinberger No Budget 'Knife' Today," *Indianapolis Star*, October 13, 1985, 35. Marianne Means also made the quip about Reagan in her syndicated column in April 1987. See the *Asheville Citizen-Times*, April 13, 1987, 4.

62. Will Bunch, *Tear Down This Myth: How the Reagan Legacy Has Distorted Our Politics and Haunts Our Future* (New York: Free Press, 2009), 81. For the Pentagon figure, see George C. Herring, "The Cold War: Ending by Inadvertence," in *Between War and Peace: How America Ends Its Wars*, ed. Matthew Moten (New York: Free Press, 2011), 289, and Michael Schaller, *Reckoning with Reagan: America and Its President in the 1980s* (New York: Oxford University Press, 1994), 126. Schaller actually puts the figure at $30 million. Other accounts pinpoint that amount being spent in 1984 specifically. For example, see Michael Schaller, Robert D. Schulzinger, and Karen Anderson, *Present Tense: The United States since 1945*, 3rd ed. (New York: Houghton Mifflin, 2003), 464.

63. Anatoly Dobrynin, *In Confidence: Moscow's Ambassador to America's Six Cold War Presidents* (New York: Crown, 1995), 478, 532.

64. Matthew J. Ouimet, *The Rise and Fall of the Brezhnev Doctrine in Soviet Foreign Policy* (Chapel Hill: University of North Carolina Press, 1990), 95.

65. Fred Kaplan, "Missile Poker Game Gets Serious," *Boston Globe*, November 20, 1983, A33, A34.

66. Seymour M. Hersh, "007's Last Minutes," *New York Times*, August 11, 1986, E15.

67. Joseph H. Campos II, *The State and Terrorism: National Security and the Mobilization of Power* (New York: Routledge, 2016), 51–52.

68. Ambinder, *The Brink*, 171.

69. *Orlando Sentinel*, September 6, 1983, A-4.

70. *Hartford Courant*, September 8, 1983, A14.

71. Five years after KAL 007, on July 3, 1988, the American cruiser USS *Vincennes* shot down Iran Air Flight 655, an Airbus A300 civilian airliner, killing all 290 people on board. Iran Air 655 was flying over Iranian territory when the U.S. ship in the Strait of Hormuz mistook it for an F-14 Tomcat, a type of fighter jet that Washington had sent to Tehran in the 1970s while the Shah of Iran was still in power. In the days leading up to the incident, tensions had been running high in the region. Even though the Soviet Union condemned the downing of Flight 655, the attack did not provoke the same level of outrage in the U.S. media and among world leaders as the KAL 007 incident. Ultimately, President Reagan apologized on behalf of the United States for the downing Iran Air 655. However, the commander of the *Vincennes*, Captain William C. Rogers III, was awarded the Legion of Merit in 1990 for "outstanding service as commanding officer," which left the families and loved ones of the crash victims embittered. See David Evans, "One Must Question the Current Value of Military Medals," *Chicago Tribune*, April 6, 1990, 23.

72. The literature on the 1979 New Jewel Movement revolution in Grenada, as well as the 1983 American invasion of the island, is slim. Among the few academic titles on the topic are Peter Clegg, Patsy Lewis, and Gary Williams, eds., *Grenada: Revolution and Invasion* (Kingston, Jamaica: University of the West Indies Press, 2015); Manning Marable, *African and Caribbean Politics from Kwame Nkrumah to Maurice Bishop* (New York: Verso, 1987); and Ronald H. Spector, *U.S. Marines in Grenada, 1983* (Washington, D.C.: History and Museums Division Headquarters, United States Marine Corps, 1987). See also Gary Williams, "Prelude to an Intervention: Grenada 1983," *Journal of Latin American Studies* 29, no. 1 (February 1997), 131–69.

73. Peter Vincent Pry, *War Scare: Russia and America on the Nuclear Brink* (Westport, CT: Praeger, 1999), 37–38.

74. Fischer, *The Reagan Reversal: Foreign Policy and the End of the Cold War* (Columbia: University of Missouri Press, 2000), 123.

75. Jones, *Able Archer 83*, 2–3.

76. Sally Bedell Smith, "ABC to Show Nuclear War Drama in November, *New York Times*, September 3, 1983, 46.

77. Connie Koenenn, "Meyer: Making the Unthinkable Thinkable," *Los Angeles Times*, November 10, 1983, Part IV, 8.

78. Julianne Hastings, "Film 'My Civic Duty,' Says Director," *Vancouver Sun*, November 19, 1983, D3.

79. *Los Angeles Times*, November 10, 1983, Part IV, 8.

80. *South Bend Tribune*, November 20, 1983, 24.

81. *Los Angeles Times*, November 10, 1983, Part IV, 8.

82. *WarGames*, directed by John Badham (New York: MGM Home Entertainment, 2008), DVD.

83. *Santa Cruz Sentinel*, August 9, 1983, A11.

84. An advertisement for this panel appeared in the *St. Louis Post-Dispatch* on the day ABC showed the film, November 30, 1983, on page 38.

85. Ronald Reagan, *An American Life* (New York: Simon & Schuster, 1990), 585.

86. *The Day After*, directed by Nicholas Meyer (New York: KL Studio Classics, 2018), DVD.

87. For the three major public opinion polls about *The Day After* and their findings, see Stanley Feldman and Lee Sigelman, "The Political Impact of Prime-Time Television: *The Day After*," *Journal of Politics* 47, no. 2 (June 1985): 556–78 (quotation on 557); Steven F. Hayward, *The Age of Reagan: The Conservative Counterrevolution, 1980–1989* (New York: Crown Forum, 2009), 335.

88. Feldman and Sigelman, "Political Impact," 557–58.

89. *Rapid City (SD) Journal*, November 18, 1983, 14.

90. Lee Winfrey, "'The Day After' Arrives as Debate Rages over Its Impact," *Philadelphia Inquirer*, November 20, 1983, 13K.

91. Ben Stein's *Los Angeles Herald Examiner* column is discussed in Marc Gunther, "ABC Wages Long Battle to Bring 'America' to TV," *Palm Springs Desert Sun*, February 14, 1987, A7.

92. Nielsen ratings show episodes 5 and 6 plunging to 41st and 44th place, respectively, during the week in which they were showing, out of a total of 64 television shows. See *Dee Moines Register*, March 1, 1987, 71.

93. Andrew Kopkind, *The Thirty Years' Wars: Dispatches and Diversions of a Radical Journalist, 1965-1994* (New York: Verso, 1995), 412.

94. Richard Rhodes, *Arsenals of Folly: The Making of the Nuclear Arms Race* (New York: Vintage Books, 2008), 170.
95. *Galveston Daily News*, November 22, 1983, 10-A.
96. Fischer, *Reagan Reversal*, 121–22.
97. Bunch, *Tear Down This Myth*, 75.
98. Nicholas Meyer, *The View from the Bridge: Memories of "Star Trek" and a Life in Hollywood* (New York: Viking, 2009), 150–56.
99. Feldman and Sigelman, "Political Impact," 557.

Chapter 6: The Wars for Central America

1. Karen DeYoung, "Nicaraguans Rejoice at War's End," *Washington Post*, July 20, 1979, A18.
2. Key works on Nicaragua and the Cold War, as well as the Sandinista Revolution of 1979, include George Black, *Triumph of the People: The Sandinista Revolution in Nicaragua* (London: Zed Books, 1983); Peter Davis, *Where Is Nicaragua?* (New York: Touchstone, 1988); David Francois, *Nicaragua, 1961–1990*, vol. 1, *The Downfall of the Somoza Dictatorship* (Warwick, U.K.: Helion and Company, 2019); Michael D. Gambone, *Capturing the Revolution: The United States, Central America, and Nicaragua, 1961–1972* (Westport, CT: Praeger, 2001); Michael D. Gambone, *Eisenhower, Somoza, and the Cold War in Nicaragua: 1953–1961* (Westport, CT: Praeger, 1997); Stephen Kinzer, *Blood of Brothers: Life and War in Nicaragua* (Cambridge, MA: Harvard University Press, 2007); Susan Meiselas, *Nicaragua* (New York: Pantheon, 1981); Mauricio Solaún, *U.S. Intervention and Regime Change in Nicaragua* (Lincoln: University of Nebraska Press, 2005); Henri Weber, *Nicaragua: The Sandinist Revolution* (London: Verso, 1981); and Matilde Zimmermann, *Sandinista: Carlos Fonseca and the Nicaraguan Revolution* (Durham, NC: Duke University Press, 2001).
3. Ray Holton, "Church Leaders Playing Important Role in New Nicaragua: Repression by Somoza Government Led to Support of Sandinistas," *Washington Post*, August 17, 1979, D16.
4. Larry Rohter, "El Salvador's Stolen Children Face a War's Darkest Secret," *New York Times*, August 5, 1996, A1; Associated Press, "El Salvador's Military Not Opening Archives for Missing Kids," Voice of America News website, February 27, 2018, https://www.voanews.com/a/el-salvador-missing-kids/4272321.html.
5. Erik Ching, *Stories of Civil War in El Salvador: A Battle over Memory* (Chapel Hill: University of North Carolina Press, 2016), 165–66.
6. Rafael Garcilazo, "An Interview with Fr. Paul Schindler," Christians for Peace in El Salvador website, https://myemail.constantcontact.com/AN-INTERVIEW-WITH-FR--PAUL-SCHINDLER.html?soid=1103630347429&aid=bvivsocPsyw.
7. David Wiley, *The Promise of Francis: The Man, the Pope, and the Challenge of Change* (New York: Gallery Books, 2015), 262.
8. There are a number of books on Archbishop Óscar Romero, nearly all of them sympathetic to the man and his teachings. The definitive account of his murder and its subsequent investigation is Matt Eisenbrandt's *Assassination of a Saint: The Plot to Murder Óscar Romero and the Quest to Bring His Killers to Justice* (Berkeley: University of California Press, 2017).

9. Russell Crandall, *The Salvador Option: The United States in El Salvador, 1977–1992* (Cambridge: Cambridge University Press, 2016), 161.

10. For more on the four American Catholic missionaries murdered in El Salvador in December 1980, see Ana Carrigan, *Salvador Witness: The Life and Calling of Jean Donovan* (Maryknoll, NY: Orbis Books, 2005); Donna Whitson Brett and Edward T. Brett, *Martyrs of Hope: Seven U.S. Missioners in Central America* (Maryknoll, NY: Orbis Books, 2018); Cynthia Glavac, *In the Fullness of Life: A Biography of Dorothy Kazel, O.S.U.* (Denville, NJ: Dimension Books, 1996); and Eileen Markey, *A Radical Faith: The Assassination of Sister Maura* (New York: Nation Books, 2016).

11. Crandall, *Salvador Option*, 163.

12. Hauke Hartmann, "U.S. Human Rights Policy under Carter and Reagan, 1977–1981," *Human Rights Quarterly* 23, no. 2 (May 2001): 419–22.

13. Jason M. Colby, "Reagan and Central American," in *A Companion to Ronald Reagan*, ed. Andrew Johns (Hoboken, NJ: Wiley-Blackwell, 2015), 434. As Colby notes, Reagan frequently referred to Central America as "our backyard" in speeches, memos, and other forms of communication.

14. Penny Lernoux, *Hearts on Fire: The Story of the Maryknoll Sisters* (Maryknoll, NY: Orbis Books, 2011), 237.

15. Doug Rossinow, *The Reagan Era: A History of the 1980s* (New York: Columbia University Press, 2015), 296–97.

16. William M. LeoGrande, *Our Own Backyard: The United States in Central America, 1977–1992* (Chapel Hill: University of North Carolina Press, 1998), 285.

17. Gerald M. Boyd, "Reagan Terms Nicaraguan Rebels 'Moral Equal of Founding Fathers,'" *New York Times*, March 2, 1985, 1.

18. Contra terrorism was extensively documented in the 1980s by human rights organizations and advocates. One of the most important books on the subject was that of Human Rights lawyer Reed Brody, *Contra Terror in Nicaragua: Report of a Fact-Finding Mission, September 1984–January 1985* (Boston: South End Press, 1985). Other important works on Contra terrorism include Americas Watch Committee, *Human Rights in Nicaragua: 1985–1986* (New York: Americas Watch Committee, 1987); Teófilo Cabestrero, *Blood of the Innocent: Victims of the Contras' War in Nicaragua* (Maryknoll, NY: Orbis Books, 1985); Edgar Chamorro, *Packaging the Contras: A Case of CIA Disinformation* (New York: Institute for Media Analysis, 1987); Leslie Cockburn, *Out of Control: The Story of the Reagan Administration's Secret War in Nicaragua, the Illegal Arms Pipeline, and the Contra Drug Connection* (New York: Atlantic Monthly Press, 1987); Roxanne Dunbar-Ortiz, *Blood on the Border: A Memoir of the Contra War* (Norman: University of Oklahoma Press, 2005); and Holly Sklar, *Washington's War on Nicaragua* (Boston: South End Press, 1988).

19. Regional histories of Central America, often with a focus on the impact of U.S. policies on the region, include Cynthia Arnson, *Crossroads: Congress, the President, and Central America, 1976–1993*, 2nd ed. (University Park: Pennsylvania State University Press, 1993); John A. Booth, Christine J. Wade, and Thomas Walker, *Understanding Central America: Global Forces, Rebellion, and Change*, 6th ed. (New York: Routledge, 2014); Walter LaFeber, *Inevitable Revolutions: The United States in Central America*, 2nd ed. (New York: W. W. Norton, 1993); William M. LeoGrande, *Our Own Backyard: The United States in Central America, 1977–1992* (Chapel Hill: University of North Carolina Press, 1998); and Thomas L. Pearcy, *The History of Central America* (New York: St. Martin's Griffin, 2006).

20. Jean-Marie Simon, *Guatemala: Eternal Spring, Eternal Tyranny* (New York: W. W. Norton, 1987), 149. For a superb snapshot of Honduras in the early 1980s, see Gordon Dillow, "Honduras, 'Even the Rich Are Poor,'" *San Francisco Examiner*, July 29, 1982, A8.

21. Julia Preston, "With U.S. Help, Honduras Is Upgrading Its Military," *Baltimore Evening Sun*, August 18, 1982, E1.

22. Rick Ratliff, "Protesters Hope Plans Will Avert Invasion," *Detroit Free Press*, December 30, 1984, 2A.

23. Bradford Martin, *The Other Eighties: A Secret History of America in the Age of Reagan* (New York: Hill and Wang, 2011), 27.

24. Christian Smith, *Resisting Reagan: The U.S. Central America Peace Movement* (Chicago: University of Chicago Press, 1996), 387. Héctor Perla Jr., a former professor of Latin American and Latino studies at the University of California, Santa Cruz, actually placed the number of such organizations at "more than 2,000," but his main citation was Smith's *Resisting Reagan*, which placed the figure between 1,500 and 2,000. See Héctor Perla Jr., "Heirs of Sandino: The Nicaraguan Revolution and the U.S.-Nicaragua Solidarity Movement," *Latin American Perspectives* 36, no. 6 (November 2009): 82.

25. Perla, "Heirs of Sandino," 86–87.

26. Sara Bentley, "Salvadoran Coalition Is Not a 'Marxist Guerilla Group,'" *La Crosse Tribune*, May 17, 1981, 7.

27. *El Salvador: Another Vietnam*, directed by Glenn Silber and Teté Vasconcellos (New York: Icarus Films, 1981), VHS.

28. Charlie Clements, *Witness to War: An American Doctor in El Salvador* (New York: Bantam, 1984); *Witness to War: Dr. Charlie Clements*, directed by Deborah Shaffer (Newburgh, NY: New Day Films, 1985), DVD; Dan Geringer, "A Tale of Two Wars," *Philadelphia Daily News*, March 17, 1986, 41.

29. Raymond Bonner, "Massacre of Hundreds Reported in Salvador Village," *New York Times*, January 27, 1982, A1; Raymond Bonner, "What Did Elliott Abrams Have to Do with the El Mozote Massacre?," *Atlantic*, February 11, 1989, https://www.theatlantic. com/ideas/archive/2019/02/ilhan-omar-elliott-abrams-and-el-mozote-massacre /582889/; Alma Guillermoprieto, "Salvadoran Peasants Describe Mass Killings," *Washington Post*, January 27, 1982, 1.

30. BBC News, "El Salvador Head Apologises for 1981 El Mozote Massacre," January 17, 2012, https://www.bbc.com/news/world-latin-america-16589757. The classic account of the large-scale bloodletting at El Mozote is Mark Danner's *The Massacre at El Mozote* (New York: Vintage, 1994). See also Leigh Binford, *The El Mozote Massacre: Anthropology and Human Rights* (Tucson: University of Arizona Press, 1996).

31. Rachel Ovryn Rivera, "A Question of Conscience: The Emergence and Development of the Sanctuary Movement in the United States" (PhD diss., City University of New York, 1987), 25, ProQuest (8708312).

32. Rivera, "Question of Conscience," 47.

33. Michael D. Matters, "The Sanctuary Movement, 1980–1988: An Organizational Analysis of Structures and Cultures" (PhD diss., University of Illinois at Chicago, 1994), viii–ix, ProQuest (9516685).

34. Andy Hall, Pete Schlueter, and Doyle Sanders, "Road to Freedom: The Flight from Central America," *Arizona Republic*, August 26, 1984, 4.

35. Martha L. Man, "They Leave behind Memories of Violence-Torn Countries," *Albuquerque Journal*, September 2, 1984, A-5.

36. Mike McLeod, "'El Norte' Is the Film That Almost Wasn't," *Cincinnati Enquirer*, May 1, 1984, D-8.

37. Roger Ebert, "'El Norte' Is Simple, Honest, Great," *Poughkeepsie Journal*, June 1, 1984, 44.

38. McLeod, "'El Norte,'" D-1.

39. *St. Louis Post-Dispatch*, July 4, 1984, 77.

40. *El Norte*, directed by Gregory Nava (New York City: Criterion Collection, 2009), DVD.

41. *St. Louis Post-Dispatch*, July 4, 1984, 77.

42. These figures come from "U.S. Aid to the Contras: The Record since '81," *New York Times*, March 20, 1986, A8. One of the few books about the Contra war that adopts the Reagan administration's position that the Contras represented an authentic, homegrown peasant army fueled by resentments against the Sandinistas is Timothy C. Brown's *The Real Contra War: Highlander Peasant Resistance in Nicaragua* (Norman: University of Oklahoma Press, 2001). Brown, a senior liaison between the State Department and the Contras from 1987 to 1990, maintains a strongly sympathetic view of the Contras in this account. Other books slanted toward a more pro–Reagan administration perspective of the conflict include Sam Dillon, *Commandos: The CIA and Nicaragua's Contra Rebels* (New York: Henry Holt, 1991); Robert Kagan, *The Twilight Struggle: American Power and Nicaragua, 1977–1990* (New York: Free Press, 1996); Roger Miranda and William Ratliff, *The Civil War in Nicaragua: Inside the Sandinistas* (New Brunswick, NJ: Transaction Publishers, 1993); and R. Pardo-Maurer, *The Contras, 1980–1989: A Special Kind of Politics* (Westport, CT: Praeger, 1990).

43. Brody, *Contra Terror in Nicaragua*, 10. The Defense Intelligence Agency description of the Contras as a "terrorist" organization was widely reported in the press in August 1983. For example, see "U.S. Report Called Nicaraguan Contras 'Terrorists,'" *Morristown Daily Record*, August 22, 1983, 5.

44. *San Francisco Examiner*, October 6, 1986, A6; Seth Rosenfeld, "Cranston Asking Senate to Probe Contra-Cocaine Link," *San Francisco Examiner*, March 19, 1986, A12.

45. *Des Moines Register*, May 31, 1984, 6A.

46. For more on the 1986 World Court ruling, see James Phillips, "When Governments Fail: Reparation, Solidarity, and Community in Nicaragua," in *Waging War, Making Peace: Reparations and Human Rights*, ed. Barbara Rose Johnson and Susan Slyomovics (Walnut Creek, CA: Left Coast Press, 2009), 57–74. Essential volumes on the Iran-Contra scandal include Robert Busby, *Reagan and the Iran-Contra Affair: The Politics of Presidential Recovery* (New York: St. Martin's Press, 1999); Malcolm Byrne, *Iran-Contra: Reagan's Scandal and the Unchecked Abuse of Presidential Power* (Lawrence: University Press of Kansas, 2014); Theodore Draper, *A Very Thin Line: The Iran-Contra Affairs* (New York: Hill and Wang, 1991); Michael E. Lynch and David Bogen, eds., *The Spectacle of History: Speech, Text, and Memory at the Iran-Contra Hearings* (Durham, NC: Duke University Press, 1996); David Thelen, *Becoming Citizens in the Age of Television: How Americans Challenged the Media and Seized Political Initiative during the Iran-Contra Debate* (Chicago: University of Chicago Press, 1996); Lawrence E. Walsh, *Firewall: The Iran-Contra Conspiracy and Cover-Up* (New York: W. W. Norton, 1998); and Ann Wroe, *Lives, Lies and the Iran-Contra Affair* (London: I. B. Tauris, 1992).

47. Patrick Hagopian, *The Vietnam War in American Memory: Veterans, Memorials, and the Politics of Healing* (Amherst: University of Massachusetts Press, 2009), 44–45.

48. Richard Sobel, *Public Opinion in U.S. Foreign Policy: The Controversy over Contra Aid* (Lanham, MD: Rowman & Littlefield, 1993), 80–88; quotation is on page 80.

49. Sobel, *Public Opinion*, 80.

50. Roger Peace, *A Call to Conscience: The Anti-Contra War Campaign* (Amherst: University of Massachusetts Press, 2012), 51–52. A Media General–Associated Press poll taken in December 1986 registered the highest level of support for the Contra War among the American public, climbing to 19 percent. See the *Philadelphia Daily News*, December 15, 1986, 36. See also Brad Lockerbie and Stephen A. Borrelli, "Question Wording and Public Support for Contra Aid, 1983–1986," *Public Opinion Quarterly* 54, no. 2 (Summer 1990): 195–97.

51. Richard Sobel, "A Report: Public Opinion about United States Intervention in El Salvador and Nicaragua," *Public Opinion Quarterly* 53, no. 1 (Spring 1989): 117–18.

52. Perla, "Heirs of Sandino," 84.

53. Patt Morrison, "Contras Aim to Scare Off Americans, Group Says," *Los Angeles Times*, May 2, 1987, 20.

54. Rose Gelbspan, "Volunteers Defy U.S. Policy on Nicaragua," *Boston Globe*, February 2, 1986, 34.

55. Kathleen McClain, "Tristaters Witness Woes of Nicaragua Firsthand," *Cincinnati Enquirer*, December 2, 1984, 4.

56. David Kirp, "Doing Justice," *San Francisco Examiner*, *Image* magazine insert, April 19, 1987, 26.

57. Bill Osinski, "Disobedience in the Name of Peace," *Akron Beacon Journal*, April 15, 1985, A3; Phil Haslanger, "Kasten's Choosy Policy on Office Visitors Irks Group," *Capital Times* (Madison, WI), June 13, 1985, 8.

58. In December 1980, the beloved British punk band The Clash released a triple album titled *Sandinista!*, which paid homage to the Nicaraguan revolution. The album turned out to be the opening salvo among antiwar musicians who wrote and recorded numerous songs about Central America, including the following incomplete list: "All She Wants to Do Is Dance," by ex-Eagle Don Henley; "The Big Stick," by California punkers The Minutemen; "Nicaragua," by Canadian folksinger Bruce Cockburn; "Please Forgive Us," by indie favorites 10,000 Maniacs; "Fragile," by former Police front man Sting; and "Bullet the Blue Sky," by Irish rockers U2. Perhaps the most overtly political Central America song was "Lives in the Balance," by Jackson Browne, the title track of his eighth studio album, released in 1986. "Lives in the Balance," a heartfelt warning about the looming prospect of war in Central America, could be heard on two *Miami Vice* episodes: "Stone's War" (season 3, episode 2, October 3, 1986) and the final episode in the series, "Freefall" (season 5, episode 17, May 21, 1989).

59. Unlike Jan-Michael Vincent's portrayal of him in *Last Plane Out*, the real Jack Cox was a World War II veteran, former Republican state legislator from Texas, and consultant to U.S. businesses in Latin America. The "globe-hopping . . . foe of communism," as he was once described, became friends with Anastasio Somoza and traveled to Nicaragua around the time of the Sandinista Revolution with plans to make a documentary. Calling Cox a "journalist" would be a stretch. Yet, at a time when movies were celebrating news correspondents covering conflicts in exotic locales, such as Peter Weir's successful *The Year of Living Dangerously* from 1982, *Last Plane Out* recasts Cox—who was 61 when the film was released—as a much younger newspaper reporter. The film, if anything, downplays his close bond with Somoza. The Nicaraguan dictator actually dictated his memoir to Cox, which was published as *Nicaragua Betrayed* in 1980 by Western Islands, a Boston-based publishing company owned by the John Birch Society. Eight years later, Cox cowrote the "autobiography"

196 · NOTES TO PAGES 135–140

of Imelda Marcos, wife of the repressive Filipino dictator Ferdinand Marcos. For more on Cox, see the *Los Angeles Times*, October 19, 1983, 81, and the *Lincoln (NE) Journal Star*, June 19, 1988, 2A. For the "globe-hopping . . . foe of communism" quote, see *Honolulu Star-Bulletin*, September 5, 1990, A-3.

60. *Last Plane Out*, directed by David Nelson (New York: Kino Lorber, 2017), DVD.

61. Examples of poor reviews in Florida newspapers include Jay Boyar, "'Last Plane Out' Never Manages to Get Off the Ground," *Orlando Sentinel*, September 28, 1983, 41; John Eldridge, "Plot Focus Knocks Out This 'Plane,'" *Miami News*, September 23, 1983, 43; and Terry Kelleher, "'Last Plane Out' Tells the New Right's Side, Badly," *South Florida Sun Sentinel*, September 27, 1983, 43. The number of theaters in Florida where *Last Plane Out* was shown is mentioned in Pam Platt, "Airport Gives Vero Runway to Stardom," *Florida Today*, September 20, 1983, 1D.

62. In 2017, director Doug Liman's film *American Made*, starring Tom Cruise, presented a viewpoint highly critical of the Sandinistas, portraying them largely as opportunistic drug dealers. But *American Made* is a dark film, full of black humor and violence, with a plague-on-all-houses approach that also implicates the Central Intelligence Agency in drug running, depicting it as treating its own operatives as expendable. Thus, while anti-Sandinista, *American Made* is hardly a celebration of U.S. foreign policy or American exceptionalism.

63. *Invasion U.S.A.*, directed by Joseph Zito (New York: MGM Home Entertainment, 2006), DVD.

64. *Missing*, directed by Costa-Gavras (New York: Universal Pictures Home Entertainment, 2004), DVD.

65. Kevin Thomas, "Costa-Gavras: Politics Is Never Missing," *Los Angeles Times*, March 1, 1982, Part VI, 9.

66. The State Department's side of the story is found in "U.S. Takes Issue with Costa-Gavras Film on Chile," *New York Times*, February 10, 1982, C22.

67. Larry Kart, "Another Controversy for Films' Nonaggressive Good Guy," Arts and Books, *Chicago Tribune*, March 14, 1982, 7.

68. *Salvador*, directed by Oliver Stone (New York: MGM Home Entertainment, 2001), DVD.

69. *Under Fire*, directed by Roger Spottiswoode (New York: MGM Home Entertainment, 2001), DVD.

70. Bart Mills, "'Salvador' Film a Risky Venture," TGIF, *Palm Beach Post*, April 18, 1986, 34.

71. *Austin American-Statesman*, February 12, 1987, Section C, 1. *Under Fire* was also nominated for an Oscar in the category of best original score, composed by Jerry Goldsmith. Parts of the score were later reused in Quentin Tarantino's *Django Unchained* (2012).

72. *Latino: America's Secret War in Nicaragua*, directed by Haskell Wexler (Burbank, CA: Cinema Libre Studio, 2011), DVD. The original film was titled simply *Latino*. The subtitle was later added to the DVD version.

73. Judy Stone, "Haskell Wexler's Double Cinematic Pedigree," Datebook, *San Francisco Chronicle*, November 17, 1985, 29.

74. Poor reviews did not help the film either. Typical of the handful of critics who even acknowledged the film's existence was Michael Sragow's review for the *San Francisco Examiner*, headlined "Wexler's New 'Latino' Is Agit-Prop without Passion or Punch," November 23, 1985, B1.

75. Ben Sachs, "An Interview with Director Alex Cox about *Walker*, One of the Most Audacious American Films of the 1980s," *Chicago Reader*, August 31, 2017, https://

www.chicagoreader.com/Bleader/archives/2017/08/31/an-interview-with-director
-alex-cox-about-walker-one-of-the-most-audacious-american-films-of-the-1980s.

76. *Walker*, directed by Alex Cox (New York: Criterion Collection, 2008), DVD. Over the years, Walker has amassed a cult following, which may account for the fancy version of the DVD released by the Criterion Collection, a company that specializes in acclaimed classic, foreign, and art house films. For Cox's comment about being "blacklisted," see Sachs, "Interview with Director Alex Cox."

77. *Romero*, directed by John Duigan (Worcester, PA: *Vision Video, 2013), DVD; Windsor Star*, November 24, 1989, C3.

78. Stephen Hunter, "Priest Films a Eulogy to Slain Archbishop Romero," Maryland Live, *Baltimore Sun*, November 24, 1989, 14.

79. *Santa Fe New Mexican*, September 21, 1989, 80.

80. Surprisingly, at this date, one of the few informative books on the landmark show is Trish Janeshutz's *The Making of "Miami Vice"* (New York: Ballantine Books, 1986), published shortly after the show's second season ended.

81. "Smuggler's Blues," *Miami Vice*, directed by Paul Michael Glaser, season 1, episode 16 (New York: Universal Pictures Home Entertainment, 2005), DVD, disc 3.

82. "Back in the World," *Miami Vice*, directed by Don Johnson, season 2, episode 11 (New York: Universal Pictures Home Entertainment, 2005), DVD, disc 2.

83. Sonny Crockett's previous car, a 1972 Ferrari Daytona Spyder, was blown up by a rogue arms dealer (Jeff Fahey) in season 3, episode 1, "When Irish Eyes Are Crying," airdate September 26, 1986.

84. "Stone's War," *Miami Vice*, directed by David Jackson, season 3, episode 2 (New York: Universal Pictures Home Entertainment, 2007), DVD, disc 1.

85. Stuart A. Kallen, *The Aftermath of the Sandinista Revolution* (Minneapolis, MN: Twenty-First Century Books/Lerner Publishing, 2009), 97.

86. David Thelen, *Becoming Citizens in the Age of Television: How Americans Challenged the Media and Seized Political Initiative during the Iran-Contra Debate* (Chicago: University of Chicago Press, 1996), 15–16.

87. Joan Kruckewitt, *The Death of Ben Linder: The Story of a North American in Sandinista Nicaragua* (New York: Seven Stories Press, 1999), 315–29.

88. Kruckewitt, *Death of Ben Linder*, 328.

89. Peter Collier and David Horowitz, "Hang Down Your Head, Ben Linder," *Tampa Tribune*, June 14, 1987, 7C.

90. Mike Connolly, "Navy Report Calls Maiming an 'Accident,'" *San Francisco Examiner*, November 18, 1987, A-1, A-14.

91. Garry Abrams, "A 'Peace Warrior's' Journey from Obscurity," *Los Angeles Times*, September 20, 1987, Part IV, 8.

92. *Springfield (MO) News-Leader*, February 3, 1988, 9.

93. Storer H. Rowley, "Reagan Seeking Contra-Aid Options," *Chicago Tribune*, February 5, 1988, 2.

Chapter 7: The End of the Line

1. Key histories of the Reagan-Gorbachev summit meetings and the final years of the Cold War include Ken Adelman, *Reagan at Reykjavik: Forty-Eight Hours That Ended the Cold War* (New York: Broadside Books, 2014); Michael Beschloss and Strobe Talbott, *At the Highest Levels: The Inside Story of the End of the Cold War* (Boston:

Little Brown, 1994); Jeffrey A. Engel, *When the World Seemed New: George H. W. Bush and the End of the Cold War* (Boston: Houghton Mifflin Harcourt); Andrei Grachev, *Gorbachev's Gamble: Soviet Foreign Policy and the End of the Cold War* (Cambridge, U.K.: Polity Press, 2008); David Hoffman, *The Dead Hand: The Untold Story of the Cold War Arms Race and Its Dangerous Legacy* (New York: Anchor, 2010); Melvyn P. Leffler, *For the Soul of Mankind: The United States, the Soviet Union, and the Cold War* (New York: Hill and Wang, 2008); James Mann, *The Rebellion of Ronald Reagan: A History of the End of the Cold War* (New York: Penguin Books, 2010); Jack Matlock, *Reagan and Gorbachev: How the Cold War Ended* (New York: Random House, 2004); and Robert Service, *The End of the Cold War: 1985–1991* (New York: PublicAffairs, 2015).

2.   George P. Shultz, *Turmoil and Triumph: My Years as Secretary of State* (New York: Charles Scribner's Sons, 1993), 606.

3.   Hoffman, *Dead Hand*, 264.

4.   Ronald Reagan, *An American Life: The Autobiography* (New York: Simon & Schuster, 1990), 683.

5.   Will Bunch, *Tear Down This Myth: The Right-Wing Distortion of the Reagan Legacy* (New York: Free Press, 2010), 26.

6.   George F. Will, "The Illusion of Arms Control," *Newsweek*, October 13, 1986, 102.

7.   Richard Nixon and Henry Kissinger, "A Real Peace," *National Review*, May 22, 1987, 32–34; James Gerstenzang and Robert Shogan, "Conservatives Hit Reagan on Treaty," *Los Angeles Times*, December 5, 1987, Part I, 1.

8.   Gerstenzang and Shogan, "Conservatives Hit Reagan on Treaty," 12.

9.   Stephen R. Rock, *Appeasement in International Politics* (Lexington: University Press of Kentucky, 2000), 3; *National Review*, May 22, 1987; Robert Samuel, "Conservative Intellectuals and the Reagan–Gorbachev Summits," *Cold War History* 12, no. 1 (February 2012): 149.

10.   For example, see Lee Sigelman, "Disarming the Opposition: The President, the Public, and the INF Treaty," *Public Opinion Quarterly* 54, no. 1 (Spring 1990): 39–41.

11.   Samuel, "Conservative Intellectuals," 149.

12.   Samuel, 150.

13.   Samuel, 149.

14.   Mikhail Gorbachev, *Perestroika: New Thinking for Our Country and the World* (New York: HarperCollins, 1987), 30, 18.

15.   Wilbur G. Landrey, "Both Sides in Summit Put Off Hard Decisions," *Tampa Bay Times*, December 11, 1987, 20.

16.   John Robinson, "A Soviet Émigré Assesses Superstar Gorbachev," *Santa Cruz Sentinel*, December 10, 1987, 5. See also *Asbury Park Press*, October 21, 1988, C9.

17.   Susan Baer, "Raisa's Wardrobe: Smashing Success or Pseudo-Chic?," *Baltimore Sun*, December 11, 1987, 8E.

18.   *Camden Courier Post*, December 2, 1987, 3; Landrey, "Both Sides in Summit," *Tampa Bay Times*, December 11, 1987, 20; *Indianapolis Star*, May 16, 1988, 4.

19.   Douglas C. Walker, *Congress and the Nuclear Freeze: An Inside Look at the Politics of a Mass Movement* (Amherst: University of Massachusetts Press, 1987), x.

20.   Bradford Martin, *The Other Eighties: A Secret History of America in the Age of Reagan* (New York: Hill and Wang, 2011), 22–23; David S. Meyer, "The United States Structure of Political Opportunity and the End of the Nuclear Freeze Movement," *Political Research Quarterly* 46, no. 3 (September 1993): 173.

21. In the early months of 1984, most freeze activists initially supported the candidacy of Senator Alan Cranston of California. But when Cranston dropped out of the race in the spring, the activists shifted to Walter Mondale's campaign. See the *Akron Beacon-Journal*, February 19, 1984, D1.

22. *Pittsburgh Press*, March 29, 1984, 8; *Murfreesboro (TN) Daily News-Journal*, July 13, 1987, 4.

23. The number of freeze campaign "affiliates" actually grew between 1983 and 1986, from 1,333 to 1,824, according to historian Lawrence Wittner. Despite this growth spurt, the movement was—by the admission of many of its activists—suffering from burnout, poor leadership, and a general lack of direction. See Lawrence S. Wittner, *Toward Nuclear Abolition: A History of the World Nuclear Disarmament Movement, 1971 to the Present* (Stanford, CA: Stanford University Press, 2003), 340–43.

24. Mark Hume, "Caldicott Quitting 16-Year Peace Fight," *Vancouver Sun*, April 4, 1986, 17; *Arizona Daily Star*, May 15, 1986, B13.

25. Robert Jay Lifton and Richard A. Falk, *Indefensible Weapons: The Political and Psychological Case against Nuclearism* (New York: Basic Books, 1982), 109–10.

26. Keith Graham, "Nuclear Disarmament Activist Is Just About out of Energy," *Atlanta Constitution*, April 15, 1986, B2. While Helen Caldicott did disappear from the public spotlight for a few years, she eventually returned to antinuclear advocacy and activism, continuing to write books, speak out, and travel extensively in support of disarmament and peace.

27. *Philadelphia Inquirer*, February 23, 1987, 7.

28. For example, see *Florida Today*, June 24, 1986, 19.

29. *Austin American-Statesman*, June 27, 1986, C33; Gary Stahl, "Footsteps on the March toward Peace," *Washington Post*, March 23, 1986, K1.

30. Interview with David Mixner, conducted by Randy Shulman, July 28, 2004, Metro Weekly website, Washington, D.C., https://www.metroweekly.com/2004/07/david-mixner/.

31. Dain TePoel, "Endurance Activism: Transcontinental Walking, the Great Peace March and the Politics of Movement Culture" (PhD diss., University of Iowa, 2018), 53–54, ProQuest(10837201), 1–5; Laura Haferd, "The Tough Are Still Going," *Akron Beacon Journal*, March 18, 1986, B1.

32. *Salem Statesman Journal*, June 27, 1986, 35.

33. Gordon Anderson, "What Happened to the Great Peace March," *International Journal on World Peace* 4, no. 1 (January–March 1987): 113–14.

34. For a superb account of the Nevada Test Site protests, see Ken Butigan, *Pilgrimage through a Burning World: Spiritual Practice and Nonviolent Protest at the Nevada Test Site* (Albany: State University of New York Press, 2003).

35. Randolph Ryan, "In Nicaragua, a Win but Not a Victory," *Boston Globe*, February 28, 1990, 11.

36. For a superb account of the dramatic decline solidarity activism in Nicaragua after the country's 1990 general elections, see Chris Hedges, "Sandinistas' U.S. Friends: Case of Dashed Ideals," *New York Times*, July 21, 1990, 23.

37. Ross Gelbspan, "Credibility of Ex-Agent Is Key Factor in Probe of FBI," *Boston Globe*, July 26, 1988, 9.

38. Paul Weingarten, "FBI Broke into Group's Office, Informant Tells Subcommittee," *Chicago Tribune*, February 22, 1987, 21; Philip Shenon, "F.B.I. Papers Show Wide Surveillance of Reagan Critics," *New York Times*, January 28, 1988, A1.

39. Ross Gelbspan, "Sessions Said He Disciplined Six Agents in CISPES Probe," *Boston Globe*, September 15, 1988, 15.

40. For more on the government's campaigns of infiltration, surveillance, and harassment, see Ross Gelbspan, *Break-ins, Death Threats, and the FBI: The Covert War against the Central America Movement* (Boston: South End Press, 1991).

41. Ross Gelbspan, "Right-Wing Groups Spied on Reagan's Foes for FBI," *Boston Globe*, March 21, 1988, 7.

42. Christian Smith, *Resisting Reagan: The U.S. Central America Peace Movement* (Chicago: University of Chicago Press, 1996), 296.

43. Countless examples of Reagan-era repression can be found in Smith, *Resisting Reagan*, 280–324. Smith devotes a lengthy chapter to the subject. Gelbspan's *Break-ins, Death Threats* similarly documents such abuses. See also David Cole and James Dempsey, *Terrorism and the Constitution: Sacrificing Civil Liberties in the Name of National Security* (New York: New Press, 2006), 25–40.

44. On grassroots resistance against apartheid, see Gavin Brown and Helen Yaffe, *Youth Activism and Solidarity: The Non-Stop Picket against Apartheid* (New York: Routledge, 2018); Charles Cobb Jr., Gail Hovey, and William Minter, eds., *No Easy Victories: African Liberation and American Activists over a Half Century, 1950–2000* (Trenton, NJ: Africa World Press, 2007); Anna Konieczna and Rob Skinner, eds., *A Global History of Anti-Apartheid: 'Forward to Freedom' in South Africa* (London: Palgrave Macmillan, 2019); and Francis Njubi Nesbitt, *Race for Sanctions: African Americans against Apartheid, 1946–1994* (Bloomington: Indiana University Press, 2004). As of 2020, the literature on the antiapartheid movement in the United States is surprisingly sparse. The best short account is in Martin, *The Other Eighties*, chap. 3, "'Unsightly Huts': Shanties and the Divestment Movement," 45–66.

45. Donald R. Culverson, "The Politics of the Anti-Apartheid Movement in the United States, 1969–1986," *Political Science Quarterly* 111, no. 1 (Spring 1996): 145.

46. The most balanced single history of the long, violent civil war in Angola is Justin Pearce, *Political Identity and Conflict in Central Angola, 1975–2002* (Cambridge: Cambridge University Press, 2015). A fine account of South Africa's role in the Angolan civil war is William Minter, *Apartheid's Contras: An Inquiry into the Roots of War in Angola and Mozambique* (London: Zed Books, 1994).

47. *Allentown Morning Call*, April 6, 1986, A19; *Rochester Democrat and Chronicle*, November 9, 1986, 28A.

48. Philip G. Altbach and Robert Cohen, "Student Activism: The Post-Sixties Transformation," *Journal of Higher Education* 61, no. 1 (January–February 1990): 45. For University of Texas, see Monty Jones, "Anti-Apartheid Shanty at UT Is Rammed by Stolen Scooter," *Austin American-Statesman*, October 14, 1986, B3. For the University of Pittsburgh shanty arson incident, see *Indiana Gazette*, November 25, 1986, 5. For the University of Missouri at St. Louis, see Dale Singer, "Fire Consumes Anti-Apartheid Shanty at UMSL," *St. Louis Post-Dispatch*, February 25, 1986, 1. For the University of Washington, see *Salem Statesman Journal*, May 12, 1986, 10.

49. Mike Adams, "Lawyer Cites Racism in Arson Case," *Baltimore Evening Sun*, September 11, 1986, D1.

50. William B. Collins, "A Master's Play of Tragic Import Is Brought Here," *Philadelphia Inquirer*, March 21, 1982, 10-M.

51. *Cry Freedom*, directed by Richard Attenborough (New York: Universal Pictures Home Entertainment, 1999), DVD; *A World Apart*, directed by Chris Menges (New York:

MGM Home Entertainment, 2005), DVD; *A Dry White Season*, directed by Euzhan Palcy (New York: Criterion Collection, 2017), DVD.

52. *Lethal Weapon 2*, directed by Richard Donner (New York: Warner Home Video, 2006), DVD.

53. *Detroit Free Press*, July 7, 1989, 4C.

54. Artists United against Apartheid, "Sun City," track 1 on *Sun City*, produced by Steven Van Zandt and Arthur Baker (New York: EMI Manhattan Records, 1985), LP; Michael Drewett, "The Cultural Boycott against Apartheid South Africa: A Case of Defensible Censorship?," in *Popular Music Censorship in Africa*, ed. Martin Cloonan and Michael Drewett (New York: Routledge, 2016), 26–28.

55. Marc Eliot, *Paul Simon: A Life* (Hoboken, NJ: John Wiley & Sons, 2010), 189–96.

56. Charles M. Young, "It Takes a Worried Man," Fall Preview, *New York Daily News*, August 24, 1986, 24.

57. See, for example, Unity in Action Boycott Linda Ronstadt leaflet, advertising a protest on June 7, 1988, the Pantages Theater, Hollywood and Vine, Los Angeles, courtesy of the African Activist Archive, http://africanactivist.msu.edu/document_metadata .php?objectid=32-130-1673.

58. Louise Meintjes, "Paul Simon's Graceland, South Africa, and the Mediation of Musical Meaning," *Ethnomusicology* 34, no. 1 (Winter 1990): 47–48. The author of this piece is not necessarily making the argument that *Graceland* is cultural appropriation, but she draws attention to such arguments made by other critics.

59. Fall Preview, *New York Daily News*, August 24, 1986, 24.

60. Culverson, "Politics of the Anti-Apartheid Movement," 146.

61. In July 1989, conservative syndicated columnist and *National Review* contributor Joseph Sobran wrote the perfect example of a column that danced around the issue of apartheid without strongly endorsing the Pretoria government. Sobran criticized the movie *Lethal Weapon 2* for its not-so-subtle attack on apartheid. Specifically, he takes the summer blockbuster to task for demonizing white South Africans and faults Mel Gibson's character, Martin Riggs, for likening the bad guys in the film to Nazis, which he refers to as "libel." He calls the movie "propaganda," describing the experience of watching it as "chilling." But even as he slams *Lethal Weapon 2* for vilifying the white Afrikaner bad guys in the movie, Sobran says nothing about the apartheid regime and its lengthy catalog of crimes against humanity. See Joseph Sobran, "Casting South Africa as Villain of a Blockbuster," *Indianapolis Star*, July 26, 1989, 10.

62. With regard to public opinion and apartheid, political scientist Donald R. Culverson writes: "Substantial growth in public support for movement objectives occurred from 1977 to 1985 and 1986. A 1977 Harris Poll asked if the United States and other Western nations should pressure South Africa to give Black people greater freedom and political participation. Forty-six percent responded yes, while 26 percent responded no. However, as the follow-up question indicates, Americans expected the initiative to come primarily from the corporate sector. Forty-six percent of those surveyed felt that the U.S. government should encourage U.S. companies in South Africa to pressure the South African government, and 28 percent opposed this measure. A similar Gallup Poll conducted in September 1985 revealed that 47 percent of respondents favored the U.S. placing more pressure on the South African government. Fifteen percent favored less, and 37 percent said that no change in the amount of pressure was necessary. Asked the same question a year later, 55 percent

felt that the U.S. should apply more pressure on Pretoria, 14 percent said less, and 24 percent approved of the current level." Culverson, "Politics of the Anti-Apartheid Movement," 146.

63. Matthew Countryman, "Lessons of the Divestment Drive," *Nation*, March 26, 1988, 406; *Wilkes-Barre Citizens' Voice*, May 30, 1988, 22.

64. Nicholas M. Horrock, "U.S.-Soviet Talks May End Final Chapter of Cold War," *Chicago Tribune*, May 29, 1989, 11.

65. *Hartford Courant*, October 19, 1988, A16.

66. Don Oberdorfer, "Thatcher Says Cold War Has Come to an End: Briton Calls for Support of Gorbachev," *Washington Post*, November 18, 1988; Shultz, *Turmoil and Triumph*, 1131, 1138; John Mueller, "What Was the Cold War About? Evidence from Its Ending," *Political Science Quarterly* 119, no. 4 (Winter 2004/2005): 612–13; Chris Black, "Gorbachev's Popularity Rivals Bush's," *Boston Globe*, November 16, 1989, 21.

67. Francis Fukuyama, "The End of History?," *National Interest*, no. 16 (Summer 1989): 3–18.

68. Francis Fukuyama, *The End of History and the Last Man* (New York: Free Press, 1992).

69. Mueller, "Cold War," 614; *Honolulu Star-Bulletin*, September 30, 1988, 3; *Dayton Daily News*, December 28, 1989, 15; *Arizona Daily Star*, July 5, 1989, 21.

70. So said Ben Wattenberg in his syndicated column, which ran in the *Lancaster New Era*, January 14, 1989, 12.

71. William Safire argues this in his column, *Salina (KS) Journal*, June 7, 1990, 4.

72. Editorial page editor Ray Jenkins gave FDR credit in the *Baltimore Sun*, November 18, 1989, 11A.

73. Tom Teepen advances this point in the *Atlanta Constitution*, December 29, 1991, D11.

74. David Abshire, former U.S. Ambassador to NATO, made this assertion in the *St. Louis Post-Dispatch*, March 26, 1990, 28.

75. Russian historian Howard Hurlbut's verdict stated in the *San Bernardino County Sun*, October 21, 1990, D3.

76. Not surprisingly, the Bush campaign adopted this position in 1992, *Minneapolis Star-Tribune*, August 19, 1992, 1A.

77. Dick Ochs, a longtime Students for a Democratic Society activist in the 1960s, asserted this position. See the *Baltimore Sun*, March 18, 1990, 3E.

Conclusion

1. William H. Hill, *No Place for Russia: European Security Institutions since 1989* (New York: Columbia University Press, 2018), 67.

2. H. Stuart Hughes, "On 'The End of History and the Last Man,'" Book Review, *Los Angeles Times*, November 8, 1992, 13.

3. Peter Beinart, "Think Again: Ronald Reagan," *Foreign Policy*, no. 180 (July/August 2010): 30.

4. Key works in the Reagan triumphalist school include Martin Anderson and Annelise Anderson, *Reagan's Secret War: The Untold Story of His Fight to Save the World from Nuclear Disaster* (New York: Crown Archetype, 2009); Paul Kengor, *The Crusader: Ronald Reagan and the Fall of Communism* (New York: Harper, 2006); Paul Lettow, *Ronald Reagan and His Quest to Abolish Nuclear Weapons* (New York: Random House, 2005); and Peter Schweizer, *Reagan's War: The Epic Story of His Forty Year Struggle and Final Triumph over Communism* (New York: Doubleday, 2002).

5. A growing number of books have emphasized the importance of dissent in the Reagan years. Essential titles in this category include Michael Stewart Foley, *Front Porch Politics: The Forgotten Heyday of American Activism in the 1970s and 1980s* (New York: Hill and Wang, 2013); Kyle Harvey, *American Antinuclear Activism, 1975–1990: The Challenge of Peace* (New York: Palgrave Macmillan, 2014); William Knoblauch, *Nuclear Freeze in a Cold War: The Reagan Administration, Cultural Activism, and the End of the Arms Race* (Amherst: University of Massachusetts Press, 2018); Bradford Martin, *The Other Eighties: A Secret History of America in the Age of Reagan* (New York: Hill and Wang, 2011); Kevin Mattson, *We're Not Here to Entertain: Punk Rock, Ronald Reagan, and the Real Culture War of 1980s America* (New York: Oxford University Press, 2020); Roger Peace, *A Call to Conscience: The Anti-Contra War Campaign* (Amherst: University of Massachusetts Press, 2012); Christian Smith, *Resisting Reagan: The U.S. Central America Peace Movement* (Chicago: University of Chicago Press, 1996); and Nick Witham, *The Cultural Left and the Reagan Era: U.S. Protest and Central American Revolution* (London: I. B. Tauris, 2015).

Index

Page numbers in *italics* refer to illustrations.